Dear Doctor

Dr. Saul Levine and Dr. Kathleen Wilcox

Sensitive, sensible
answers to teenagers'
most troubling questions

Lothrop, Lee & Shepard Books   New York

**To David
and to Jaime, Mischa, and Zachary,
who each day reaffirm our faith in our youth**

1 2 3 4 5 6 7 8 9 10

Library of Congress Cataloging in Publication Data Levine, Saul, Dr. Dear doctor. Includes index. 1. Youth—Health and hygiene—Miscellanea. 2. Youth—Miscellanea. I. Wilcox, Kathleen, Dr. II. Title. RA777.L48 1987 613'.0433 86-21335 ISBN 0-688-07094-9 (pbk.) ISBN 0-688-07095-7 (lib. bdg.)

The material contained in *Dear Doctor* is based on the column "Youth Clinic" originally published by Toronto Star Newspapers Limited.

CONTENTS

ACKNOWLEDGMENTS

This book would not have seen the light of day were it not for the existence of the column "Youth Clinic," initiated by the *Toronto Star* and distributed by the Toronto Star Syndicate. We are therefore indebted to Shelley Robertson, *Toronto Star* Life Section editor, and her staff, and to Jim Cherrier, managing director of the syndicate. Their enthusiastic featuring of the column gave us exposure to thousands of young people and their parents. They also contributed to the excitement the column generated in us and in our readers.

While we had been actively discussing writing the book, the actual impetus to do it came from Valerie Hussey and Ricky Englander of Kids Can Press. They initiated the project, pushed and cajoled, supported and encouraged us, and were delightful to work with. Their editor Kathy Vanderlinden needs to be congratulated for bringing some semblance of order to the chaos of hundreds of letters.

Valerie Wine's yeomanly performance of typing and organizing our manuscript (and us), and her perpetual good cheer in the face of it, were remarkable, especially in light of an otherwise exceptionally heavy workload. We are in awe.

Special thanks are also due to Pat and Peggy McGregor who tirelessly read through reams of dusty pages to find the "antique" advice that heads each chapter. Their enthusiasm and support made this task a joy.

We are grateful to those colleagues and friends who encouraged us and who tolerated our preoccupation with the project. Over the years we have used colleagues, experts, and seers for advice and guidance on difficult questions. Their ideas and help have always been appreciated. Some of these silent contributors are Neil Shear, Bob Schemmer, Pat Latner, Rick Comisarow, Sandi Leibovici, Susan MacKinnon, Pat Kelley, Mary McKenzie, Howard Donsky, Bill Mindell, Bill Harris, P. L. Chan, Paul Garfinkel, Dianna Chalupa, Alan Kaplan, and Judy Verbeeten.

Lastly, doing a book of any kind has to take some toll in time, energy, and involvement on the part of those closest to the writers. Our families were always unequivocally and enthusiastically supportive. To them we can only express gratitude and love.

INTRODUCTION

This is a book written by you as much as by the two of us. It is made up of letters written by young people to "Youth Clinic," a nationally syndicated column we've been writing for several years. The letters reflect the concerns that arise during the years of growing up, and our answers are an attempt to help you resolve, cope with, and/or understand these concerns.

While we've organized the letters into sections based on the most common issues raised, categories often overlap. Because of this, we suggest that you read all letters that might pertain to your own question, rather than hunting only for *the* letter that most closely describes it. (Advice about birth control, for example, may require reading about condoms, the Pill, menstrual cycles, and relationships to get a full picture of all the issues.) Use the index, table of contents, subject headings on each page, and the references to other letters or sections given with some letters—these guides will help you get much more out of the book.

All medical information has been reviewed and updated just prior to press time, but in those areas where new discoveries seem to occur overnight (especially regarding infections), remember that these letters will form a solid base of information but your family doctor can add new details.

You, our correspondents, have taught us a great deal about adolescents. Along with the wonderings and worries so eloquently expressed, you have revealed inner strengths, resources, and aspirations that are exciting and reassuring. Our contacts with so many of you over the years through the column, our clinical work, and through personal involvement have indeed filled us with optimism about youth and, by extension, about the future of society.

ONE:

Your Body

*In the good old grandmother days of girls help-
ing with work of household, warm but loose
clothing, plain food, good thick-soled shoes and
absence of novels to excite sexual thoughts, etc.,
such a thing as a debilitated woman or girl was
hardly known.*

A. W. Chase
Dr. Chase's Recipes *(1903)*

Adolescence is a time of tremendous physical change
that occurs at a faster and more dramatic rate
than any you've previously experienced. Even the
change from a wriggling, screaming newborn to a walking,
talking two-year-old is no match for the transformation your
body is now undergoing. And the question that always seems
to accompany this transformation is: Am I normal, or am I
the only person with (take your pick) small breasts/large
breasts/no muscles/irregular periods/a high voice/a low
voice/too much body hair?

This section contains common general questions about
the physical changes accompanying puberty. Questions
about more specific problems (for example, heavy thighs,
spontaneous erections, acne) are included in later sections
(for these examples: *Weight, Fitness, and Body Image*; *Sex
and Sexuality*; *Skin*). You may also find the information
you need scattered through other parts of the book—the
cross-references and index will guide you. The letters in this
part should help you realize you're not alone in the changes
that now engulf you, and that the concerns you feel are just
a normal part of growing up.

G I R L S

**Dear Dr. Wilcox: I am a girl, almost twelve, and don't
have hair in two places that I think I should have.** **1**

I'm also short. Am I going to be slow in puberty, or is it normal? Most of my friends talk about puberty, and I'm always left out.

Although the age at which one's body begins to mature varies from one person to another, the order in which these events occur is fairly set. Often if a girl seems to be maturing a bit later than average, it will turn out that her mother and other female relatives also tended to be "late," since these trends seem to run in families. The same is true for boys and their male relatives.

At almost twelve, you still have plenty of time for your body to begin to mature. In most cases (96 to 98 percent), the events of a girl's puberty occur in the following order and age ranges:

- For the very first hint of breast development (thelarche), the average age is about 11 or 11½, but the normal range is from about 9 to more than 13.
- For the beginning of the growth of pubic and underarm hair (adrenarche), the average is about 11½, but again the normal range is from about 9 to nearly 14.
- The beginning of menstruation or "periods" (menarche) occurs later than the other two stages. Menstruation begins at about age 12 years 4 months, but the normal age range is very wide, from 9 to 17. The vast majority, though, are between 11 and 15. If a girl has not yet had periods by sixteen, she would generally have evidence of adrenarche and thelarche. The height "growth spurt" occurs sometime during these events, often just months prior to the onset of menstruation.

2 **Dear Dr. Wilcox: I read in a magazine that after a girl has had her period she only grows less than one more inch (about two more centimeters). Is this true?**

No. The statement is an oversimplification of a complicated process and is also inaccurate.

I assume the point the magazine was trying to make is that girls grow the fastest shortly *before* menstruation starts. This is true. This time of rapid growth is called the growth spurt. It usually occurs around age twelve for girls, although it can start before ten or even after thirteen. During this year a girl may grow taller by 2 to 4 in (6 to 11 cm). After menstruation starts, on average a bit after twelve, the average girl will grow only about 1 in (3 cm) by fourteen, and would have achieved most of her adult height by age sixteen.

The growth spurt is stimulated by increased amounts of "growth hormone" from the pituitary gland and by increased levels of androgens, hormones we usually think of as being male, although they are responsible for many of the changes both boys and girls experience during adolescence.

The growth spurt doesn't affect all parts of the body equally or at the same time. For example, most of the height increase is caused by rapid lengthening of the trunk rather than the legs. The legs usually grow fastest before the width of the hips and chest begins to increase. Shoulders get wider even later. Eventually there are growth spurts in head circumference, size of the internal organs (including heart, lungs, and reproductive organs), bones, muscles, and glands such as the thyroid and pituitary.

Dear Dr. Wilcox: I am a fifteen-year-old girl who is 3 worried about her growth. I am only 5 ft (152 cm) tall and weigh only 90 lb (41 kg). Perhaps it is because of my Asian heritage. For the past few years my height has remained the same, and there is only a small increase in weight. My arms, feet, fingers, and legs are not growing either.

Have you heard of anything like this? Is this hormone deficiency? Is there any way to make me grow normally again? You might suggest that it's malnutrition, but I feel that I eat a fairly well balanced diet. The most common cause of short stature is the height potential one has inherited from one's parents. If your parents and relatives are small, the likelihood of your also being petite is quite high. Hormone deficiencies are rarer causes and are often associated with being markedly short—less than your height—and/or with delayed puberty. Remember that most girls experience their growth spurt between ages ten and thirteen, and that by fifteen increase in height can be minimal: you may be experiencing the normal slowing and cessation of growth.

Your doctor is the best person to tell if you if your height is normal for you; make an appointment to discuss your concerns.

Dear Dr. Wilcox: I am almost thirteen. When I was 4 younger my parents were divorced, so I live with my father. I have lumps in my breasts, but I find it im-

possible to tell my father even though we get along
great and have always communicated well. What are
the chances of a girl my age having cancer?
At your age the most common breast lumps are "breast
buds," which are a normal part of early breast development.
The onset of breast development may occur at any age between 8 and 14½ (average: 11.2). During breast development, the breast bud may be noted as a ½-in (1-cm) button
of firm tissue beneath the nipple. It may be tender, and one
side may develop before the other. The buds are needed for
normal breast development and therefore are never removed.

A doctor can easily identify breast buds, and you should
check with one to make sure that this is the cause of your
lumps. Breast cancer is very rare during adolescence.

5 **Dear Dr. Wilcox: I am fourteen years old. I know some
girls who, like me, are flat-chested. Our breasts are
like little bumps. I am wondering why we are flat. I
think it's not fair that we don't have breasts. We
should have something, don't you think? Do you
think we should wear bras in high school this fall?
Could wearing a bra too soon prevent breasts from
growing?**
People mature at very different rates and all are normal.
Breast development may just be beginning in some girls at
fourteen but in others may have started as early as age eight.
The number of years it takes for the breasts to completely
mature also varies greatly. Each person's body has its own
timetable for developing, and there is no way to speed the
process up or slow it down.

Whether you choose to wear a bra or not is a personal
choice; wearing or not wearing a bra has no effect on breast
development. But if most of your friends are wearing bras,
you may feel more comfortable if you do so as well. Before
deciding, you may want to try on several sizes and styles. In
the earlier growth stages, very soft, expandable bras made
especially for girls in their teens are the most comfortable.
Your mother, an older sister, or friends can help you shop
for one when you're ready.

6 **Dear Dr. Wilcox: How important is it, really, to wear
a bra? I am fifteen years old and have very small
breasts. I do not wear a bra for this reason but am
concerned about the effects of not doing so. I am
physically active and very slim.**

Whether to wear, or not wear, a bra is a personal choice and a matter of comfort. Many women find *not* wearing a bra very comfortable, particularly if the breasts are small. It is often fashion, not health, that dictates whether or not a bra "should" be worn. Nevertheless, everyone is affected by gravity, and eventually gravity will win out and cause breasts of any size to sag to some degree, especially if they've had no support for years. (Young women can probably go without the support of a bra for several years without any long-term effects.)

Women with heavier breasts may be uncomfortable without a bra, particularly when they participate in sports and other physical activities.

Dear Dr. Wilcox: I am almost sixteen. You could never tell if you saw my body. It looks like that of a twelve-year-old. I am tall, 5 ft 6 in (168 cm), and I guess that's why people know I'm older. My problem is that I am very, very flat-chested. Will I ever grow? Why are some girls so much bigger than others? Is there any way I could increase my bustline?

7

P.S. Being flat-chested is not hereditary in either of my parents' families. Also, I started to grow in about sixth grade but never got past a size 34AA.

Speed of breast development and ultimate breast size vary greatly from one female to the next; both pattern of development and size are influenced by heredity, as you know, but there are other factors as well. If, for example, you are thin, there will be less adipose tissue (fat) available for the breasts, and it is the amount of fat deposited in the breasts that determines size. Some very athletic women with little extra fat on their bodies find that, although they aren't underweight, their breasts also tend to be small.

At your age, however, you may not yet have completed puberty. If besides having little or no breast development, you have not begun to menstruate, you should see your doctor to find out if there is an endocrine (glandular) problem delaying the onset. If you are menstruating, the amount of breast development present is normal for you at this stage of life.

Dear Dr. Wilcox: I am a seventeen-year-old girl who has an embarrassing question to ask you. Is there any way one can increase one's bust size without going through surgery? I have read in some magazine ads of a cream that has ten thousand units of

8

estrogenic hormones that supposedly increase one's bust. Does it really work? What are estrogenic hormones?

Breast size is determined by the amount of fat tissue in the breasts, and this in turn is primarily determined by heredity. Creams, lotions, and other methods for supposedly increasing breast size do *not* work. There is no available method of increasing breast size other than surgery. Women may, however, notice an increase or decrease in breast size with variations in their total body weight, and a woman whose chest muscles are well toned through exercise may feel that her breasts are higher and firmer. Good posture may also emphasize the bust, whereas slouching de-emphasizes it. Overall fitness, although it won't actually increase breast size, can often help one appreciate and become comfortable with one's own body.

Do estrogens play a role in breast development? Yes, but trying to increase the amount or effect of estrogen with medication or creams is not a way to grow bigger breasts— it just doesn't work that way (incidentally, though, some women do notice a small amount of breast enlargement when they take birth control pills, which *do* contain estrogen). Estrogens are one of the female hormones in your body; they work internally as part of a complicated hormonal system. They have a number of effects, one of which is to initiate breast development. Fat is deposited in the breasts, the support tissue enlarges, and the milk duct system within the breast grows. But the degree of response of the breast to the hormone is part of your heredity, and your breast size will most likely be similar to that of other women in your family.

9 **Dear Dr. Wilcox: I am seventeen years old and have a flat chest. It really bothers me, especially when I am wearing a bathing suit. Everyone stares at me, and I do have big hips so I look out of proportion. I saw on TV once that they can enlarge breasts with an operation. Do you think it would be wise to do this? How much would it cost?**

Augmentation mammoplasty is a surgical procedure for enlarging the breasts. The cost ranges from about $800 to $1,500. Breast-shaped implants—bags of a saline (salt-water) solution and gel—are inserted beneath the natural breast tissue. The patient and plastic surgeon choose the size and shape of the implant prior to surgery and base this choice on the patient's body build and desired result.

The plastic surgeon always carefully evaluates his or her patient's health, expectations, and alternatives prior to agreeing to operate. As with any operation, there are certain associated risks (such as reaction to the anesthetic and risk of infection) that will be discussed. Perhaps more important, however, is discussing the patient's expectations; plastic surgery doesn't cure all of one's problems, nor can it completely alter one's body. And because one's feelings about one's body may change greatly during adolescence, many plastic surgeons will not perform augmentation surgery until a woman is in her twenties, although they may be willing to *discuss* it earlier.

Think carefully about your reasons for considering surgery, evaluate your options (improved fitness, for example), and then, if you are still interested, discuss it with your family doctor, who could refer you to a surgeon. But keep in mind that it may well be several years before you can have the operation performed.

Dear Dr. Wilcox: I have a problem that is embarrassing. I am a fairly attractive sixteen-year-old girl, 5 ft 8 in (173 cm), 125 lb (57 kg). The problem is that I am flat-chested.

10

I've heard that the only way to enlarge the breasts is through surgery, but is it true your breasts will begin to sag and hang two or three years later? If it is true that gaining weight enlarges the breasts, then perhaps I could gain the weight needed, then lose it only in the places wanted, leaving the breasts larger. Augmentation mammoplasty is the surgical procedure used to enlarge the breasts, and a well-performed mammoplasty will not lead to ptosis (sagging).

As for gaining weight, it will often increase breast size because of increased fat deposits in the breasts. If weight decreases, however, breast size usually does as well, regardless of attempts to "spot reduce" only. Good posture, too, helps emphasize the bust. Perhaps the easiest way to solve your problem is to work on becoming generally physically fit. Being fit can increase your feeling of well-being, confidence, and appreciation of your own body. And becoming comfortable with your body can greatly increase its attractiveness.

Dear Dr. Wilcox: I am thirteen years old, 5 ft 4 in (163 cm) tall, and weigh 115 lb (52 kg). I have very large breasts. I envy girls in my school who are small,

11

look fragile, and are flat-chested. When I'm with them, I feel so big and so old because nobody else looks like that. I want to lose weight so maybe my breasts will grow smaller. Will that work? Mostly I wear large, loose clothing, and sometimes that makes me feel safe. But I know that isn't the answer. I also started to slouch, which suddenly became a habit. My parents get very disgusted. Can you help me?

It is true that if you lose weight, your breasts will *probably* become somewhat smaller (when you lose weight, you lose it everywhere). But you are not overweight, and weight reduction is a drastic and hazardous solution that endangers your health and does not guarantee the results you want.

At thirteen, you already have fully mature breasts. This is perfectly normal, though only about 10 percent of girls your age have reached this stage. More than 90 percent will have at least some hint of breast development at thirteen, and 50 percent will have significantly but not fully developed breasts. You are well within the normal range but slightly ahead of some of the other girls your age. Within the next year many of them will catch up.

Clothes that fit well and are comfortable can help you feel more confident. There are also bras available called "minimizers" that de-emphasize breast size yet provide good support. Perhaps at this stage, this style might help you feel more comfortable.

If you can share your feelings with someone you trust (your mother?), you may be surprised how helpful she can be. Just remember, you are not alone with the type of feelings you are experiencing.

12 Dear Dr. Wilcox: I have a very close friend who is planning to have a breast reduction operation. She is 5 ft 2 in (157 cm) tall and weighs 170 lb (77 kg). Her bra size is DD. She expects that this operation will make her a size B. Frankly, I can't see what more this operation could do that dieting wouldn't accomplish, and the arguing that we have been doing has really hurt our relationship. Do you have any suggestions?

Although weight reduction may often decrease the size of the breasts to some degree, it might not solve all the problems your friend may be experiencing. With very large breasts, drooping may be a problem, and even if the size is reduced, the normal supporting tissue may have been so damaged that drooping persists. Surgery can correct this and other more immediate problems such as backache, shoulder pain, skin damage from bra straps, skin eruptions under the breasts, breast pain, and problems with posture, all of which can be associated with having very heavy breasts.

Each case is individual, and the pros and cons of surgery must be weighed in each situation. Sometimes surgery offers the best solution.

Dear Dr. Wilcox: I am a fourteen-year-old girl. One of my breasts is two bra sizes bigger than the other, so it is very hard to find a bra to fit. But worst of all, it is very visible. I always have my arms crossed and wear baggy clothing. I am terribly scared to wear bathing suits. I have seen breast enlarging creams but never tried them. I have tried exercises but none work. I don't think that I am the only one to have this extremely embarrassing problem.

13

You are right that you aren't alone with this problem. Human beings simply aren't perfectly symmetrical. When breast development begins, the breasts may develop at different rates, and a size difference may occur that is quite dramatic though temporary. Once the body has matured to its adult configuration, the breasts become more equal in size. If you've not fully matured yet, your breasts may become more symmetrical. In the meantime, don't bother trying exercises or creams, as there are none available that will equalize the breasts. What you can do is fit your bra to the larger breast and pad the cup on the smaller side. Under comfortably fitting clothes, the difference should be unnoticeable. Look for a bathing suit with which you could use a similar padding-one-side technique. One girl I know (her size difference was greater than yours) tried a store that specialized in lingerie for women who have had a mastectomy (a breast removed surgically for medical reasons). She found a swimsuit that completely camouflaged the difference.

If the size difference still bothers you once your body is fully mature, the only way to make the breasts equal in size is through surgery: either the larger breast is reduced or the smaller one made larger. You could explore this alternative with your doctor in a few years if it were something you wanted to consider.

Dear Dr. Wilcox: I have what are called inverted nipples. I thought that by the time I finished developing this would change, but it hasn't. I'm now eighteen

14

years old and have stopped growing, so I gather that
if it hasn't changed by now, it never will.

When showering after physical education class in
school, I get really embarrassed and feel like a freak!
I came across this condition in a medical book, and
it was listed under "sexual deviations." Is there anything that can be done to make my breasts normal?
I hope the medical book you saw was an old, out-of-date
one, because inverted nipples are *not* in themselves considered abnormal or pathological. Only when a previously
erect nipple becomes inverted permanently does the inversion signify a medical abnormality; when this happens, a
doctor should be consulted because this change may mean
there is a growth in the breast that is pulling the nipple
inward.

In your case, however, the inversion is not abnormal. The
ability of the nipple to become erect (point outward) depends upon the amount of erectile tissue present. This is a
special, very elastic tissue with many nerve endings. The
amount of erectile tissue present varies normally from person to person, and there is no way to change it. Your breasts
are perfectly normal.

15 Dear Dr. Wilcox: I'm a seventeen-year-old female with
a hidden problem only my mother and I know about.
My nipples are not normal. They sink in and ten
minutes later they jut out. If I ever married, I don't
know how I'd face this terrible situation. I don't know
how my husband would react. Is it hereditary, and is
this a common abnormality? Will I be able to nurse
babies?
What you describe sounds completely normal. The areola is
the circle of skin that surrounds the nipple and is darker
(or pinker) than the skin of the breast itself. Nipples can lie
flat, so they just look like a little circle in the middle of the
areola, they may stick out, or they may turn inward, looking like little craters (the nipples are then said to be inverted). But in most women, if the nipple is stimulated by,
say, touch, cold, or sexual arousal, the nipple will become
erect: it will stick out more than before and feel stiffer.

Erectile tissue is what allows the nipple to stick out when
stimulated. The amount of erectile tissue present in the
nipples varies from one woman to the next. If there is very
little or none, the nipples are always inverted and never be-

come erect. Trying to breast-feed might be more complicated for these women, but otherwise it causes no problems.

Dear Dr. Wilcox: I am fourteen years old and have not started menstruating yet. I do not have a flat chest. All of my friends have started already, and I feel abnormal and alone. **16**
Each person's body has its own internal timetable that can't be speeded up or slowed down. Often a girl's age at the start of menstruation is similar to what her mother's was: if her mother experienced it later than average, she is more likely to begin later too. Because twelve is just an average age for starting to menstruate, you at fourteen are still well within the normal age range (nine to seventeen). Your breast development shows that your body is producing the appropriate hormones necessary for menstruation.

Your periods probably will start within the next two years or so. Try not to worry, and if you have further questions, your family doctor will be very willing to answer them.

Dear Dr. Wilcox: I am fifteen years old, and I have had my period for three years. For the past year it has been coming about every fifty days instead of twenty-eight. I know it varies from person to person, but is fifty days too long apart? **17**
At least 25 percent of all girls experience some irregularity of their menstrual cycles in the four years after their periods first begin. This is particularly common during the first two years, when the system of hormones (body chemicals) responsible for regulating menstruation is not yet fully mature. Some girls may find it takes as long as seven years for the system to become stable.

As you know, the length of time from the beginning of one period to the beginning of the next varies from person to person but usually averages twenty-one to thirty-five days. Regardless of the length of the cycle, ovulation usually occurs about two weeks before the start of the next period.

When periods are more than forty days apart, the pattern is called oligomenorrhea, which means infrequent periods. If periods actually stop, it's called amenorrhea. If a person ever misses three periods, she should see a doctor, because amenorrhea may be a symptom of serious health problems. However, if a woman is having sexual intercourse and misses just one period, she may be pregnant and should see her doctor immediately.

As I mentioned, your fifty-day cycle could just be a sign that the system is not yet fully mature. But it can also mean that a medical problem is affecting the hormones, particularly if your periods were regular at first and then became irregular. Stress, illness, and major weight loss or gain are common factors that can interfere with normal cycles. Problems with the thyroid or pituitary gland or with the ovaries are just a few other possibilities.

When irregular periods have a medical cause, there may be other symptoms as well. For example, weight change, intolerance of heat or cold, and diarrhea or constipation can be further signs of thyroid problems; headaches or breast discharge may be the result of problems with the pituitary gland (a tiny gland in your head that regulates all kinds of hormones), and excessive body and facial hair may signal problems with the ovaries. See your doctor to discuss your particular situation.

18 **Dear Dr. Wilcox: I have a problem I am too embarrassed to ask anyone about, and I am literally getting tired of it. I am twenty-one years old now, and ever since I got my period at thirteen it has been fairly heavy, it has lasted eight days, and it has come roughly every thirty days. Over the last year or so it has been coming every twenty-four days, still lasting for a heavy eight days. This means that I am menstruating exactly one-third of the time, or 122 days per year. I feel that this is too much!**

I usually feel tired, and I thought that inactivity was the cause, so I started exercising more. Unfortunately, this seems to make me even more tired. Do you have any suggestions for me?

The length of the normal menstrual cycle can vary greatly, from twenty-one to thirty-eight days; only one-sixth of all women will have the classic twenty-eight-day cycle.

Most women will experience three to seven days of bleeding during menstruation. Average blood loss is around 1 to 1¼ oz (30 to 35 ml), with women under twenty having lighter flows and those over thirty having heavier flows. More than three-quarters of the blood is lost during the first two days of the period.

Menstrual discharge contains not only blood but vaginal and cervical cells, mucus and secretions, endometrial tissue (the spongy lining from the uterus), plus a wide variety of enzymes (body chemicals). Because iron is lost in the menstrual blood, an iron-deficiency anemia may result. This is particularly true when the blood loss has been heavy, as yours appears to be, with the average loss greater than 2 oz (60 ml) each period. A heavy blood loss is particularly likely to lead to anemia when few iron-rich foods are eaten; teenage girls are notorious for eating iron-poor diets. Fatigue can be a symptom of anemia.

You should see your doctor to have your problem examined more thoroughly and have appropriate blood tests performed. Although you feel sensitive about it, yours is a very legitimate concern.

Dear Dr. Wilcox: I am a seventeen-year-old who has a major problem with her period. In my first year I was always fairly regular. In my second and third years I was more irregular and would skip a few months at a time. Then I would have a longer and heavier period the next month.

19

In the last five or six months I have been having my period nonstop, like a five-month period with the bleeding becoming stronger at the top of every month. When menstrual periods come regularly, it is easy to forget that this seemingly simple event is actually the result of a very complicated process. This simple regularity depends upon very intricate, delicately balanced systems of hormones. Trouble in any part of the system upsets the schedule, and it is not uncommon for women to miss a period, or even two, at various times. Stress can affect the hormone system and is the most common cause of temporary disruptions in menstrual cycles.

Your excessive bleeding is most likely a sign of a problem somewhere in your hormone system. For example, there may be an imbalance in the series of chemicals directly responsible for the regularity of your periods. Problems with other kinds of hormones, such as thyroid hormones, can also cause irregular bleeding.

Your problem needs to be sorted through by a doctor. He or she can determine the cause.

Dear Dr. Wilcox: In the last year I have lost a fair amount of weight. Because of this (and the fact that I'm relatively athletic), I have not had my period for about ten months now. I got my period when I was eleven and it has always been right on time. I'm fif-

20

**teen now. Could I get pregnant if I were to have in-
tercourse? And if so, what are my chances of it?**

For menstruation to occur, there is a critical weight and
percentage of body fat that must be reached and maintained (generally, 22 percent of body weight in fat is needed
for regular cycles to be maintained). Because of this, *some*
very athletic women with extremely low levels of body fat do
experience menstrual irregularities.

Of concern in your case is that you have lost a significant
amount of weight and are now experiencing amenorrhea (lack
of periods). Although menstrual patterns may alter with
weight reduction, amenorrhea can be a sign of a serious
weight-loss problem such as anorexia nervosa. There are
other medical causes as well (thyroid problems, pregnancy,
etc.), and you should see your doctor soon to have your
problem checked out.

In answer to your question: yes, pregnancy can occur
during an episode of amenorrhea. The problem is that when
your body is re-establishing its normal monthly cycle, ovulation—and therefore the fertile part of the cycle—occurs
before any period returns. If you have intercourse around
this time, pregnancy can result, and when you skip your
next period because of the pregnancy, you may think it is
just part of your problem with amenorrhea. When a woman
is sexually active, birth control methods must therefore be
used during an episode of amenorrhea to prevent unplanned pregnancy, just as they must be used when a woman
has regular periods.

It is very important for you to see your doctor. Make an
appointment soon.

See 53.

21 **Dear Dr. Wilcox: Every month during my period I get
very painful cramps. They sometimes get so bad I
have to stay in bed for a whole day. What can I do?
Also, because of the cramps would it be unwise to
wear a tampon?**

Dysmenorrhea, or menstrual cramps, is an extremely common problem. More than half of all women experience some
discomfort during menstruation, and 10 percent have pain
that is severe enough to interfere with their normal daily
activities.

So-called primary dysmenorrhea is what women generally
experience and is part of the normal process of menstruation. Secondary dysmenorrhea is much less common and is

caused by a medical problem, with the pain often getting worse period after period. Primary dysmenorrhea is probably the cause of your problem.

The pain of dysmenorrhea usually starts when the period begins, although many women may notice a feeling of heaviness or a dull ache in the lower abdomen the day or so before the bleeding actually starts. The pain usually lasts hours but can last several days and often increases and decreases in waves. Although it is usually centered in the lower mid-abdomen, it can also spread to the lower back and thighs. It may be accompanied by such symptoms as nausea, loss of appetite, fatigue, abdominal bloating, breast tenderness, headache, or diarrhea.

Fortunately, these symptoms tend to get less and less severe as women get older. The question, of course, is what to do in the meantime.

For years, "painkillers," heat, rest, and exercises were the mainstays of treatment and may still be sufficient for moderate symptoms. But for severe pain, much more effective medications are now available. It has been found that women who have very painful periods have in the lining of the uterus higher than average amounts of prostaglandins, body chemicals that increase the amount of "spasm" in the uterus and thereby increase pain. But antiprostaglandin medications can block these effects, and taken early in the period before the pain becomes established they may greatly decrease discomfort.

If they're not effective, the birth control pill may be prescribed. (The Pill prevents ovulation, the release of an egg from the ovary. Periods that occur without ovulation first taking place hurt less.) See your doctor soon.

In answer to your second question, tampons have no effect on dysmenorrhea.

Dear Dr. Wilcox: I just started to menstruate a little while ago, and there's just one problem: I don't get cramps or any other pain at all. I talked to my mom about it, but she didn't help much. She just said "don't worry" and that it was very rare. I don't want to get cramps, so I think I am lucky, but could you explain why I don't get them? **22**

The amount of discomfort experienced during menstruation varies from person to person and also from period to period. In most women it rarely interferes with normal activities.

When cramping does occur, it is always during what we call ovulatory periods, the type most adult women have; this means that approximately two weeks before menstruation starts, an ovum (egg) is released from the ovary to set off hormonal changes in the body that lead to a period. These hormones stimulate the lining of the uterus (womb) to grow, and the blood you pass during menstruation is this lining being shed.

When you've just started to menstruate, it is very normal to have periods even when an egg has not been released; these are called anovulatory periods. Because they lack the hormone shifts of ovulatory periods, they don't produce cramps during menstruation.

23 **Dear Dr. Wilcox: I have been encountering problems with my period for about six months. The trouble arises after my period has ostensibly stopped. About a week after it has ended, I've been experiencing a light discharge that is very similar to my period. There is no pain accompanying the discharge, but it usually occurs every two months or so and lasts a few days. When it happens I wear a sanitary napkin.**
It is possible that the discharge you describe is a normal event that many women experience, but you should see your doctor to make sure.

There are two conditions that are linked to ovulation (the release of the egg from the ovary): mid-cycle pain, called Mittelschmerz, and mid-cycle bleeding or discharge, called Kleine Regel. They may occur together or separately.

For the woman who menstruates every twenty-eight days, ovulation occurs around day 14 of her monthly cycle (the first day of her period is considered day 1). If your period lasts about five days and the discharge occurs about a week later, then it is occurring around mid-cycle, at the time of ovulation.

Kleine Regel ("little period") can be a brownish discharge or bright red bleeding and can last an hour or two or three days. In some cases the discharge is so heavy the woman may think she menstruates twice a month. Why some women experience this discharge is not known. It is thought that in these cases the endometrium (lining of the uterus) may be especially sensitive to the temporary decrease in estrogen (a female hormone) that accompanies ovulation. This small drop in estrogen level is enough to make the endometrium unstable and some of it is shed. It can be an annoying event but is not harmful.

Mittelschmerz, or mid-cycle pain, is more common than Kleine Regel. It can last hours or several days. It is thought the pain may be caused by tiny amounts of internal bleeding that can accompany the release of the egg from the ovary. Again, no treatment is needed.

Although these events are normal and may apply to you, you have experienced a change in your menstrual pattern. Discuss it with your doctor to make sure it is normal for you.

Dear Dr. Wilcox: What kind of protection do you recommend? Maxipads can be so uncomfortable, and I'm scared of getting that disease if I wear tampons. **24**
I assume the disease you are concerned about is toxic shock syndrome (TSS), a serious but rare infection caused by bacteria called *Staphylococcus aureus.* Before discussing ways to minimize one's risk of contracting this rare condition, it is important to put the situation into perspective.

Across North America, it is estimated that of every one hundred thousand women of menstrual age, only six will develop toxic shock syndrome each year. However, 4 percent of TSS cases occur in men and 8 percent among women *not* menstruating. TSS during menstruation has been associated with tampon use and particularly with continuous use during the period. Some super-absorbent brands of tampons—now off the market—apparently greatly increased the risk because they may have lowered the magnesium level in the vagina, and somehow this allowed the staphylococci to produce more toxin, or poison.

Obviously, the risk of developing TSS is very small indeed, and there are ways of using tampons that may further reduce the already small risk. The major recommendation is to use tampons for only part of the period, occasionally substituting pads; for example, minipads on a light-flow day or a pad at night. Other suggestions include changing tampons every four hours and avoiding both deodorant-containing tampons (deodorant isn't needed anyway) and the extra-super-absorbent tampons. Pads that are made of super-absorbent material, on the other hand, are safe and are often thinner than ordinary pads.

Choosing to use primarily pads or tampons is really a case of personal preference. The risk of TSS is very small, but using the tampon wisely and as directed may further lower this already small risk.

25 **Dear Dr. Wilcox: I am a victim of premenstrual syndrome. I suffer from all the classic symptoms: water retention, food cravings, depression, and a short temper. My purpose in writing to you is that I know there are many girls who are not aware that PMS exists and who may think they are abnormal or going crazy because of their symptoms. Can you discuss PMS a bit?**

Premenstrual syndrome (PMS) is a complex group of symptoms that many women experience recurrently, starting ten to fourteen days prior to each menstrual period. Authorities suggest that 25 to 35 percent of all women experience some form of PMS at some time in their lives, and if those who experience only changes in mood premenstrually are added, the percentage rises to 75 percent.

PMS is real and isn't just "all in your head." The range of symptoms of PMS is vast—more than 150 have been catalogued over the years. The most common include mood swings and irritability, headache, breast discomfort and swelling, abdominal bloating, cravings for sweets or salt, and menstrual cramps (dysmenorrhea). There are many theories about the causes of PMS, but it now seems to be a problem involving hormones called endorphins and vasopressin.

Before diagnosing PMS, it is important to make sure the symptoms do correlate with the menstrual cycle. Keeping a calendar record of symptoms, menstruation, and even your temperature (taken first thing in the morning for five minutes before getting out of bed) can help your doctor make the diagnosis.

No cure-all is yet available, but treatment is aimed at the dominant symptoms. Much of it is controversial at present. Discussing your own particular case with your doctor will help him or her decide if you might benefit from treatment, which can include vitamin B_6, specific hormones, or special diuretics ("water pills") that, unlike most diuretics, help keep the element potassium in the body.

As for menstrual cramps, an antiprostaglandin drug has also been tried. (In PMS there seems to be an excess of prostaglandin, a body chemical that, incidentally, has nothing to do with the prostate gland.)

Regular exercise can help and is something you can institute on your own. Having someone supportive to count on will also help, as will remembering that PMS is real, that it will get better with time, and that research will eventually find definite help.

Dear Dr. Wilcox: I am a teenage girl with a problem that I am too embarrassed to go to a doctor about. One side of my labia is quite a bit larger than the other side, which is barely existent. I am worried.   **26**

Just as a person may have one hand, one foot, or one breast that's larger than the other, so can the right and left labia differ in size.

A woman's external genitals include two sets of labia. The labia majora are the thicker, outer folds of skin, or lips, and are covered with pubic hair; the labia minora are the smaller, thinner, hairless skin folds that are on either side of the vagina. Although the right and left sides of both sets of labia tend to be similar in size, there is often a size difference. It generally is not the sign of any kind of medical problem.

A recent or increasing unexplained change in any area of one's body is, however, a different matter. And that includes unusual changes *anywhere,* including your big toe, left breast, or labia. Such a change can be a sign of a medical problem and should be checked out.

BOYS

Dear Dr. Wilcox: I am twelve years old. My penis hasn't grown yet, but I think my testicles have, and the skin covering them is darker. Is this normal?   **27**

Yes. The first change that occurs when a boy begins to mature physically is exactly what you describe. This happens usually around age twelve but can occur as early as nine or as late as fourteen. Very soon after, the penis gradually increases in length, usually reaching adult size an average of three years after growth begins. Pubic hair generally starts to grow around age 12½, and if it does start then, adult amounts are present by age 15 or 16. Just before the pubic hair reaches an adult distribution, hair begins to grow in the axilla (underarms) and on the face, first at the corners of the upper lip, then on the chin, and finally on the cheeks, usually when the genitals are reaching adult proportions.

Each person has his own built-in timetable that determines just when these changes will occur. The sequence, too, may vary but generally follows the pattern described.

28 **Dear Dr. Wilcox: I am a male of almost twenty years of age. My problem is that my body is so far behind in development. It is very embarrassing since I get my ID doublechecked everywhere I go. I have heard that females who have a sex change are given some type of hormone so that they get facial hair growth. If this is true, what is it called and where could I buy it? If it isn't true, what could I do to speed things up?**

Delay of maturation is a more common complaint among males than females. The most common cause is "constitutional delay." Basically, this means that, although the timing of body changes is later than average, the timetable is *normal* for that individual; maturation will be completed, but later than average. In such situations there will often be a family history of late development with either a brother or father having a similar pattern, even achieving adult height after twenty.

After a thorough evaluation your doctor can tell you whether or not what you are experiencing is a constitutional delay. There are also many medical problems that can cause delayed maturation, although these are quite rare. Depending on initial results, your doctor may want you to see an endocrinologist, a specialist in problems involving hormones and glands.

The hormones you refer to are types of androgens, or male hormones. They must be prescribed and used only with a doctor's supervision. They would only be used in very specific cases of delayed maturation (for example, where there is evidence of true failure of the body to produce the hormones).

29 **Dear Dr. Wilcox: I am a fifteen-year-old male who is 5 ft 5 in (165 cm) tall. Although this height may not be considered too short for my age, I am fully convinced that I will not grow any taller. My father is 5 ft 8 in (173 cm). I believe I had my growth spurt quite early in life and have grown only ¼ in (6 mm) since last year.**

Do you know of anything I can do to increase my height? I have heard of numerous things from dif-

ferent sources. Some are: taking vitamin B$_{12}$, getting hormone shots, hanging upside-down from one's feet every day for half an hour (a doctor claims this has increased his height by 3 in/8 cm), sending away for books that tell you how to increase your height (one has a money-back guarantee that you will grow 3 to 4 in/5 to 10 cm in ten weeks or less), and playing basketball.

Please help. I seem to have developed an inferiority complex over this problem and fall into deep depression constantly.

The growth spurt for boys occurs between 12½ and 15, when a boy may grow as much as 3 to 5 in (7 to 12 cm) in height in one year. Most of this increase in height is due to increased length of the trunk (main body) rather than to increased leg length. After the spurt is over, growth continues but more and more slowly until age seventeen or eighteen, when a boy is very close to his adult height.

At fifteen, you may not yet have reached your full height. But in any case, aside from making sure to get good nutrition, there really is nothing a normal, healthy person can do to increase his or her ultimate height because this potential is genetically determined. Unfortunately, there is no scientific evidence that the remedies you list have a significant impact on growth. Good posture and good muscle tone, however, can make anyone of any height look healthier, and these can be achieved through regular exercise.

It is important to discuss your concerns with your physician. The depression you feel should not be ignored because it sounds as though it is interfering with your confidence and your enjoyment of life. Arrange for an appointment so there will be plenty of time to talk.

Dear Dr. Wilcox: I am a nineteen-year-old male. Even though I act and feel my age, I know I don't look it. I have a skinny body, practically hairless. This is an embarrassing problem, and because of it I always decline any swimming or hot-tub invitations. I feel as though I'm missing out on the fun and I've developed quite a complex. Ever since seventh or eighth grade I've been behind other guys my age in physical development. I've started working out on weights, but that won't put hair on my chest. What's wrong with

30

me? Is this a common problem? And is there anything I can do to speed up my physical development?

The amount of body hair you will ultimately have is primarily determined by heredity, so there isn't much you can do
to change it. Many adult men have very little body hair. Your
basic body build is also genetically determined, but it *can*
be altered to some degree by body building and exercise.

During the teen years the arms and legs lengthen before
muscle size increases. As a result, after one's great spurt in
height that occurs around age fourteen, there is often a time
of looking rather long, lean, and gangly.

Between the ages of twelve and sixteen, a boy's measurable strength may more than double. The peak increase in
strength happens about one and a half years after the growth
spurt in height. It is often recommended that boys wanting
to intensively build muscles and strength wait until they
reach this stage. Since you probably are reaching the end
of the natural increase in musculature, it would be an entirely appropriate time to try to improve your fitness.

Joining a good fitness club with experienced instructors
can help you improve your fitness, muscle strength, and body
image. To ensure that you are eating a balanced diet, go to
your library and borrow a book on basic nutrition. *(See 39.)*

31 Dear Dr. Wilcox: I am a fifteen-year-old boy and I'm
very embarrassed because I have this high-pitched
voice. Most kids don't mind, but there are always a
few people who bug me about it. It has now got so
bad that I am ashamed to talk, afraid of what people
might think. I was wondering, could my voice be
changing? If not, and I'm stuck with this forever, is
there an operation, perhaps plastic surgery, that could
deepen my voice?

Deepening of the voice occurs relatively late in adolescence.
The timing of the voice change varies greatly from person
to person. Although one boy may have a deep voice at fifteen
and another a high voice, *both* are normal; they just have
different timetables for this change. The people who are
bugging you are obviously ignorant of this fact, and I would
put very little value on their opinions!

Voice change is a gradual process. As the levels of testos-
terone (a male hormone) increase, the voice box gradually
enlarges, and the vocal cords lengthen. Once fully mature,
this larger apparatus produces a deeper voice. But when the

process first starts, boys may find they experience sudden changes in pitch (cracking) while talking. Eventually, this effect resolves.

Plastic surgery has no role in altering one's voice. For adults who do wish to change their voices, speech therapists and coaches, widely used by actors and actresses, can be of great help. Your current problem, however, sounds as though it is one that will resolve as your larynx matures. Give it time.

Dear Dr. Wilcox: I am an eighteen-year-old male and a virgin. When we are showering, the guys in the gym make fun of the small size of my penis. I am afraid to get intimate with a girl because of its size. What is the average size of an erect and nonerect penis? **32**

The teasing that characterizes the teen years—and that you are experiencing now—is a product of the discomfort adolescents feel with their own bodies; when everyone grows up a bit and becomes more confident and comfortable with his body, the teasing stops.

When flaccid (not erect), the average length of an adult penis is 3 to 4 in (7 to 10 cm) with a diameter of 1 to 1½ in (2.5 to 4 cm). But the range of "normal" varies greatly, and a penis can be longer or shorter (or wider or narrower) than this and still be completely normal.

The size when flaccid also may have little bearing on the size when erect. A "smaller" penis might enlarge quite a bit with an erection, whereas a "larger" one may become firm with erection but not necessarily that much bigger. When erect, the length of the average adult penis is somewhere around 6 in (15 cm), but again there is great variation in what is normal. And furthermore, penis size has nothing to do with one's ability to enjoy sexual intercourse or with the enjoyment one's sexual partner will experience.

Dear Dr. Wilcox: I am a nineteen-year-old male. I have noticed that my testicles can elevate to the base of my penis. I also find that when I need to clear my bowels or when I have an erection, they usually elevate even higher (almost inside me). There is no abnormal discrepancy between the sizes of my testicles. I don't have an empty scrotum. Could this all be the result of tension, or is there possibly a greater problem that I should be aware of? **33**

The scrotum (the pouch that contains the testicles) has the ability to contract or relax and can bring the testicles close to the body (with contraction) or can suspend them away from the body when the muscles in the scrotum relax. The scrotum's "job" is to keep the temperature of the testicles constant. If you have a fever or if the weather is hot, the scrotal muscles relax, and the testicles are kept cooler by hanging away from your body. If you are cold, the scrotum pulls the testicles up to your body to keep them warm. This is important because if the temperature of the testicles is inappropriate, sperm production can be adversely affected.

Other stimuli can also cause the testicles to be brought close to the body. Erection of the penis, rectal stimulation (the feeling of needing to have a bowel movement), and fear can all cause the scrotum to contract. Even a gentle stroke on the inside of the thigh can cause the testicles to elevate within the scrotum; this is called the cremasteric reflex. Some men note that with extreme elevation of the testicles, one or both may seem to be temporarily up inside the body; when this occurs, the testicles are said to be retractile.

The scrotum can, then, keep the testicles very close to the body at times, just as you describe. If you notice that the scrotum can also be very loose, such as when you've had a hot bath, then it is doing its job, and the elevation you notice at other times is entirely normal.

34 **Dear Dr. Wilcox: My scrotum seems like it's covered with lots of little goose pimples. Is this normal?**
Yes. There are actually many tiny hair follicles scattered over the surface of the scrotum, and this can give it the appearance you describe.

35 **Dear Dr. Wilcox: I am sixteen years old and until now have never given much thought to my foreskin not being able to retract or even be pulled back on my penis, even though there is some pain during erection. Is this common? I would like to have it corrected.**
Usually by the time an uncircumcised male is four, his foreskin can be gently pulled back to expose the head of the penis. This is important for good hygiene and prevention of infection in the area.

Phimosis is the medical term for the condition in which the foreskin is too tight to allow it to be retracted. It is estimated that 2 to 10 percent of all uncircumcised males develop phimosis. (In circumcision all or part of the foreskin is removed so that the head of the penis is always exposed.)

If phimosis leads to infection, adhesions or scar tissue may result that can make the phimosis more pronounced. Phimosis can interfere with erection. If the opening at the tip of the foreskin becomes very small, it can obstruct urination.

The condition can be easily corrected. Your family doctor can refer you to a urologist, a specialist who can deal with the problem.

Dear Dr. Wilcox: I would like your advice on a problem. Unlike most other infant boys, I was not circumcised at birth. Now that I am seventeen, I am seriously considering the operation. Do you feel, from a medical viewpoint, that circumcision is necessary? I am healthy and have no irritation or problem with my penis. **36**

The frequency and popularity of circumcision, the surgical removal of the foreskin, has varied greatly over the years and also from culture to culture. From the late 1940s to the early 1970s circumcision was routinely performed on most newborn males born in North America because the procedure was thought to provide a number of health benefits, such as helping to prevent cancer of the penis and, for the sexual partners of circumcised males, cancer of the cervix. These benefits, however, have since been questioned, and from the mid-1970s on, the official medical position was that there was no medical necessity for routine circumcision. (There is, of course, a deep religious basis for the procedure that makes circumcision a very important tradition in certain religions.)

Interestingly, however, some new studies indicate that the risk of urinary system infections may be greater in uncircumcised than in circumcised males. The medical debate, then, is hardly over.

In any case, there are two medical conditions that, it is generally agreed, definitely require circumcision. One is phimosis, a narrowing of the foreskin that interferes with erection and/or urination. The other is paraphimosis, in which the retracted foreskin is so tight that it cannot be moved and can actually interfere with the blood supply to the head of the penis. If you do not have either of these problems, then there is probably no *medical* reason for the procedure. If you want to discuss the question further, however, a urologist is the specialist to see.

TWO:

Weight, Fitness, and Body Image

The best exercise is that which employs the mind pleasantly. A good dose of exercise may be obtained in housework, and, if conducted with pleasure in work, may be of great physical advantage.

Mary Wood
What a Young Woman Ought to Know *(1898)*

From movie stars selling fitness books to doctors hawking magic diets they claim will help transform us into clones of Jamie Lee Curtis, we are surrounded by people telling us fit is fabulous, fat is scandalous, and the major goal of life should be to develop the perfect body.

Being fit *is* healthy—a person who is fit has more energy, a greater sense of well-being, and higher resistance to many diseases. But the body-conscious society we live in can also create stress: self-hatred if we vary from an unattainable ideal and frustration if we believe the myth that weight loss is the path to ultimate happiness and the faster we proceed along it, the better ("Never mind a balanced diet, just take these pills!"). The fitness craze, when carried to an extreme, may be just a repackaged version of our culture's old and unacceptable demand that people—particularly girls and women—must look a certain way.

The letters in this section reflect these fitness concerns, and the answers try to separate fitness fact from fads. We have purposely not included a height/weight chart. It is very difficult to describe ideal weights for anyone, let alone teenagers, who vary not only in bone structure and build but also in physical maturity. For example, one fourteen-year-old boy may be a 5 ft 8 in (173 cm), broad-shouldered, physically mature adult, while another may be in the midst of a growth spurt (en route to 6 ft 1 in/185 cm) and have the physique of a long-legged child: the first may be about 20 lb

(9 kg) heavier than the second, yet each is at a "normal" weight.

You and your weight needs can't be reduced to a series of numbers. It is much more complicated than that. If you think you are overweight or underweight, discuss it with a professional (school nurse, nutritionist, doctor), who can help you work out a realistic program based on sound nutrition and exercise.

Dear Dr. Wilcox: I'm a fourteen-year-old boy, 5 ft 7 in (170 cm) and 143 lb (65 kg). I am very large-boned and my arms are big because I lift weights. Would you please tell me how much I should weigh? Am I fat? **37**

"Should" is a dangerous word. Each person is so individual—with his or her own height, build, and level of activity—that it is difficult to make a blanket statement. What one can do, however, is look at average ranges of weight and height for specific age groups.

Although these ranges vary according to the population studied, the following ranges can be used for North American fourteen-year-old boys: 90 percent will be about 57 to 69 in (142 to 175 cm) in height, with 5 percent shorter and 5 percent taller; 90 percent will weigh about 77 to 160 lb (35 to 75 kg).

You are at the taller end of the height range for fourteen-year-olds, large-framed and obviously interested in fitness. From the information you give, it hardly sounds as though you are "fat." Perhaps a more useful question might be how "fit" you are; weight and percentage of body fat are just factors in this analysis. Your physical education teacher, school nurse, or doctor can tell you more about how to fully evaluate your fitness.

Dear Dr. Wilcox: I am twelve years old and 5 ft 2 in (159 cm) tall. My problem is my weight. I weigh 112 lb (51 kg). All my friends gasp when I tell them how much I weigh. They all weigh 85 lb (39 kg) or less. My parents tell me I am not one bit fat and I am not to worry about it. I am extremely strong for a girl, and my mom tells me all my weight is muscle. **38**

I know I can trust you to tell me if I am fat, because I am sick and tired of all this gasping from my skinny friends. I don't think I am that fat. But I think

I will quit exercising with my dad morning and night, because I don't need muscles, do I?

From the information you provide, it sounds as though you most certainly are not fat.

During adolescence, one's body changes very rapidly, but the age at which the major growth spurt occurs varies from person to person. Because of this, one twelve-year-old girl might, for example, be 4 ft 7 in (140 cm), weigh 67 lb (30 kg), and have no breast development; another might be 5 ft 5 in (165 cm), weigh 130 lb (59 kg), and look fully mature—and both are completely normal.

Among normal, healthy twelve-year-old girls 10 percent may be shorter and lighter or taller and heavier than these two examples. Your friends, therefore, may be simply maturing and growing at a different rate, and their lower weights don't mean that yours is too high for you.

But deciding whether someone is fat or not requires knowing more than just her height and weight. Bone structure (or build) and the ratio of fat to lean body mass are also important. Because you sound very physically fit and strong, you probably do not have excess fat on board (after puberty, girls' bodies are 20 percent fat and boys' are 10 percent). Muscle is heavier than fat, so a healthy, well-toned person may, in some cases, weigh more than he or she did before becoming fit.

Being healthy with well-toned muscles is desirable for both men and women. Enjoy your exercise, enjoy being fit, and don't let your friends worry you.

39 **Dear Dr. Wilcox: I am a sixteen-year-old girl. I think I am perfectly healthy, yet my mom and others think that I don't eat enough or eat the proper things. I agree that I don't eat much, and I usually don't like to eat good things (the only vegetables I eat are corn and peas). Because I don't eat much of the proper things, I thought you could suggest good vitamins or something to give me some of the nutrition I miss out on.**

You are right to be concerned about good nutrition, because it is essential to maintaining good health. More important, the eating habits you establish now will form the basis of a lifelong pattern that will help assure your good health in the future.

Vitamin pills are not the answer. Although we all require certain amounts of each vitamin every day to maintain our health, we also require minerals, such as iron, and need to balance the kinds of foods we eat so that we get the proper amount of protein, carbohydrates, fats, and fiber. Only food—not pills—can supply everything the body needs.

How do you learn about good nutrition? You can see your doctor. (He or she can, if necessary, refer you to a nutrition-ist or dietitian for review of your eating habits.) You can read about nutrition; there are many good books available in libraries and at bookstores. Or you can begin to establish healthy eating patterns by following the recommendations below; if you do, your diet will be balanced, and you will get all the vitamins and minerals you need.

The following are daily requirements during adolescence. Eat a variety of foods from each group.

1. Milk and milk products (such as cheese, yogurt): 3 to 4 servings.

2. Meat, fish, poultry, and "meat alternatives" (such as eggs, cheese, peanut butter, nuts, seeds, legumes—lentils, kidney beans, chick peas, etc.): 2 servings.

3. Whole-grain or enriched cereals and breads (includes pasta, muffins): 3 to 5 servings.

4. Fruit and vegetables (include green, leafy, yellow-or-ange, citrus fruits): 4 to 5 servings, at least 2 of which should be vegetables.

Dear Dr. Levine: I am an overweight fifteen-year-old girl, and lately my life has been pure hell. I moved into a new community and a new school, and as if it isn't hard enough for me to adjust to my new sur-roundings, my so-called baby fat has to further com-plicate things for me.

40

The boys in my grade (ninth) act like little fifth-graders. They bug me and taunt me in the halls. It never fails, and at the beginning of the year I cried every day. Every time I move away (which has been pretty often all my life), I always think that maybe the boys in my new school will be more mature, but they never are.

The area I moved into is one where everybody has gone to the same elementary schools and has known everybody else since they were very young. Since I am fairly new and also chubby, I feel alien and awk-ward. I have no trouble with girls. They either are nice and friendly or simply accept my presence. But

I also want guys to like me. If any of them are reading this, I hope they will see how immature they are. I am aware of my weight problem, and I do not need to be reminded every time I walk down the hall. Why can't they just accept me for who I am instead of getting hung up on how fat I am?

You are obviously a very bright and sensitive girl. Your letter, while painfully honest, shows exceptional understanding. Of course, the easiest answer to toss off would be to say: lose weight. And that is also the most difficult thing for you to do. Obesity is a highly complex problem—it involves heredity, constitution, psychology, and social pressures, to name but a few factors that affect it. I am sure that it is something you are wrestling with, possibly under considerable family pressure.

I am pleased, however, that the girls are more tolerant, or even more accepting. This may have something to do with their relative maturity, and that augurs well for the future. As the boys get older, their need to insult and gang up will diminish markedly. All your moves and recent changes have made things worse for you. Perhaps a stabilizing period can now set in.

In the meantime, you will have to pursue your interests, skills, and above all relationships that do give you satisfaction, enhancement, and recognition. I am confident you can do it.

41 **Dear Dr. Wilcox: I'm an eighteen-year-old female, 5 ft 4 in (163 cm) tall, and when I started dieting about a year ago I was 123 lb (56 kg). My goal was 115 lb (52 kg), but not much has changed since I started except that my eating habits are worse. After a few days of dieting, I feel so deprived I pig out. I end up eating more than I did when I wasn't on a diet.**

If you can change your approach to food, you can benefit not only physically but emotionally and nutritionally as well. Right now you see food simply as a source of calories. A great deal of effort is spent fighting this "enemy." If you can refocus all this work on learning to follow a sound diet that meets your body's vitamin, mineral, nutrient, *and* energy requirements, you can be healthier—and much less frustrated.

Your family doctor can help you find a nutritionist to review your diet and help you learn what your body needs not only to be "normal" weight but to be healthy as well. She or he can also help you decide what weight is realistic for you. *(See 39.)*

You certainly aren't alone in your extreme concern about weight. This overconcern is a real and potentially very dangerous problem that many teenage girls face. Studies have shown that many girls who *think* they are too fat are in fact *below* the average expected weight for their age, sex, height, and build.

Dear Dr. Wilcox: I am an eighteen-year-old girl. Right now I feel like I'm going completely out of my mind. The problem is my weight. I am far from fat (5 ft 3 in/160 cm, 118 lb/54 kg), but I would like to weigh 110 lb (50 kg). At the present time I am maintaining a six-hundred-calorie-a-day diet. Yesterday I had nine hundred calories and gained 2.2 lb (1 kg). Every time this happens, I feel like telling everyone I know that I hate them and crawling into a closet to hide. Sometimes my calorie intake can suddenly return to normal (about thirteen hundred calories) without my gaining weight. This will last for a few days, and then I might have to go an entire month on six hundred to seven hundred calories a day. What makes me more upset is that now nobody, except my mother, believes that I am not overeating or cares anymore. **42**

Your letter conveys the desperation you are feeling, and I agree with you that you must have help. There is more to the problem than just the battle with your weight. The tremendous distress you feel over your weight and your efforts to control your calorie intake are very important and must be dealt with. You need help in understanding why it affects you so deeply.

Just from a medical standpoint, you should remember, first, that daily weight fluctuations may not reflect overall weight loss patterns. Fluid intake or loss and amount of activity may (or may not) cause weight changes over a twenty-four-hour period. When you diet, weigh yourself *once per week.*

Secondly, many scientists believe we each have a natural "set point" for our weight, and as we approach it, weight gets harder and harder to lose. Someone your height could have a set point of 110 lb (50 kg), while someone else's could be higher or lower. In theory, if a person is "average" in activity level, he or she needs to eat at least eighteen to twenty calories per pound (40 to 44 per kg) just to *maintain* weight (for a 120 lb/54 kg average woman, that would be two thousand two hundred calories per day). In theory, the more active you are, the more calories you need. In theory too, if you are overeating just two hundred calories every day for one year, you'll gain more than 20 lb (9 kg).

Obviously, however, the situation is far more complex than this, and some people lose weight eating higher-calorie diets than can be tolerated by their desperately dieting friends.

See your doctor soon. Whether or not you are caught at your set point or have a medical problem that is causing you not to lose weight are just two issues. The others are your deep distress and the fact that your present diet, as described, cannot be adequate to maintain good health.

43 **Dear Dr. Levine: I have just started college, which I enjoy very much and find fulfilling. My problem is that along with this new life has come an increase in stress. The method I have adopted (not consciously) to counteract this stress is eating.**

I am 15 lb (7 kg) overweight and not yet unattractive, but I fear that my gorging will soon render me so and that my self-esteem will suffer too. I need some advice on what I should do to turn this harmful habit into a more positive one. I should also note that I am a diabetic, which probably adds a new dimension to my problem.

You are correct when you surmise that your diabetes adds further complexity to your situation. Overeating in response to stress is extremely common, but in a diabetic there is an added element of self-destructiveness involved.

There are many kinds of approaches you could take—tranquilizers, diets, biofeedback, nutritional counseling, educational counselors, relaxation therapy, hypnotism, psychotherapy, to name a few. Your first step should be to discuss your dilemma with your family doctor, who can assess the damage the stress is doing to your body and psyche.

It is early enough in the game that your relatively recent problems can be handled in a more appropriate and constructive manner. But act now, before a downward spiral begins.

44 **Dear Dr. Wilcox: I know that my problem doesn't seem desperate, but it is to me. I have very fat legs, especially my upper thighs. And they are driving me in-**

sane. It is very embarrassing on hot days when everybody is wearing shorts while I sit in my humid jeans facing the question, "Why aren't you in your shorts? It must be 90° F (32° C) outside!" So I skulk home to isolation. I find myself withdrawing from my friends more and more because of this.

Could you please tell me of some exercises or something to help? I am entering a new high school next year and I will need to make new friends. I know I won't be able to with these gross legs.

Many women and girls complain that their legs are too heavy, whereas it is an uncommon problem among males. Part of the reason is that estrogen (one of the female hormones) causes fat to be deposited on the hips, thighs, and buttocks in women. Many adolescent girls may think they are getting fat when this happens during puberty, when in fact it is just part of the body maturing into its adult female form. Later, however, some women find that their legs seem heavier and not in proportion to the rest of their bodies. This tendency seems to be determined by heredity and does, indeed, run in families.

You can slim your legs in several ways. First, check your overall weight. If you are overweight, this will aggravate the situation. Your doctor can help you plan a healthy reducing diet. If your weight is normal, exercise can improve the muscle tone of your legs. Cross-country skiing, swimming, bicycling, and jazz dancing are safe and effective forms of exercise that will help your legs and general fitness. If you are interested in more specific exercises, many exercise books are available through your local library or bookstore. In the meantime, remember that choosing clothes that fit well and are not tight will de-emphasize leg heaviness.

Dear Dr. Wilcox: I am 5 ft 3 in (160 cm) and weigh 115 lb (52 kg). My problem is that my waist is big. My sisters aren't fat but have big waists too. Both are *very* fit. I don't know whether to diet and get very thin or just not gain any more. Do you know of a suitable diet plan that would take my excess weight off my waist? I run regularly.

45

The way people carry their weight—having heavy thighs or thick waists, for example—tends to run in families, and these tendencies are difficult to overcome. Becoming too thin is a poor solution and is potentially dangerous. Following good nutrition and exercising regularly to keep your body well toned are the best ways to maintain your best weight, although they will not give you a tiny waist. You may want to check out an exercise book from the library to see if there are specific exercises you could do in addition to your running.

46 **Dear Dr. Wilcox: Can you tell me the various ways to remove fat from the face area (around cheeks)?**

There aren't really any specific methods available to remove fatty tissue on one's face. General weight reduction will lead to weight loss from all parts of the body, including the face. Some people find, in fact, that weight loss is apparent first in a slimming of the face.

The other general change that can alter the chubbiness of one's face is age. The hormone changes that cause a person's body to begin to mature at puberty also alter the way fat is distributed. Because of these changes, someone who has a round baby-face at age ten may have a slim, more mature look at sixteen.

47 **Dear Dr. Wilcox: I am an eighteen-year-old girl who has a problem with cellulite. When I was sixteen I started to notice that the skin on my thighs, buttocks, and hips was lumpy. Could you please tell me what causes these terrible bumps to appear and if there is anything that will get rid of them! I am 5 ft (152 cm) tall and weigh 98 lb (44 kg), and I try to eat the right kinds of food and try to exercise a lot.**

Although much has been written about cellulite in popular magazines, and many anticellulite products have been promoted, cellulite is simply fat or, in medical terms, adipose tissue. Giving the fat on the hips, thighs, and buttocks a different name just because it may have a distinctively bumpy, soft, and uneven appearance rather than a smooth, firmer look doesn't change what it is.

Under the influence of estrogen, a female hormone, fat is deposited in greater quantity on women's frames than on men's, particularly on the thighs, hips, buttocks, and breasts. The overall ratio of fat to muscle is also higher for women than for men.

In the high-deposition areas of the lower body, the tissue can look very uneven and lumpy. This appearance can be accentuated by overweight, although this is certainly not a factor in your case. In your situation, improving body tone and thereby increasing the proportion of muscle to fat through exercise may be helpful. Although you say you exercise a lot, this might be a chance to review your knowledge of fitness and exercise. Your physical education teacher at school or fitness instructor at the local Y, for example, can review your exercise program with you and help you design one to meet your needs. Reading up on exercise and fitness might also be useful, and many books are available at libraries and bookstores.

Dear Dr. Wilcox: To keep my weight stable, I am abusing laxatives. I take about fifty to sixty a day so food I eat will be expelled. I am afraid. If I stop them all at once, is that safe? Will I be able to go the bathroom without their assistance? **48**

Because laxatives can be purchased right off the counter, they are among the most commonly abused drugs. It's very important that you recognize that what you're doing is dangerous to your health. You need help: first, to retrain your bowels to function on their own, and second, to learn healthy ways to maintain your weight as well as a good nutritional status.

The side effects of laxative abuse vary with the type of laxative used, but all laxatives can have serious ones. These include imbalance of body chemicals (such as potassium), which can be severe enough to cause death; malabsorption of important nutrients; and addiction of your bowels to the laxatives so that eventually they can't work without the stimulation of the laxatives. *(See 318.)*

See your doctor *immediately*. He or she can help you.

Dear Dr. Wilcox: I am about 50 lb (23 kg) overweight and have tried many diets. I read recently that a woman had her mouth wired shut and drank liquids for a couple of months and lost 30 lb (14 kg). Is this a good way to lose weight? **49**

For all problems, but particularly long-term ones like obesity, everyone would like to find a "once and for all" solution. Unfortunately, as with most chronic problems, the solution involves long-term effort, and the one-shot treatment of having teeth wired shut to induce an initial weight loss doesn't answer the basic question: how can you keep the weight off once the wires are off?

The problem is that, although the immediate weight loss might be dramatic, the chances of keeping the weight off are not good, because wiring the teeth doesn't help you change your usual eating habits into healthy patterns that will help you maintain your ideal weight.

Put your effort instead into finding a good weight control program in your area, perhaps through your doctor. Here are some questions you should ask when trying to decide if such a program is safe and effective:

- Is your doctor aware that you are considering this program (or diet)?
- Is there a registered professional dietitian with the program who is available to consult with you?
- Are your personal eating habits and nutritional status assessed before the diet is designed for you?
- Are your food likes and dislikes, activity patterns, income, and lifestyle considered when the diet is planned?
- Does the diet provide at least one thousand calories a day?
- Does the program recommend regular physical activity suited to your lifestyle and physical condition?

50 **Dear Dr. Wilcox: I know you don't think that wiring a person's teeth shut is a good way to lose weight. What about stomach-shrinking operations?**

Gastroplasty, or "stomach stapling," is a radical surgical approach to the treatment of massive obesity. During surgery, the stomach is stapled and reduced in size to a 1¾-oz (50-ml) pouch. The hope is that, because the pouch is small, patients will feel full and satisfied after small meals and will therefore not overeat and will lose weight. How successful the operation is in helping patients lose weight and keep it off is controversial, since studies have shown variable results.

After surgery, moreover, patients may not be able to eat anything they want. With certain styles of gastroplasty, they can't drink anything with meals because liquids might wash the food out of the pouch or make them vomit. They can eat only when they are hungry, must chew thoroughly, eat slowly, and eat only small amounts. If these rules aren't followed, the pouch may stretch and they'll start overeating again.

There are also potential complications associated with the operation, and up to 4 percent of patients die from the surgery. On the other hand, the health dangers for the "morbidly obese" (more than 100 lb/45 kg overweight) are also serious.

Surgery for obesity is a radical treatment, therefore, and would be appropriate only for a very select few. Patients considered for such an approach are generally *at least* twice their ideal weight, have made previous serious attempts to lose weight through dieting (and have had some short-term success with diets), are otherwise in good health, and are emotionally stable. Surgery would rarely, if ever, be appropriate for a teenage patient.

Dear Dr. Wilcox: Most kids seem to have a problem being overweight. I'm just the opposite; I happen to be underweight. I am a 5 ft 1 in (155 cm), fourteen-year-old girl and weigh about 90 lb (41 kg), and I look as though I weigh only 80 lb (36 kg). I really hate it!

51

Are there any types of drug to make me gain weight? I was thinking possibly hormone pills. But that's not all. My biggest problem is my legs: they look like toothpicks! So I was wondering if there is such a thing as injecting fat cells to fatten my legs— or any other method to solve my problem.

There are no pills, drugs, or other specific medical treatments to induce weight gain. Instead, our basic body builds are influenced by heredity (what we genetically inherit from our families) as well as by the balance between the energy we take in (calories) and the energy we use up in our daily activities, in addition to muscles we firm and strengthen by exercise. And although we *tend* to have builds similar to those of other members of our families, we are still unique individuals with our own metabolic makeup. Illness, of course, can alter weight, and significant illness occurring during childhood can decrease one's height.

Age and physical maturity also affect body build, since one's body becomes heavier and more mature during adolescence. Have you matured physically yet (have your breasts developed and are you having periods)? If not, the curves you want may be yet to come.

What can you do from a medical standpoint? First of all, ensure that you are eating a nturitionally balanced diet. Next, see your doctor. He or she can help in a number of ways. First, your doctor can review your diet with you or refer you to a dietitian/nutritionist who can. Secondly, he or she can tell you whether your height and weight are normal and can also give you some idea of what further growth you can expect. At the same time, any medical problems could be diagnosed and treated. Finally, your doctor (or someone he or she refers you to) can help design a program to maximize your muscle tone and overall fitness. Feeling fit will help you feel better in general.

52 **Dear Dr. Wilcox: I am too embarrassed to talk to anyone about my problem, which is that I am obsessed with food and my weight. I am 5 ft 5 in (165 cm) tall and weigh 105 lb (48 kg), but I feel I am too fat and would like to weigh 95 lb (43 kg). I try to keep my daily food intake to 450–500 calories, but I can't lose enough weight fast enough.**

When I get depressed about being too fat I do something really stupid—I pig out. Then I feel really guilty, and the next day I won't eat at all or I'll really cut back on my calories.

Often I take a lot of laxatives to help lose weight, but I don't think I'll ever be able to reach my ideal weight at the rate I'm going. Have you got any ideas about how I can stop being so obsessed with food and my weight? I am desperate.

You are describing an increasingly common phenomenon. I can't tell you the number of young women I have seen in the past year or two who have exactly the same obsession with food, calories, and weight as you have. Some of them lose considerable weight, look sickly, can't eat (anorexia); others gorge themselves and then use laxatives or induce vomiting (bulimia). And there are thousands in between who are always watching their diets and weight.

Anorexia nervosa and bulimia are serious eating disorders that afflict, to some degree, between 1 and 10 percent of the adolescent/young adult female population. Characterized by a preoccupation with thinness and a distorted body image (thinking of oneself as "fat" when one is not), anorexia/bulimia can cause very serious health problems. Malnutrition and chemical imbalances can result from restricting food intake, inducing vomiting, and/or abusing laxatives and diuretics. Hormone systems are also disrupted and menstruation may cease.

Teenage girls comprise 90 to 95 percent of anorexics. As a result of their prolonged voluntary restriction of food intake, 10 percent of anorexics die, often because potassium, an important body chemical, becomes very low and this affects the heart's function.

Bulimia, a subtype of anorexia, is characterized more by alternating binging with purging (self-induced vomiting, abuse of laxatives or diuretics) than by simple food restriction (starving oneself). Often there is a mixture of both types of symptoms.

There are no easy cures. A few visits to a doctor or psychiatrist will not be the answer. Instead, it will take a great deal of time and effort. Hospitalization may be necessary. Your family doctor should be familiar with the resources for help in your community and an appointment with him or her is one way to start. Often a department of psychiatry at a hospital has someone on staff who has special training in eating disorders. If not, they should be able to direct you to the closest source of help.

Dear Dr. Wilcox: I'm a fourteen-year-old female, 5 ft 3 in (160 cm) tall and 110 lb (50 kg). I am heavily into sports so most of my weight is muscle. My problem started when I weighed 120 lb (55 kg), and many people teased me about being fat when I told them how much I weighed. This really depressed me, so I just stopped eating. That was a mistake, and I don't know how to correct it. **53**

Everything is very rushed in the mornings, and even when I do try to eat breakfast my stomach rejects it. So I don't eat breakfast. Lunch hour at school is the only time for me to see my boyfriend, and so I never eat lunch. He sometimes insists I eat something, but I really feel like a pig when I eat. I absolutely hate eating any kind of food! When I get home from school I eat something light, and then about six I eat a very small dinner.

How can I start a regular healthy diet again without gaining weight? I'd love to lose another 10 lb (5 kg), but I know my mom would think something was wrong.

There are comments in your letter that indicate you may be in an early stage of anorexia nervosa. Your concerns, therefore, are not unfounded, but by seeking help now you can overcome this potential problem.

Anorexia nervosa is a condition in which a patient seeks marked weight loss, can become severely wasted, and has abnormal eating patterns that can lead to starvation. Early symptoms include a continuously decreasing weight goal, increasing criticism of one's body, and ignoring hunger. There often is an extreme fear of gaining weight and a lack of concern over a significant weight loss. Patients may also complain of bloating and feeling full after eating small amounts of food, may exercise more and more, and may become socially isolated because of their obsessive dieting. Twenty percent of anorexic girls and women stop menstruating. Despite these symptoms, there usually is a denial of anything being wrong.

I'm concerned about your desire to "lose another 10 lb (5 kg)," your anxiety about gaining weight, and your intense dislike of eating. You imply that you know you aren't fat, yet you want to lose more.

What can you do? Go to see your family doctor now. He or she can help you discuss your concerns and/or refer you to a counselor interested in eating problems. Now is the time to seek help. Don't delay.

See 39, 52, 54.

54 **Dear Dr. Levine: I am a nineteen-year-old girl who has been struggling with anorexia nervosa for a little over two years. I am 5 ft 7 in (170 cm) tall and weigh 99 lb (45 kg). I seem to go through stages where I eat somewhat normally, though I always seem to revert back to eating nothing. My mother watches me at dinner to make sure I eat all my meal, but I always vomit afterward. I eat no other meals during the day, though occasionally I may have an apple. I take four laxatives every night because I'm not always certain I have successfully gotten rid of all my unwanted dinner. It's not that I hate food. It's just that there seems to be some underlying force inside me that tells me I can't gain weight, that I can't get fat.**

A teacher at school phoned my mother to tell her what was going on, so I know my mother knows. However, she doesn't ever say anything about it to me. She simply gives me twice as much as the other members of my family at dinner in hopes that I will fatten up. I'm extremely sick and tired of this insane disease because it seems to be trapping me in a darkened world. I used to be quite popular at school, but now I am no longer so outgoing; in fact I'm quite the opposite.

I want to be able to eat normally again just like everyone else. I want my energy back. I used to have

so much and now I have next to none. In the past four weeks I have fainted thirteen times. I know this is getting extremely dangerous, but I don't know what to do. I can't talk to my mother because she finds it easier to deal with if she just ignores it. I have seen a doctor about it, but she only weighed me weekly and explained she couldn't help me if I didn't want to help myself. So you see I have nowhere to turn.

You are right: you sure do need help! You seem to be in an uncontrollable and serious phase of anorexia nervosa. The vomiting and laxatives are further evidence of your single-minded determination to lose weight at the expense of your health and functioning.

I must say that I am quite concerned about you, since the very people who should be instrumental in getting you help, if you cannot do it yourself, are your parents and doctor, and they have failed miserably. In all fairness to your mother, she is probably at at her wits' end and does not know what to do. She may be receiving conflicting advice that is further confusing her.

There is considerably less excuse for your doctor. You can see by the latter's reaction that anorexics often engender anger. She did make a valid point, that for treatment to succeed the patient must have some degree of motivation to improve. But there is no way at this juncture that you are going to do it all on your own.

I also agree that the illness has proceeded to the point of danger to you, and it certainly is interfering with your psychological and social life. I urge you to talk to your mother in the hope that she can confront the reality of your problem and try to help you get professional attention. Your own doctor obviously missed the boat, and I'm not sure she even knows where it docks!

Failing this, you might contact an adolescent clinic in your town or city. The people there will have seen many young women with anorexia nervosa or variations on that theme and have people on staff who can help you. You can be helped, but you shouldn't delay.

Dear Dr. Wilcox: I am fifteen years old, have lots of friends, and do very well in school. My friends say I am pretty, and I have had my share of boyfriends. It sounds like I have a pretty stable life, right?

Wrong! Everybody needs some kind of secret es-

55

cape from trying to be, or at least appear, perfect to others. For some it is alcohol, for some it is drugs, but for me it is food. I am not obese, but I would look and feel a lot better if I lost around 15 lb (7 kg). For the last few years I have often resorted to starving myself for weeks and losing a lot of weight. Then I gain it all back.

Now I have found a way to satisfy my binge urges without suffering afterward. I eat enormous amounts of food, then stick my finger down my throat and throw up. But I am still overweight, and when I'm not on a binge, I starve myself, which leads to even more binging eventually.

I have taken up to seventy-five laxatives at one time. I know that I have a very serious problem and could really harm myself. I am not a very healthy person to start with, and this could lead to even more serious damage to my health.

I really need help, but I couldn't go to see a psychiatrist or counselor. I'm sure there could be a lot of psychological reasons why I do this, such as a need to feel power over my body or to "get back" at my parents who are constantly at my throat. I have heard many reasons why people do this, but even though I realize it, I just can't stop myself. I have said to myself a thousand times, "This is the last time."

Please help me if you can. I think I now know where they got the saying "Eat your heart out" because that seems to be exactly what I am doing.

You have already made several important steps toward getting the help you need. You have recognized that the starving/binging is a serious problem, you know that you want to stop, and you have been able to tell someone about the problem by writing this letter.

You are not alone with your problem. Bulimia (the starving/binging you describe) and related eating disorders are not at all rare and appear to be becoming more and more common. Perhaps because of the increasing frequency of this problem, the number of physicians with expertise in treating eating disorders is also increasing. And although help is available at any stage, the earlier you seek help, the better.

Can you tell your family doctor what you have told me? If

not, choose an adult whom you trust and confide in him or her. That person can then help you find a doctor with whom you feel comfortable. The doctor can get to know you and help you overcome the bulimia or can refer you to an eating disorder specialist.

Remember that many people have experienced what you are now going through and that there are many resources available to help you.

Dear Dr. Levine: I am a twelve-year-old girl. I am writing to you about my sister. She is fourteen and in ninth grade. She is a very smart student and gets straight A's. She has nice friends and is kind to them, but when she gets home from school she's a monster.

56

She collects pictures of models and has over four hundred of them. Her favorite is Brooke Shields. My sister is an average-looking girl—not beautiful but certainly not ugly. She thinks her nose is fat, her eyes are small, her lips are too thin, she's got too many blackheads and pimples, and her hair is too straight. There are many more complaints, but I will not bore you with the details. Then she takes a picture of Brooke Shields and compares herself to it.

She has been complaining about herself every day since the beginning of seventh grade. My mom does her best to help. She takes her to the dermatologist and buys her creams and medications for her face, but she still complains. My mom tells her it is just a phase she is going through. But I'm afraid this phase will never end, and by the time it does, my mom and I probably will have gone crazy. Will you give my mom and me some advice that will help us deal with my sister?

Your sister, of course, is mistaken; even if she were beautiful there would be no guarantee she would be any happier with herself. It sounds like she has a lot going for her—brains, friends, popularity. She's even attractive—although no Brooke Shields.

Well, I'm no Robert Redford; so what? Very few of us reach the levels of physical attractiveness we'd like. The trick is to accept and maximize what we've got and to strengthen our other interests and talents. If we are never satisfied, we torment ourselves and others. And that is what your sister is doing.

If your mother is powerless to reach her, then perhaps somebody she likes—an aunt, grandmother, teacher, family doctor—can do the trick. A counselor at an adolescent clinic could also be of help to your sister and the rest of the family.

57 **Dear Dr. Levine: I am a nineteen-year-old female. My problem is my appearance. Because of the way I am built, guys assume that all I am after is a good time. Nothing could be further from the truth. I just want someone who will accept all of me, not just my body. At this rate I'm afraid I will never get married. Also, many people tell me that I look like I've been around. What does somebody who's been around look like, anyway? Obviously I can't change my appearance, but is there something I can do? I am tired of thinking I've found the right guy, then getting used by him. So far I've been able to shrug off these encounters, but I am beginning to wonder if I'm the problem and not them.**

I might assume from your letter that you are exceptionally pretty, have voluptuous features (breasts, buttocks, etc), or dress somewhat provocatively. Perhaps you have a "sultry" appearance, or your eyes meet men's in an alluring or even teasing manner.

I might assume all that, but even if you were any or all of the above, it would still not excuse the lascivious and lecherous leering that you have had to endure. There are ways to dress differently, to avoid making direct extended eye contact, or to reduce subtle suggestive behavior. Some young women have even resorted to plastic surgery in order to reduce the size of breasts, for example, and not always for reasons of physical comfort.

It is unfortunate, especially if you are a total innocent, for you to have to be the one to modify your behavior in order to get these sexual predators off your trail. The truth, is, however, that there are too many of them.

Your best approach is to make sure that you are not leading anyone on, and to not give any suspicious character the time of day. Carry on with your life, and develop your own intellectual, physical, and emotional outlets and pursuits.

See 151.

THREE:

Skin

[Acne] treatment: In the morning an ointment made of olive oil, 4 ounces; white wax, 2 drams. Melt together, and then add honey, 2 drams; croton oil, 20 drops. Take a dose of sulphur and cream of tartar twice a week.

J. H. Ayers
Ayers' Every Man His Own Doctor *(1883)*

Your skin is your body's largest organ, having more surface area than your heart, lungs, liver, spleen, and stomach combined. It protects your body from such outside invaders as bacteria, helps keep your temperature stable, and is waterproof. It plays a vital role in keeping you healthy and comfortable. Because skin is such a major part of our bodies, however, it is not surprising that it can also be a major source of problems.

During adolescence, skin can cause seemingly endless aggravation: it becomes oily and irritable and often breaks out in a sea of blackheads and red bumps, usually timed to be at their peak the night of your most important party or date.

Besides acne, there are other ways skin can plague us: itchiness, stretch marks, warts, and excess perspiration are just some of them. In this section we offer suggestions for dealing with such common annoyances, as well as techniques for taking care of your skin to make it seem less like an enemy and more like a friend.

Dear Dr. Wilcox: I am a nineteen-year-old male student with a seemingly minor but irritating problem. My body produces an excess amount of oil, in my opinion. My back, chest, face, and scalp tend to be terminally oily. What is the purpose of the oil anyway? How can one prevent it besides daily showers? Does diet have any affect on oil?

58

The medical name for the oil produced by the skin is sebum. It comes from the tiny sebaceous glands that are present around the roots of the hairs on your head and body. The sebum lubricates the skin, and without it the skin would become dry, scaly, and irritated.

The amount of sebum produced varies from person to person and also with age. During the teens and early twenties, sebum production is usually at its peak because of the hormone changes that occur in the body during maturation. Dry skin—with low sebum production—is much more common in old age. By the way, if you tend to have oily skin, you usually also produce more earwax!

Soapy showers do wash the excess oil away. The warmer the water, however, and the longer the exposure to that water (as in a good soak in a nice hot bath), the drier your skin will be. There are also medications that can be applied to the skin to dry it (such as benzoyl peroxide; *see 63*) as well as medicines (such as antibiotics), taken as pills, that will alter the composition of the sebum. Both of these, however, are usually used in treating acne, not just to make skin less oily.

You can try taking showers morning and evening and after exercise. Use a nonmoisturizing soap (don't use anything made for "dry skin") and use a tar-containing shampoo for your hair (ask your pharmacist). Studies have failed to confirm that diet influences oily skin, but you will find many people who swear that it does. Therefore, if you find that your skin seems worse after eating certain foods, avoid them.

59 **Dear Dr. Wilcox: I have combination skin, but every product I use only makes it worse. My parents won't let me see a dermatologist because it costs too much. I'm wondering if you can recommend something for combination skin and suggest where I can buy it.**

By combination skin, I assume you mean that one part of your face tends to be oily while another part tends to be dry. Usually in such cases the chin, nose, and forehead are more oily and the cheeks are drier.

Whether caring for dry or oily skin, the key is to strike a balance that keeps your skin clean and yet allows enough oil to remain for comfort. If the amount of oil varies from one part of your face to another, you will have to use different cleansing techniques for each area.

Start by gently washing your face with a mild soap each morning. Remember that hot water dries the skin more than cold. During the day, rewash only the oiler areas of your skin. Some people use premoistened wipes that you can buy in a drug or grocery store. Before you go to sleep at night, wash again, removing all makeup; you may want to use only cool water and no soap on the drier areas.

Over a few weeks, by varying the temperature of the water and the frequency of washing, you should find the right combination for both your dry and oily skin.

If these general suggestions don't help, talk to your family doctor. If there are special problems you do not mention in your letter, and if your family doctor feels it is necessary, he or she can refer you to a dermatologist, whose care is covered by some health insurance plans.

Dear Dr. Wilcox: I am sixteen years old and suffer from acne. Please explain it and what I should do to control it. **60**

Acne results from the interaction of the skin with oil produced by the skin. Although people vary greatly in their susceptibility to acne, it is especially common during adolescence, when the hormones that control sebum (oil) production become much more active. The key with any treatment is to find a balance that will give you skin that is too dry to produce pimples yet has enough oil to feel comfortable.

Although there are a number of suggestions one can follow to decrease acne, treatments prescribed by doctors involve topical antiacne preparations that are applied to the skin, and/or pills. The topical medications either are designed to dry the skin or contain antibiotics that make the sebum less irritating. Some of the drying medications can be purchased without prescription but must be used with care to avoid excessive redness and irritation. (If your skin becomes temporarily too dry from using one of these, *never* apply moisturizer to try to correct it; this will just make matters worse.)

Antibiotic pills for acne are used when topical treatment is not enough. They decrease the amount of bacteria present in the oil and thereby decrease the fatty acids that are available to inflame the pores.

What can you do on your own? If you notice certain foods make your acne worse, by all means avoid them. However, there is no scientific evidence that a specific diet will help your acne. Gently washing your face at least twice a day with a soap that works well for you will also help. And, finally, don't pick your acne, cradle your chin in your hands, or touch your face unnecessarily; the picking can lead to infection and/or scarring, and the oil on your hands can make the acne worse.

61 **Dear Dr. Wilcox: I am a reasonably attractive fifteen-year-old, and I'm very happy with everything that is going on in my life. But I have just one complaint: blackheads. The problem area is usually around the nose. I eat a good diet, I get plenty of exercise, and I wash my face extremely well twice a day. I've tried to remove the blackheads with a sterile needle, but it never works. Is there a safe, easy, and painless way to remove them?**

Blackheads, or open comedones, are actually tiny plugs of fat, cells, and pigment and are one of the most common features of acne. Although it is tempting to try to remove them yourself by squeezing or poking, this is dangerous and can lead to serious infection and even scarring.

Measures that help include good daily washes, which you already do, and avoiding moisturizers and liquid makeup. And you could use a mild abrasive wash once or twice a day instead of your regular soap. Ask your pharmacist for a gentle one that contains aluminum oxide crystals. But use it carefully and stop if irritation develops.

If after several weeks there is no improvement, see your doctor, who may recommend special drying lotions or other medications.

62 **Dear Dr. Wilcox: I am an eighteen-year-old girl who is going to be maid of honor at a friend's wedding. The problem is that I have acne on my chest and back. The dresses my friend has picked out for us are off-the-shoulder style, which would not be so good for me. Are there any kinds of cream or makeup that I could apply to my skin to cover up the acne? I notice that many actresses use makeup quite successfully to cover their imperfections. If there are none, what can be done?**

As I'm sure you know, there is no quick remedy for acne. Instead, treatment needs to be long-term, a careful and consistent combination of cleansing and, in many cases, use of either topical (applied) or systemic (swallowed) medication.

What you want right now, though, is some way to get

through the wedding. It wouldn't hurt to talk to your doctor to see what you can do in the time you have, remembering, however, that *some* acne treatments may initially appear to make the skin flare up before it gets better. Because of this possibility, be sure to let your doctor know the wedding date.

Have you told your friend about your concerns? If the choice of dresses is not yet irreversible, it would certainly be worth discussing your worries and seeing what the alternatives are. If your friend knew how you felt, she would undoubtedly want to choose a style in which you'd be comfortable. Could the dress be slightly modified to better suit you?

There is such a thing as special makeup designed to cover birthmarks, scars, and discolorations. It would, however, only be a one-time solution for you, because heavy makeups can trap the skin's irritating oils in the pores and ultimately make the acne worse. If you want to use it just this once, experiment ahead of time to see if you can match your skin tone and conceal the acne. Contact the cosmetics department of a large department store and describe what you need. But even if this does work for the wedding, don't neglect a long-term solution. Contact your doctor; many effective antiacne treatments are available.

Dear Dr. Wilcox: I read in the paper that a Japanese researcher has found that benzoyl peroxide, a medicine you can buy in the drugstore to help get rid of acne, causes cancer. Please comment. **63**
Benzoyl peroxide is a useful antiacne medication that, when applied daily, makes the skin less oily by decreasing the amount of free fatty acids present. I do not feel it is unsafe when used as directed.

Benzoyl peroxide has been used in North America for years and has an impressive safety record. It can be purchased over the counter. There is no increase in cancer noted among people who have used the product.

In the Japanese study the medication was given to mice that had been bred to be highly susceptible to cancer. And it was also used in doses vastly higher than those ever used for humans. The current feeling is that this one study must be viewed with care since it is at odds with virtually all other research on benzoyl peroxide.

Dear Dr. Wilcox: I don't know if I have acne or something worse. I've got *huge*, painful, red pimples. What is it, and can I get rid of it? **64**

Cystic acne is a severe type of acne characterized by nod-
ules, clumps of "pimples," and large red cysts, any or all of
which may be sore and tender. Scarring is a major problem
with this condition. Although cystic acne can affect both
girls and boys, it occurs most frequently in boys at about
age sixteen. It can be a very persistent problem, lasting well
into adulthood, especially if it affects the back and neck.

Because it has been very difficult to treat successfully in
many cases, it is especially good news that a medication
called isotretinoin (or Accutane) is now available for the
treatment of cystic acne.

Isotretinoin is a very effective medication; nodulocystic
acne usually begins to improve during the first month of
taking the drug, and its good effects often continue for
months or years after it has been discontinued. It is usually
given for fifteen to twenty-two weeks. If the skin clears 80
percent during the course of treatment, almost complete
clearing will often occur after treatment. A second course,
if needed, can be started after an eight-week "rest period"
when no medication is taken.

Like most potent medications, isotretinoin can have significant side effects. For this reason, it should be prescribed
by a physician who knows the drug well. Dermatologists with
a special interest in acne will likely have had the most experience with the medication.

65 **Dear Dr. Wilcox: I'm a seventeen-year-old male with
an acne problem. I have been to a number of dermatologists, but they haven't helped me. I have heard
about a drug called Accutane that appears to shrink
the oil-producing glands in the face, which will in
turn make my face clear up. The drawback is the side
effects, which I'm concerned about. Can you please
tell me more about this drug?**

Accutane is the brand name for a special variant of vitamin
A called isotretinoin. It represents a tremendous advance in
the treatment of severe nodulocystic acne where other therapies have failed. In these severe, difficult cases it can bring
long-lasting improvement and relief.

Some clinicians are recommending that isotretinoin might
also be used in treating patients with less severe forms of
acne, such as those where scarring is likely to occur. But
significant side effects limit its use, and the final word is
not yet in on whether or not lower doses would be less toxic
but still effective for such patients. Anyone wishing to con-

sider the use of isotretinoin in treatment of his or her acne should consult a dermatologist thoroughly familiar with its use.

There are many side effects, but most are related to dosage and resolve once the drug is stopped. For example, 90 percent of users experience some form of skin problem while on the medication; most commonly this includes symptoms of dryness and chapping, particularly leading to cracking of the skin at the corners of the mouth. Other less common side effects include painful joints or muscles, an increase in fatty substances (triglycerides) in the blood, abnormalities of liver function, and other effects involving the central nervous system, the eyes, and the level of calcium in the blood.

A major concern, however, is that isotretinoin can cause serious birth defects if it is taken during pregnancy. It is critical, therefore, that any woman taking isotretinoin have a pregnancy test before starting the medication and use an effective form of birth control during and for at least one month after treatment.

Dear Dr. Wilcox: I'm an eighteen-year-old girl and not one of those lucky people who have beautifully smooth skin. I have acne scars. I recently read that there are a couple of methods to get rid of these scars. How is this done? I'm very self-conscious about my face, and I don't like to wear makeup all the time. 66

There are three potentially effective approaches to dealing with acne scars: makeup, dermabrasion, and collagen injections.

Although you say you don't want to wear makeup all the time, properly applied makeup can camouflage scars well— and there are no side effects! Dermatologists recommending this approach suggest you go to a professional makeup artist, such as those employed by reputable and respected establishments known for their makeovers. When you call for an appointment, be sure to ask if they have anyone on staff specially trained to deal with acne scars.

Dermabrasion is another possible solution, but it cannot be done if you are still breaking out. It works best for shallow scars in skin that heals easily. The process involves first chilling or freezing the skin to be treated and then, while the patient is sedated or under general anesthetic, planing the skin using motor-driven, rotating wire brushes. A week after the operation, the crusts (scabs) will have fallen off and the skin will be red and shiny. The redness gradually fades, but sunlight must be avoided for six to eight weeks because it can cause the treated area to become permanently darker than the surrounding skin. Other possible complications include *decreased* pigmentation in the dermabraded areas and further scarring problems.

The newer treatment, collagen injections, involves a series of injections and, like dermabrasion, is not without potential side effects. It also cannot be done if you still have active acne. Basically, it involves injecting collagen, a protein, into the deep layer of the skin. After one to six injections, there is enough collagen present to push the bottom of the scar up to the level of the surrounding skin. The injections are moderately painful, and because the collagen is from a "foreign" source there may be an allergic reaction.

You should see a dermatologist to discuss the options appropriate for your own skin type. If dermabrasion or collagen injections are suggested, checking with a second physician for a confirming opinion could help you make a decision.

67 **Dear Dr. Wilcox: I am an eighteen-year-old female with an embarrassing problem. When I was small I got a lot of flogging from my parents. I am no longer upset about the treatment; I saw a counselor and feel better. But my skin has got a lot of dark spots on it that are very noticeable. I have to live in stockings to hide the spots on my legs. Could you please recommend something that can remove them?**

Sometimes when skin has been injured, the only "scarring" that occurs is increased color, or pigment, in the injured areas. This is called postinflammatory hyperpigmentation. The deeply colored spots contain extra melanin (the substance that gives skin its color), not only in the top layer of the skin but also in the deepest part of the skin.

Special bleaches can partially lighten the dark areas if applied two or three times a day for weeks or months. They can be prescribed by a dermatologist. Your family doctor can help you find a dermatologist who can do this for you. Like any cream or lotion that's applied to the skin, bleaches will penetrate only the top layer of skin and won't have any effect on the deep skin layer. Therefore, the spots cannot be completely bleached.

A dermatologist might also suggest that you avoid exposing the spots to the sun: sunlight increases melanin in the skin (that's how people get a tan), even more so in skin with extra melanin.

Although the "floggings" are ancient history for you, many children are currently experiencing the suffering you did years ago. No child should have to endure such abuse, and any child in that situation should seek the help of a trusted adult—a teacher, friend, doctor, etc. This person can call the Children's Aid Society so that protection can be arranged. If a child feels there is no one to turn to, he or she can call Children's Aid directly and ask for help.

See 248.

Dear Dr. Wilcox: As the result of an accident a couple of years ago, I have a 1-in (2.5-cm)-long scar on my chin. I have gone through endless amounts of questioning and teasing about it. My parents won't allow me to wear much makeup to school, and therefore the scar remains clearly visible. Are there any medical treatments available to fade the scar? Even though it's been there a while, it is still very red in color, a sharp contrast to my fair skin.
68

The skin consists of two layers, the epidermis and the underlying dermis, often referred to as the "true skin." The dermis is made up of so-called connective tissue, including elastic fibers that allow the skin to give and stretch. Scars are new formations of connective tissue that replace substance lost when the dermis is injured.

If you want to make a scar less noticeable, you can either camouflage it with special makeup or seek medical help. It sounds as if you are more interested in the latter. You will have to see either a dermatologist or a plastic surgeon for any of the following treatments. Your family doctor can refer you to the appropriate specialist, who can carefully evaluate your specific scar and skin type.

If the scar is flat, it could be excised (cut out) and the skin neatly sewn back together. If the scar is raised, however, the healing from the surgery can leave another scar that is just as big as or bigger than the one that's been removed.

If the scar is raised, injections of steroids once a month for three or four months may "dissolve" the scar tissue and reduce the scar. These steroids are *not* the ones that some athletes use in an attempt to build up muscle; they are made up of a different compound known for its ability to decrease inflammation and are given only in very tiny amounts right into the scar itself.

Much smaller, depressed scars, like those from acne, are sometimes injected with collagen. Collagen is a natural protein (one brand is derived from calfskin). Like any foreign protein, it may cause the body to produce antibodies against it and may cause inflammation. Injected into the dermis, it raises the scar, filling in the tiny crater. Because the collagen is absorbed gradually by body tissues, its effects last only one to three years so that retouching may be needed. Camouflaging scars with special makeups is a topic in itself. Many department stores carry special brands, and a salesperson could explain the techniques to you. (See 62.)

You need to discuss your alternatives with your parents. Feeling good about your appearance is important to your self-esteem.

69 **Dear Dr. Wilcox: I have red hair and fair skin that causes me to get freckles. I can't stand them. I have them on my face, hands, arms, and legs. I can't even go outside all summer. Is there anything that will help me tan and also stop my freckles?**

Freckles, or ephelides, are areas in the skin where the production of melanin, the brownish skin pigment, is concentrated. As you know, freckling is particularly common in blonds, redheads, and people with fair skin, and trying to get a tan only increases freckling.

A good sunscreen rated 15 can block the effects of the sun. It will not allow tanning. Someone as fair as you needs a sunscreen any time you are outside. Some dermatologists recommend using one when you are outdoors during the day, however briefly, from the end of February through October. This means using it on cloudy as well as sunny days.

Although the idea of having a tan may be appealing, keeping pale may not only help prevent the freckling you dislike but will in the long run keep your skin healthier and younger-looking. The same rays that tan the skin can also damage and age it and can lead to skin cancer.

There are a few skin bleaches that dermatologists occasionally prescribe and use with care to try to fade freckles, but you would have to be evaluated by a dermatologist to see if this were even a possibility. Even then, exposure to the sun would cause the freckles to recur.

70 **Dear Dr. Wilcox: My family has just bought a sunlamp, and I would like to know the disadvantages of**

getting a tan this way. Also, if there are some dangers, would it be okay if I just used it sometimes?
Ultraviolet light is the type of sunlight that causes sunburns and tans. So-called UVB light is the subdivision of this band of the spectrum of rays found in sunlight that is most responsible for burning and tanning and is generally emitted by the sunlamps one can buy in the store. Carefully designed sunlamps have been used for many years in treating specific, serious skin conditions, but routine use of sunlamps for tanning should be discouraged; chronic exposure to UVB light causes the skin to age and may lead to skin cancer.

There are short-term problems too, mostly because people underestimate the effect of the exposure. Although there is some immediate redness (or erythema) of the skin after exposure, this fades quickly. The true burn appears two to four hours later and reaches its peak in fourteen to twenty hours.

In addition, being too close to the light intensifies the possible damage. Care must be taken not to fall asleep under the light (which may lead to severe burns), and special goggles must be worn to prevent injury to the eyes.

Tanning salons have become increasingly popular and advertise what "gentle rays" they use. Although sunburns are rare in this setting, dermatologists still warn that artificial tanning, just like natural suntanning, will probably increase risk of prematurely aging the skin *and* of developing skin cancer.

Dear Dr. Wilcox: My problem started about four years ago, when I was ten. I scratched my bottom raw one night and the next day I had a couple of scabs. I picked at them and continued to scratch. What's so embarrassing is that at sleepovers people say, "How come you have a rash on your rear end?" I come up with some flimsy excuse. I'm embarrassed to talk to my mom, for we don't get along, and I'm also embarrassed to see a doctor. Is there some kind of cream I could use? **71**
Unfortunately, this is one of those problems that really needs to be seen to be accurately diagnosed. I'll make a few suggestions, but to get the help you need you'll have to let a doctor take a look. Perhaps your friends or family have a doctor they really like and with whom you can be comfortable. Remember that doctors deal with a multitude of "pri-

vate" problems every day, and for them these problems are routine.

What are the possible causes of your continuing rash? Neurodermatitis and an acnelike rash are just two possibilities. The treatment for each is different—which is another reason you need to see a doctor. Neurodermatitis and related rashes are basically chronic irritations caused by continual, often unconscious, scratching. If there are a few scabs present, there must still be some scratching going on. Creams and sometimes pills are prescribed to soothe the skin and relieve subtle itching that may be initiating the scratching. Other rashes that look a bit like acne may be an acne variant or a low-grade chronic skin infection for which there are several possible causes. Antibiotics may help but must be prescribed by a doctor.

72 **Dear Dr. Wilcox: I am a sixteen-year-old girl who has a rash that won't go away. It is red and itches some of the time. The embarrassing part is that it's in the front where my leg joins my torso. I've had it for months, and taking lots of baths doesn't help and sometimes even makes it worse. I used some old cortisone cream, but it only helped a little bit. What do you think it is and what can I do about it?**

What you describe may be a skin rash called intertrigo. This rash occurs in so-called intertriginous areas of the body, areas where there are creases in the skin. Such areas include the inguinal area (where the leg joins the front of the torso), the axillae (underarms), and, in women, under the breasts. These areas can become irritated because they tend to be warmer and moister than other parts of the body. Keeping them as cool and dry as possible can prevent the problem.

Sometimes it can be hard to tell if irritation alone is the problem or if there is also a fungal infection present. Cortisone cream will ease irritation but will not remedy infection. Special antifungal creams are available.

73 **Dear Dr. Wilcox: I have an extremely embarrassing problem. I am very much overweight, about 100 lb (45 kg), and on my inner thighs I have a lot of blackheads and pimples. I have always been overweight and have had this problem for a number of years. Is this because I am overweight? I have started a diet that I intend to stick to. Will this problem clear up**

when I reach my proper weight? Please help me; I'm much too embarrassed to go to my own doctor.

What you describe sounds like folliculitis, an infection or inflammation of the hair follicles. Follicles, which contain tiny oil-secreting glands, are located at the base of each hair. There are a number of causes of folliculitis, and without seeing you it is impossible to say for sure which form you have. The treatment varies with the cause, so it is important to make an accurate diagnosis.

One of the most common forms is caused by an infection of the follicles by bacteria called *Staphylococcus aureus*. It most frequently occurs on the legs and arms, particularly in areas where the skin is especially warm and moist. It can also occur on the face. If you are overweight, you may have a problem keeping certain areas of your skin cool, which can contribute to your susceptibility to this type of folliculitis. Losing weight, however, won't cure it. Washing the areas with an antibacterial soap, then applying an antibiotic ointment, and in stubborn cases taking antibiotic pills will get rid of it. Antibiotics must be prescribed by a physician, although a pharmacist can suggest antibacterial soaps.

Folliculitis may be superficial or deep. Deep infection can lead to scarring and is most common as a result of plucking hairs, shaving too closely against the direction of hair growth, or using greasy creams—contributing factors in the development of the folliculitis. Other causes include reactions to medications or irritating chemicals, fungal infections, parasitic infections (such as scabies), and ingrown hairs. Obviously, each type of problem will require its own specific treatment.

Folliculitis is quite a common problem and your doctor will undoubtedly have treated many cases. Please make an appointment to see him or her so that a proper diagnosis can be made and appropriate treatment begun.

Dear Dr. Wilcox: Since I was ten years old, I have had a problem with cold sores on my lips and nose. I don't mean just one small cold sore, I mean about six to ten all at the same time. I get them about once a year and am forced to stay away from school for up to a week for fear of embarrassment!

74

Is there any known quick cure for cold sores? Does something specific cause them? Do only some people get them? How long does one usually take to go away?

Cold sores are a common and annoying problem for which there is currently no quick cure. Caused by a virus, the first infection may occur without symptoms while the susceptible person is very young (not everyone gets this infection). The virus then remains in the nerve endings close to the site of the first infection, and in 75 percent of people who have the virus it periodically reactivates, causing cold sores. Factors that trigger the reactivation vary from person to person but include emotional stress, physical stresses such as injury to the skin where the sores usually appear, sunburn, and fever. The recurrent cold sores usually take seven to ten days to heal. When the cold sore is present, the virus is too. Be careful about spreading the virus. Wash your hands after touching your mouth, and obviously kissing is out when you have the sores.

Some people suggest that putting ice on the area several times per hour when you feel the tingling or burning sensation that usually precedes the development of the sore will prevent its formation. Others suggest that keeping the sore dry will speed healing. See your doctor if the sores ever develop a yellow crust, because this may indicate the presence of bacterial infection, which can be easily treated.

There is much research in the field, and for more serious forms of the infection new antiviral medications are being tried. Ideally, we will develop a medication that not only promotes healing but can eliminate the virus from the nerve endings. Your doctor can keep you posted about new developments and treatments.

75 **Dear Dr. Wilcox: I have had warts for the past few years, but until recently I haven't done much about them. I bought something that's supposed to remove warts, but it did nothing for me. I went to see a dermatologist, and he burned a bit of them off. It was painful. I didn't go back. Is there anything I can use that is not so painful?**
Warts, or verrucae, are caused by the papilloma virus, of which six or seven different types have been identified. They can occur anyplace on the skin, even the lips or nose, but are most common on the hands during childhood and adolescence.

Some warts respond to simple treatment, some may suddenly disappear on their own, whereas others stubbornly recur. It has been estimated that over the years more than one thousand different ways of treating warts have been de-

scribed. There is even statistical evidence that hypnosis can
be effective. The choice of treatment depends upon the location of the warts, their size and number, how tender they
are, results of previous treatment, and the age of the patient (among other factors). The most widely accepted treatments used and found helpful in North America include
prescribed lotions (often containing salicylic acid), electro-
desiccation (burning), and cryotherapy (freezing with liquid
nitrogen). Discomfort has been reported with each.

It sounds as though you were treated with electrodesic-
cation. Before you give up, remember that it can take four
to five weeks before healing is complete. In the meantime,
you should see your dermatologist to discuss your concerns
and the amount of discomfort you experienced. He or she
can then gauge treatment accordingly.

Dear Dr. Wilcox: Ever since I was in fourth grade I've **76**
had these bumps on my arms and legs that look like
goosebumps. I eat lots of whole grains, fruits, and
vegetables. I don't know why they won't go away. I
feel very self-conscious. I also feel depressed be-
cause everyone can wear shorts and short-sleeved
tops and I have to wear jeans and long-sleeved shirts.
I feel very embarrassed about going to the doctor. I
can't talk to my mother about this; we've never been
able to talk about girl stuff.

What you describe sounds like a skin problem called keratosis pilaris. But without seeing you it is impossible to say
for sure. Keratin is a protein that helps make the epidermis, or top layer of skin, sturdy. Too much keratin makes
the skin rough and hard (calluses are an example of extra
keratin forming in response to chronic traumatization of
the skin by, for example, a poorly fitting shoe).

In keratosis pilaris, extra keratin is, for unknown reasons, deposited around the skin's tiny hairs, usually on the
arms and thighs. It gives the appearance of chronic goosebumps. Diet has no influence. Doctors prescribe a number
of medications to try to reduce the roughness of the skin.
Some of these preparations promote peeling away of extra
roughness, others decrease any inflammation present, and
still others moisturize the skin.

You shouldn't be embarrassed to see a doctor about this
problem. Doctors (especially skin specialists) will have had
experience trying to help others who've had it too. See your
doctor to make sure this is the correct diagnosis.

77 Dear Dr. Wilcox: I have been using tweezers to remove a hair growing from a raised mole. Since I
started, more hairs have grown from the mole. I have
recently read two articles about removing unwanted
hair. Both said never pull a hair from a mole but did
not explain why. Is this dangerous? Could you suggest other methods of removal?

The reason people have been told never to pluck hair from
a mole, or nevus, is that there was fear that irritation from
the plucking could make the nevus become malignant (can-
cerous) or that careless tweezing could lead to infection.
Probably only the fear of infection is legitimate.

A mole is a small area of skin that is darker than the surrounding skin. It contains cells sometimes called nevocytes.
Some experts think these are a variation of melanocytes,
the cells in our skin responsible for producing melanin,
the substance that gives skin its color.

Most people have at least a few moles. We are thought to
have the highest number when we're twenty to twenty-five—
often as many as forty! After age twenty-five, many moles
may flatten and fade until they disappear.

Signs of cancer in a mole can include sudden enlargement, changes in color or surface (scaliness, oozing, bleeding), itching, pain, swelling, the appearance of a "new" mole
near an old one, or a leaking of color beyond its previous
boundaries. If you ever notice such a change, consult a doctor. The development of a new mole in someone over thirty-
five also may be of concern.

The type of mole you describe is generally benign and needs
to be removed only if it develops one of the above danger
signs or if it is so unsightly that even an unsatisfactory scar,
which could occur if there were problems with removal, is
preferable. Interestingly, removing the mole may not remove the hair; it might well continue to grow.

If you want a permanent solution to the problem, the hair
could be removed by electrolysis. You should check first with
a dermatologist, who can direct you to a good electrolysist.
If you want to try this, you should stop tweezing, because
tweezed hairs don't respond as well to electrolysis as do those
that have never been plucked. Electrolysists destroy the hair
root by inserting a tiny needle into it and running electric
current through the needle.

You could try clipping the hair very short or continue to
pluck, being extremely careful to avoid infection by cleaning

the skin first, using scrupulously clean tweezers, and taking care not to nick the skin with the tweezers.

Dear Dr. Wilcox: Is it possible for a guy to get stretch marks? Although I've never been overweight and I'm in excellent shape, I've noticed an increasing number of horizontal lines on my buttocks over the past year. Is this common in guys? What causes it? **78**

Stretch marks can and do occur in both males and females. They are, in fact, common. Known medically as striae distensae or striae atrophicae, they are most common in areas of the body where the skin is stretched by rapid weight change or growth, and the microscopic elastic fibers in the skin are broken. They are common on the buttocks and thighs and, in women, on the breasts and, especially during pregnancy, the abdomen.

Interestingly, striae frequently occur without apparent cause on the buttocks and thighs and even over the knees and elbows, especially in children aged nine to thirteen. Very rarely, they can be caused by medications (steroids) that weaken the skin's elastic fibers as a side effect, or by medical problems such as Cushing's syndrome, where the body produces too much steroid; there are always many other signs of illness if this is the case.

There is no product available that will remove stretch marks. One big problem in trying to come up with one is that the damaged elastic fibers are in the dermis, the deep layer of the skin. Creams, lotions, and ointments simply do not penetrate that deeply, and so the broken fibers remain unreachable.

Fortunately, stretch marks, pink or purple when they first occur, gradually fade and in time become a pearly, often unnoticeable white.

Dear Dr. Wilcox: I am a seventeen-year-old male and have a problem with psoriasis of the scalp. Can you suggest anything I can buy that might help? **79**

Psoriasis is a condition characterized by scattered patches of red, scaling, itchy skin, often primarily affecting the scalp. Because other conditions can also cause scalp scaling, however, it is important that the final diagnosis be made by a doctor.

There are very effective treatments available for psoriasis of the scalp. Usually, treatment starts with the use of so-

called tar shampoos, which can be purchased at any drugstore. Use of further medicated lotions must be prescribed
and supervised by a doctor. Your family doctor or a dermatologist will be able to help you.

80 **Dear Dr. Wilcox: I have never had a real problem with
acne, but in the last couple of years I have been constantly plagued by whiteheads that just won't disappear. No amount of cleansers has any effect on them.
They mostly develop around the eye area, which I
know is extremely sensitive. Do you have any suggestions?**
What you describe sounds like milia, tiny collections of oil
trapped in the skin; however, the surrounding skin is not
irritated and red, as it is in acne.

Moisturizers and creams are prime causes. Gently cleansing the skin, using cool rather than hot water, and then
applying a small amount of light moisturizer to damp skin
only in the areas that would otherwise feel uncomfortably
dry are the best ways to avoid overusing moisturizers and
ending up with milia.

Once milia are there, however, there is no safe way to remove them yourself. If you stop applying lotions to the area,
they may eventually resolve. Alternatively, a physician who
is familiar with milia could easily remove them for you.

81 **Dear Dr. Wilcox: In the past year, bluish purple "spi-
der" veins have become apparent on the backs and
sides of my legs. I know that this is hereditary because my mother also has them. I am afraid that they
will become more apparent as I get older, and I definitely do not want that to happen. Is there any way
to get rid of these veins safely?**
What you describe sounds like telangiectasias, which are
tiny blood vessels in the skin that have become dilated.

The tiny ones that occur on the face can be treated with
electrocautery. This involves briefly touching them with an
electric pointer through which a very low current is passed.
It eliminates the vessel essentially by burning it, but the
voltage is kept low to avoid scarring. Discomfort, if any, lasts
only a few seconds.

The same treatment can be tried on the larger ones that
occur on the legs, but it may not completely eliminate them.
Sclerotherapy, injection of the veins with a substance that

"dries" them up, may also work but must be done by some-one very skilled with this technique.

You can see a dermatologist to discuss the veins. But re-member, they may well be more noticeable to you than to others. Ignoring them or camouflaging them with clothes or, if you really want to, using tiny amounts of body makeup (available from cosmetic departments) might be alternative solutions.

Dear Dr. Wilcox: I am a thirteen-year-old girl, and I have dark circles under my eyes. They've been there a long time even though I'm so young. Why do I have them, and what can I do to get rid of them? **82**

Dark circles under the eyes are a common cosmetic com-plaint. It is said that being sick or overtired can make them worse, and they are also frequently seen in children with allergies (these are called "allergic shiners").

Outside of these semimedical causes, there are few health conditions that cause them. Generally, significant surgical conditions (such as a defect in blood vessels in the area) would cause only *one* side to be deeply discolored. And sig-nificant medical problems leading to excessive bruising would also cause bruising elsewhere on the body, not just under the eyes.

What, then, is the most likely cause in a healthy thirteen-year-old? It's usually an inherited tendency, occurring more frequently in brunets than in blonds or redheads. If you look closely at some of your relatives, you will probably notice that they too tend to have shadows.

The many cosmetics available to camouflage dark circles testify to how common a problem it is. An older sister or relative might be able to suggest a coverup to try. Salespeo-ple in cosmetic departments could also make suggestions.

Dear Dr. Wilcox: I have a serious problem with sweaty palms. Whenever I hold hands with a boy or square dance in school, they just drip. It's really humiliat-ing when someone tells you that your hands are sweaty. It's all I ever think about. Do I have to go through life like this? **83**

Palmar hyperhidrosis, or sweaty hands, is a common prob-lem, particularly during adolescence. The palms have some five hundred sweat glands per square half-inch (square cen-timeter)! Probably because it is so common, there are a number of do-it-yourself remedies, many of which may be quite effective.

One of the oldest remedies is soaking the palms in cooled tea for ten minutes each day. The tannic acid in the tea may decrease the sweating. The only drawback is that the tea may slightly stain the palms.

Another fairly easy solution is to buy an *unscented* antiperspirant containing aluminum chlorohydrate or aluminum chloride (listed on the label) and apply it to your palms once a day for a week. If any irritation develops, discontinue it immediately. If there is no irritation after a week's use, increase the applications to twice a day. After several weeks you can adjust the frequency of application until you find what works for you.

If a regular antiperspirant doesn't work after you have tried it for a full month, you could ask your doctor to prescribe a "super" antiperspirant solution made of 20 percent aluminum chloride in 80 percent absolute anhydrous ethyl alcohol (Drysol). This solution may cause irritation, so be sure to test it first on a small area of skin, leaving it on overnight, before trying it on your palms.

If the test is fine, you can then apply the solution to your *completely dry* hands at bedtime, approximately two hours after washing them. Do this nightly for several weeks, then use it less and less often until you determine how many times per week you need to use it to keep your hands dry. Again, however, if any irritation occurs, you must stop using it.

Iontophoresis is a newer procedure that involves placing the hands on a special machine that emits enough electrical current to ultimately block the action of the sweat glands. Treatments take twenty minutes each, are given three times per week at first, and effectively decrease sweating after two to ten treatments. To maintain the effect, repeated sessions are needed once a week or less often. It is important to consult a dermatologist before even considering iontophoresis.

These are just a few of many possible solutions. If necessary, your doctor can give you more suggestions.

84 Dear Dr. Wilcox: I am a seventeen-year-old male, and in hot weather the seat of my pants gets damp. This is very embarrassing. When I sit on vinyl or walk for about five minutes, I can feel the seat of my pants getting wet.

When moisture evaporates from the surface of the skin, the body is cooled. The body perspires in hot weather as a way of keeping its temperature normal. People vary in the degree to which they perspire when exposed to excessive heat.

When air does not circulate to allow the perspiration to evaporate, the moisture will accumulate on the skin and subsequently be absorbed by one's clothes. Vinyl tends to get hot and also does not allow the air to circulate; these two factors make perspiration more pronounced.

Wearing looser clothing made of natural fibers such as cotton will improve the air circulation and help keep you more comfortable. Tight clothes and those made of synthetic fibers can make your problem worse. If you are overweight, you may find the problem decreases if you lose weight.

Dear Dr. Wilcox: My problem is that my underarms perspire very heavily, and it seems to be getting worse. I have tried every antiperspirant on the market, but none has worked. My sister is getting married soon, and I have bought a taffeta dress, which stains very easily.

85

Axillary hyperhidrosis (excessive underarm perspiration) is a common problem, especially during adolescence. For your immediate problem, the best and safest solution may be a nonmedical one. Go to a dressmaker or tailor and ask that dress shields be designed for your dress and then sewn into place. These will provide material to absorb the perspiration before it reaches the dress.

Well before the wedding, you could also try experimenting with roll-on antiperspirants that contain either 12 percent aluminum chlorohydrate or 23 percent aluminum zirconium tetrachlorohydrex glycine (check the labels). If you are having problems with staining, avoid stick antiperspirants, which contain an ingredient that can stain clothing.

You could also ask your doctor about a product called Drysol. It's a 20 percent solution of aluminum chloride in 80 percent anhydrous ethyl alcohol that can provide dramatic relief. Drysol must be carefully applied following very specific directions, as it may cause some skin irritation. First, apply it to a small area on your arm and leave it on overnight. If no irritation occurs, apply it to your absolutely dry underarms at bedtime the next night and cover with plastic wrap. Use cloth, not tape, to hold the wrap in place. Leave this on for six to eight hours overnight and wash the medication off thoroughly in the morning. Repeat for two or more consecutive nights for the first week until the desired dryness is achieved, then use only one to three times per week to maintain the dryness.

In extreme cases people have had surgery to stop excessive perspiration, if it persists beyond adolescence. One technique is removal of the sweat glands. Another somewhat more complicated one involves severing the nerves that stimulate the glands to sweat. Neither remedy should be undertaken lightly, and surgery should only be considered if all else fails.

86 **Dear Dr. Wilcox: I am a sixteen-year-old girl and have a terrible perspiration problem. This is not just a little water on the nose, it means my whole face and body get wet when I do even a little strenuous work. When I am hot, my face becomes dripping wet, even if I go to sit down. It feels and looks as if someone splashed water on my face. Is there some sort of surgery or any way to cover up this unbearable problem?**

Excessive, widespread sweating is known in medical jargon as generalized hyperhidrosis. There are many causes.

In some situations, it may be normal. Many people perspire a lot if they are exposed to a hot, humid environment, if they develop a fever, or if they participate in unusually vigorous exercise. This is normal hyperhidrosis and is the body's attempt to keep cool in unusual circumstances. How vigorously the body responds to these challenges varies from person to person.

Emotions can also trigger hyperhidrosis. Situations causing marked anxiety or fear can induce excessive sweating, which again is something everyone will probably experience at some time. Some people, however, find that even minor stress can set off their hyperhidrosis; these people may also find that caffeine in coffee, tea, and cola drinks makes their problem worse.

There are also a number of medical causes of hyperhidrosis. Hormonal disturbances, such as those that occur in hyperthyroidism, diabetes, and pregnancy, can cause unusual sweating. Disturbances of the part of the nervous system that regulates sweating can also induce hyperhidrosis. Some drugs may cause it and even some foods may induce it in individuals with unusual sensitivities. The list of causes goes on and on.

Treatment depends upon the cause, and your doctor would have to carefully review your particular case to make a diagnosis. The most common cause is a particular sensitivity to the factors that make everyone perspire to some degree (exercise, heat). Wearing clothes that keep the body cool, avoiding stimulants such as caffeine, and giving yourself time—many adolescents find the problem decreases as they get older—are the simplest "treatments" to try in these cases. But check with your doctor to see what treatment is appropriate for you.

Dear Dr. Wilcox: I have a very embarrassing problem that's causing me to have suicidal thoughts. Since I was a preteen I have had a problem with a sulphurous body odor that seems to be totally unrelated to how often I bathe or what kind of deodorant I use. I am desperate and becoming totally reclusive.

87

I asked my doctor about this, and he suggested an operation to have my sweat glands removed. What do you suggest? I don't think the operation is the answer. I am desperate. Is there someone who specializes in this sort of disorder?

Your obvious deep distress concerns me even more than any medical problem you may have. No matter what professional you turn to, it is essential that you tell him or her just how upset you are.

Removal of the sweat glands from under the arms can be an effective treatment for people who have unusual and uncontrollable underarm perspiration. Other treatments that don't require surgery can also be effective.

Your letter implies that excessive sweating is not the whole issue, but perhaps this is the easiest place to start. Dermatologists can be of great help with this problem. They would also be aware of the various medical problems that can cause unusual odors.

Ask your family doctor to suggest a dermatologist and make an appointment. When you are there, let him or her know just how worried you are so that your feelings, as well as any medical problem, can be thoroughly addressed.

FOUR:

Hair

*I*n the adult human there is hair on every part of the
body surface except the palms of the hands, the soles
of the feet, and areas of the genitals. And anything that
much a part of us is bound to be a source of worry at one
time or another. Often there seems to be too much in the
wrong places and too little in the right places, and to top
that off it goes gray.

This section is about those "too much" and "too little"
concerns as well as the normal changes in hair distribution
that occur as one becomes more physically mature; the cav-
alcade of hormones that makes a boy's voice change, contributes to growth spurts, and stimulates the skin's oil glands
also affects the growth of body hair, making it suddenly seem
to sprout everywhere.

The letters that follow will help you learn what's normal,
what isn't, what can be treated, what can't, and how you
can understand and (sometimes) solve the problems you have
with your own hair.

88 **Dear Dr. Wilcox: I am a twelve-year-old girl. I first
noticed my facial hair when I was ten, and now it is
darker and longer. Will it grow still longer and darker
as I get older, or will it fade a bit and stop growing?
Is there any way of removing unwanted hair permanently?**
Because facial hair increases during puberty, many girls
complain about having moustaches. The amount of facial

hair you will ultimately have will be similar to that of other women in your family. The darker your coloring, the more noticeable this hair tends to be.

Shaving may lead to a coarse-feeling stubble when the hair grows back, as may plucking (which has the added disadvantage of possibly leading to infection). Depilatories (cream hair removers) may irritate the skin and also do not avoid a stubbly regrowth. As soon as any hint of stubble appears, however, you could just remove it again, using your chosen method.

The simplest solution may be to bleach the hair, which can make it virtually unnoticeable. Use a gentle bleach made especially for lightening facial hair. The bleach must be tested on a small, inconspicuous patch of skin (on your inner arm, for instance) twenty-four hours before being used on the face, to make sure no irritation will occur. Pharmacists can suggest good brands. If your complexion is dark, however, the new blond hair may provide too strong a contrast, and you'll have to find another solution.

Electrolysis can permanently remove the hair but must be done by a well-trained technician. It is expensive and time-consuming and may cause scarring if not properly done. But for women who have tried other remedies without success and have the go-ahead from their doctors, it can be an effective treatment. *(See 92.)*

Dear Dr. Wilcox: For the past few years I have had the problem of excess pubic hair. My thighs are very hairy, but worst of all is my bikini line. **89**

There are several ways to remove unwanted hair, and all have pros and cons. Shaving with a razor and shaving cream is quick and effective and does *not* make hair grow more rapidly or abundantly; it must, however, be repeated every few days. Depilatories (cream removers) "dissolve" the hair, but regrowth does occur in days; these products can also irritate the skin. *Never* shave and use a depilatory at the same time because this is very hard on your skin.

Electrolysis can permanently remove hair but is costly and time-consuming and must be expertly done to prevent scarring. *(See 92.)* Waxing, done professionally (often through department store salons), is like widespread plucking and involves placing warm wax on the skin, allowing it to harden, and then peeling it off so that the hair is pulled out. It may be effective for four to six weeks but can occasionally irritate the skin or cause scabbing and is more expensive than shaving or depilatories. *(See 91.)*

90 Dear Dr. Wilcox: About a year ago, I used a facial hair remover. When I tested the product on my arm, there was no reaction but when I used it on my face, it caused a rash and left two dark areas. I have used cover-up cosmetics, but they either did not cover completely or looked obvious. Would fade creams even out my skin?

Using any product on the skin requires care. You were right to test it before applying it to your face, but your experience illustrates a problem that can occur: the test on one area of the skin doesn't ensure that the product won't cause a reaction when applied to more sensitive skin. One way to decrease the chances of this happening is to do two tests, twenty-four hours apart, one on the soft, hairless skin on the inside of your arm and, if that's okay, the second test on a small, inconspicuous area of the face, such as near your hairline or under your chin. Only if there's no problem twenty-four hours after the second test should you use the product.

The darker areas you describe are probably caused by postinflammatory hyperpigmentation, which is a dark "stain" left after the redness of irritation is gone. These areas of skin have more melanin (skin pigment) than do surrounding areas. The darkening will often gradually fade. You can camouflage it by using a light-colored cover-up cream on the dark areas before applying your regular liquid makeup (which you have to apply to your entire face for it to look even).

Some dermatologists feel that skin bleaches, used only under a doctor's supervision, can lighten these darkened areas. Ask your family doctor to refer you to a skin specialist if you choose to try to lighten the areas. *(See 67.)*

91 Dear Dr. Wilcox: A year ago I started to use leg wax to remove the hair on my legs. I found using it no problem until I noticed that some hairs were growing back under my skin. I started to take the hair out with tweezers, and in every place where I'd pulled out a hair, a scab developed. Now I have scabs all over my legs, and I fear I may get permanent scars.

Waxing can be an effective method of temporarily removing unwanted hair. Like tweezing, waxing pulls out the hairs without affecting the hair root—the root will continue to produce hair, growing at a rate that leads to reappearance of hair on the waxed area four to six weeks after waxing.

One problem that can occur with waxing is that the hair may bend while growing, so that instead of finding its way back out to the surface, it curls up under the skin, resulting in an ingrown hair. This is more common in people with very curly hair and also in certain areas of the body such as the "bikini" area, where the waxing is removing an extension of the coarser, curlier pubic hair.

In your case the ingrown hairs have become inflamed and scabs have formed. Touching and trying to remove the scabs will make the problem worse and increase the likelihood of scarring, so it is critical that you leave your skin alone. Some dermatologists suggest that ingrown hairs be gently pulled up through the skin, but you've developed scabs by trying to do this yourself. Also, breaking the skin with the tweezers can lead to infection, which will increase the damage to the skin and the risk of scarring.

You should see your family doctor or a dermatologist who can help you work out a safe method of dealing with these ingrown hairs.

Dear Dr. Wilcox: I am a teenage female, and I would really appreciate more information on electrolysis. What does the treatment involve? Is it painful, and will the hair grow back? Could you also give a rough estimate of how much it costs?

92

Simply put, electrolysis eliminates unwanted hair by the insertion of a tiny electrical needle into the root of a hair. The electrical current from the needle causes the root to decompose. Because of the risk of scarring, it is important to go to a competent electrolysist. Your family doctor or dermatologist can help you find one.

The time required to eliminate hair varies according to where it is, how thick it is, and the reason for the excess growth. The sensitivity of the area being treated and the tolerance of the individual for feeling the little "sharp jabs" are two determinants of how many hairs can be treated during one session. For sensitive areas, such as the upper lip, local anesthetic (similar to the "freezing" dentists sometimes inject) may be used. Usually, 50 percent of the treated hairs are eliminated with the first treatment. With each new treatment 50 percent more of the treated hairs will be permanently eliminated until most of the hair is gone. Usually, people return for one-hour treatments at weekly intervals for several months until they attain the results they desire.

If the cause of the excessive hair persists, however, new

growth will continue despite treatments. Before choosing electrolysis, it is important that you see your doctor to determine if any significant medical problem is causing the excessive hair growth. This should, if possible, be treated; a few underlying illnesses can be serious.

Electrolysists charge by the hour, many about forty to fifty dollars an hour, though charges vary greatly. Health insurance may pay if the excessive hair growth is caused by a hormone imbalance or a medication the patient must take for other health problems.

Electrolysis can be an effective treatment for permanently eliminating unwanted hair. It takes time and can be expensive and uncomfortable, but many patients feel it is worth these costs. Before embarking upon a course of treatment, however, be sure to first consult your doctor.

93 **Dear Dr. Wilcox: I am a nineteen-year-old girl with an embarrassing problem. In the past three years I have developed lots of facial hair, primarily around my neck and chin. It is now beginning to grow around the nipples of my breasts too. It is dark and thick. My periods are normal.**

Most women have at least some facial hair, and the amount tends to be similar for women in the same family.

Hirsutism is the medical name for a truly excessive hair growth that is influenced by hormones called androgens; this includes hair on the face, underarms, chest, lower abdomen, and pubic area. The excessive hair growth you are experiencing does sound as if it could be called hirsutism. In some cases this condition is caused by a significant endocrine or hormonal disorder that needs treatment, which would be more likely if your periods were irregular too.

The most common type of excessive hair growth, however, is idiopathic hirsutism, where the level of androgens is normally not high, but the hair is unusually sensitive to them. Medically, this isn't a serious problem. Treatment is removal of the hair by the easiest method (waxing, depilatories, or electrolysis) and sometimes using medication that decreases the effects of the androgens (the one used most often is called spironolactone). Although idiopathic hirsutism may be the cause of your symptoms, you should see your doctor to rule out a more serious health problem.

94 **Dear Dr. Wilcox: I was reading a response of yours to a girl who was embarrassed because of her mous-**

tache. You mentioned that this symptom plus irregular periods could indicate a health problem. I am eighteen years old and I know something is wrong. Could you tell me the kind of health problems a person with those symptoms might have?

Unwanted hair is very common and in most cases is a cosmetic rather than medical problem. However, in a small number of cases excessive hair on the face, chest, and abdomen is caused by a significant health problem. If it occurs along with other symptoms, such as irregularity or complete cessation of menses (periods), then the chances of a medical problem are increased.

Because the endocrine system (which is composed of the glands in the body that put out hormones) influences both periods and hair growth in the areas described, problems somewhere in this system may be the cause.

The list of the different endocrine causes of irregular or absent periods and hirsutism is a very long one, and I'm not sure how helpful it would be to give you a string of possible diagnoses. They can range, however, from rare but very serious tumors to more common but less dangerous problems such as polycystic ovary disease (PCO). The main problem with PCO is that women with this condition tend to have difficulty becoming pregnant and need medication so that they will have periods at least four times per year. Treatment to improve fertility also is available.

If you have irregular menses and hirsutism, you should see your doctor. By finding out what other symptoms are present, by examining you, and by doing blood, urine, and possibly other tests, he or she can make a diagnosis and provide the appropriate treatment.

Dear Dr. Wilcox: I am a sixteen-year-old female, and my hair is getting quite thin and fragile. It has been permed twice and slightly bleached. After graduation I was planning to shave my head and get some kind of scalp treatment (if there is any for my case) to get my hair to grow thicker and stronger. Would shaving help to make it grow in thicker, or is that an old wives' tale?

95

Shaving hair does *not* make it thicker when it grows in and therefore would not be a solution to your problem. Perhaps the myth about shaving is based on the appearance of the hair when it grows in: because it is so short, it feels and looks coarser and more bristly. Once the hair is long enough to lie flat, however, it will look just like it did before shaving—no thicker or faster-growing.

Hairs can be classified according to what growth phase they are in. About 90 percent of the hairs on your head are actively growing at any given time. Fewer than 10 percent have finished growing and are ready to be shed. These are the hairs you find on your pillow after a night's sleep or in your brush after you've gently brushed your hair.

The change from growing or anagen hair to resting, soon-to-be shed telogen hair is not abrupt. After growing for an average of three years, the hair enters a transitional phase (three or four months) and finally the telogen stage. Usually fewer than one hundred hairs are lost each day. If you lose more than three hundred hairs in seventy-two hours, hair loss is abnormal. (You can collect the hair shed over three days and show the collection to your doctor; this will give him or her an idea of whether or not the loss is excessive.)

If hair is injured by rough handling—such as rolling it too tightly on curlers, overstraightening curly hair using a hot comb and hot petroleum jelly, wearing hair continually in tight braids, or twisting it around the fingers as part of a nervous habit—more can be pulled out than is ready to shed. Some people experience a thinning of hair after repeatedly perming, straightening, coloring, or curling it.

Split ends may also result from rough handling that damages the hair shaft, which is made up of three layers. Conditioners can temporarily "glue" the split ends together or fill in the tiny nicks and cracks in the hair shaft to make it look shiny, but the only way to get rid of split ends is to cut them off.

Preventing further damage is the most important thing you can do. Try to choose a style that requires little handling—one that can be air-dried would be good. If your hair isn't shiny, be sure to rinse it very thoroughly before applying conditioner; if you don't, soap trapped under the conditioner will make your hair look dull. If you condition your hair daily and the hair seems limp, it could be "too much of a good thing": condition only after every other shampoo. Be gentle when you wash and brush your hair.

Although rough handling can certainly cause the problems you describe, there are also many medical causes of hair changes and loss. See your doctor to make sure nothing else is contributing to your difficulties.

Dear Dr. Wilcox: I'm a nineteen-year-old male in- **96**
volved in many sports. My major concern is that I
wash my hair a lot, sometimes twice a day. My hair
is fine, and I'm wondering if all that combing and
brushing will cause my hairline to recede. No one in
my family has any problem with their hair.
If you exercise to the point of perspiring heavily, you'll need
to wash your hair afterward so that it will look and feel clean.
Lathering up only once per shampooing will help prevent
your scalp and hair from drying out. Gentle combing should
not cause a problem, but you could minimize even this by
choosing a style that doesn't require blow-drying your hair
as you brush and brush.

Dear Dr. Wilcox: I am nineteen years old. Recently I **97**
went on a diet and lost forty-five pounds. Everyone
says I look fantastic and I have never felt better. The
problem is my hair; it used to be long, thick, and
very healthy, but now it falls out a lot and has be-
come very thin-looking. My hairdresser says not to
worry, that hair can often thin out as a result of di-
eting. When will it stop falling out? Will it grow back
to its original thickness? And, most important, how
long will it take?
Your hairdresser is probably correct; like any major medical
change, dramatic weight loss can be followed by thinning
of the hair. Regrowth takes three to nine months or longer.
Hair grows only ½ in (1 cm) per month, so it will be at least
three months before you notice a significant rethickening.
Usually one can expect to regain 80 percent (maybe more)
of the original thickness, but if there is a family tendency
toward baldness or hair thinning, the regrowth could be less.
   What you are experiencing, then, is not unusual and will
generally right itself. Your doctor can examine you, however, and learn the details of your particular case to make
sure this is the correct diagnosis.

Dear Dr. Wilcox: I am a twenty-year-old male in good **98**
physical condition. My problem is that my hair is re-
ceding rapidly for a man my age. My two older broth-
ers have normal healthy heads of hair. Is there any
way to stop and cure or even just slow down this
process?

The pattern of hair loss is important in determining whether yours is a type of baldness that might benefit from treatment. If there is a generalized loss involving the entire scalp, or if there are distinct patches of baldness surrounded by healthy hair, then the baldness may have a medical cause and may respond to treatment. But if you're noticing less hair on the crown of your head and/or a receding hairline at the temples, then, unfortunately, you are experiencing typical male balding.

Although you can try to decrease wear and tear on your hair by avoiding excessive combing, brushing, and blow-drying and by gently massaging your scalp when you wash your hair, the balding itself will follow its own timetable. Fortunately, many men who experience rapid loss in the twenties find that the rate of loss stabilizes so that their hair isn't much thinner in their thirties than it was in their twenties.

In any case, at your age, you owe it to yourself to consult a dermatologist—not a hair-loss company—who can properly assess your condition.

See 99, 100.

99 **Dear Dr. Wilcox: I am a twenty-one-year-old male and am rapidly losing my hair. I have very thin hair on the top of my head and a very receding hairline. I believe I will lose all my hair in about two years. I mentioned this to my doctor, and he said there is nothing that can be done.**

I see all the advertisements in the newspapers and on television, but I'm afraid these are all rip-offs.
You are wise to be wary of rip-offs. There are, unfortunately, no creams, lotions, pills, or devices you can buy over the counter or through an ad that can reverse androgenic alopecia, the type of baldness that you and many other men experience. Hair transplants *might* be helpful. A medication called minoxidil might also help. *(See 100.)*

Premature androgenic alopecia follows the typical pattern of male balding. The hairline recedes, particularly at the sides of the forehead, and the hair on the crown of the head thins. But unlike typical balding that may start in the thirties or forties, premature balding begins, as yours has, in the early twenties. It seems to be hereditary.

It is impossible to predict how much hair will be lost, but generally the degree of baldness tends to be similar among men of the same family. Total hair loss is almost unheard of; the back and sides of the head generally retain hair throughout a man's life. Sometimes a dramatic thinning in the early twenties is followed by very slow hair loss over the next decade or more. I can assure you that you won't be completely bald, as you fear, in two or probably even in thirty years.

Some men try to improve the thickness of the hair with hair transplants, but this is far from an easy or instant solution. With this technique, small plugs of scalp containing hair roots are removed from the back of the head and transferred to the bald areas. It is a gradual process, and if the natural hairline continues to recede, the tufts of transplanted hair may stand out and have to be supplemented by new transplants. The procedure can be a bit uncomfortable and will take time to look presentable. The cost varies, depending on how much hair has to be replaced, but for a young man with mild loss, the cost would be in the hundreds of dollars rather than the thousands. If you want to know more about hair transplants, you should consult a dermatologist who specializes in the procedure. He or she can tell you the time, cost, and type of results you can expect.

Dear Dr. Wilcox: My hair is very thin at the top of my head, and I fear that it will eventually start to fall out. I find this very disturbing, considering I am a boy in my teens. Is there any medication that might help? 100

For years, people have looked for the magic cure for baldness, and probably many millions of dollars have been spent on products that made phenomenal claims but did nothing. Now, although it is definitely *not* a cure-all, there is a medication that may be helpful for *some* men with early balding problems. But two things must be remembered: the medication is just now being approved for use, and the baldness returns if the medication is ever stopped. It is also expensive: a month's supply costs about $50.

A high-blood-pressure pill called minoxidil has long been noted to increase the growth of body hair in men and women who take it. Because of this side effect, it was hoped that if the medication could be put directly on the scalp, it might be a baldness "cure."

A recent study found that of fifty-six men who applied a minoxidil lotion to their bald spots for one year, eighteen grew new hair that looked quite natural. The men who had the best results had bald areas 4 in (10 cm) or less in diameter that had been present for less than seven years. On close examination, these men had more seminormal hairs present in the bald spot before treatment than did men who didn't respond well to the medication. One person developed severe itching; none of the others reported any side effects.

If you are interested in this medication, ask your doctor or dermatologist about it.

101 **Dear Dr. Wilcox: I am a sixteen-year-old boy who has an embarrassing problem. I am prematurely graying. I'm finding every now and then that I have white hairs. Since my hair is dark, the white is very noticeable. I've had this problem for about a year, but it's just recently become conspicuous. Is there anything you could recommend?**

The age at which graying begins varies greatly from one person to another but tends to be similar among family members. The medical term for this process is canities. Premature canities refers to graying that occurs before the age of forty. Whether or not the aging of the hair and resultant graying is premature, the process is the same. Hair becomes gray as it loses its pigment (melanin). Further aging leads to the formation of air bubbles in the shaft of the hair, and then the hair becomes white. Occasional gray or white hairs are not at all unusual as early as the teen years. When we talk of canities, we mean progressively increasing graying.

It is difficult to say if you are experiencing true premature canities, but your doctor could tell you and, if necessary, refer you to a dermatologist who specializes in hair problems. If you are experiencing premature canities, the only solution may be cosmetic (camouflage, not cure). The dermatologist could suggest ways to cover up the graying very successfully.

In a few unusual cases, graying can be a result of a medical problem, such as pernicious anemia or vitiligo, a whitening of patches of skin or hair. Although it is unlikely that any of these conditions is causing your problem, your doctor can tell you for sure and can help you.

102 **Dear Dr. Wilcox: I'm a male of seventeen. About a year and a half ago I was involved in a car accident that left me with bad scars on my face. Ever since I was small I wanted to grow a beard, and now I want**

to grow one to hide my scars. Would you please tell me if there is anything that could help me grow a beard or moustache? I have heard of people getting hormone shots to increase hair growth.
To get an idea of what your beard will be like, look at your adult male relatives. As with so many characteristics, heredity plays a great role, largely determining the type and thickness of facial hair a man (or a woman, for that matter) will have. The age at which other males in your family were able to grow beards will also give you some idea of when you can expect a mature growth. Your beard may not be as thick now as it will be in later years.

Androgens are hormones your body produces that influence the growth of facial hair. Getting hormone shots, however, is not a treatment for lack of facial hair, nor is there any treatment available for increasing the thickness of one's beard.

You don't mention if you've seen a doctor, particularly a plastic surgeon, since the accident. It might be very worthwhile to do so, since there are techniques available for decreasing the obviousness of scars that might be appropriate in your case. *(See 68.)*

FIVE:

Medical Problems

*Treatment [for canker sores]: Give a gentle lax-
ative . . . give some sweating medicine which
shall also excite the skin into action; and use a
gargle of sage tea, gold-thread tea, hyssop, su-
mac berries, etc.*

A. W. Chase
Dr. Chase's Family Physician, Farrier
Bee-Keeper and Second Receipt
Book *(1875)*

Yellow teeth, bad breath, lumps on the testicles,
constipation, vaginitis—these problems and more
are discussed in this section, a smorgasbord of
medical issues not covered elsewhere. It is not an encyclo-
pedia of every health problem an adolescent may encounter
but a selection of those our readers ask about most often.

A repeated cry in this section is "See your doctor"—and
as tired as you may become of seeing it, it's a necessary
warning: no matter how complete a writer's description of
a problem may be, reading it is still a poor substitute for
seeing, examining, and talking to the patient. Diagnoses
based on a few sentences are shaky at best, totally wrong at
worst. The letters are merely takeoff points for a discussion
of specific topics. If uncertainty remains, readers are urged
to seek medical advice for their own unique problems.

103 **Dear Dr. Wilcox: I have a very embarrassing problem. My teeth are yellow even though I brush regularly. Is it the way I'm brushing?**
Very few people have the gleaming white teeth seen in
toothpaste ads. Most normal, healthy teeth are, in fact,
somewhat gray or yellow. Good oral hygiene, however, is important for health and appearance and requires regular
brushing and flossing.

Ideally, you should brush each time you eat, to remove
food particles. These particles provide the sugar that bac-

teria in the mouth ultimately break down to form an acid
that contributes to the formation of cavities. Even thorough
brushing, however, can leave particles between teeth and
near the gum line; if not removed, plaque will build up, gums
may become unhealthy, and cavities can form. Daily flossing will clean the areas the brushing misses. Your oral hygiene is not complete without it.

You should be seeing your dentist twice a year for professional cleaning. He or she can also help you with your
brushing or flossing technique, examine your teeth and
mouth, and tell you if the color of your teeth is within the
normal range or if it signifies a problem requiring special
care.

**Dear Dr. Wilcox: My teeth are yellowish brown by the
gums, on both the top and the bottom rows. It is getting so that I hate to open my mouth. I brush my
teeth twice a day and have tried all kinds of tooth-
pastes.**

104

Without seeing you, it is impossible to say whether your
teeth are within the normal color range, but your dentist
can easily tell you. There are a number of problems that can
cause tooth discoloration. For example, pigments can be in-
corporated into the enamel in some situations. Similarly,
before birth and during the tooth-forming years of infancy
and childhood, exposure to the antibiotic tetracycline can
lead to a yellow or brown discoloration. Finally, defects in
the development of the enamel, often caused by serious vitamin and mineral deficiencies, can lead to pitting of the
enamel and uneven color.

Far more common, however, is staining from smoking,
chemicals, or foods. If smoking is a factor in your case, the
best solution—and the best thing for your long-term health—
is to quit. Another very common cause is apparent discoloration where there has been excessive plaque buildup and
the plaque has been calcified. Do not use so-called stain-
removing tooth polishes; they can damage the tooth enamel.

If your dentist feels your teeth are truly discolored, there
are treatments available. The simplest approach is bonding:
the discolored teeth are painted with a colored material that
has the desired tint. This color will last for several years but
will then gradually wear away and need to be reapplied.

A more costly, complicated, but permanent solution is
capping, or applying crowns. Teeth are ground down and a
cap (artificial tooth) is slipped on to each. Crowns are es-

pecially helpful if large cavities have weakened the teeth, but they can also be applied simply to improve appearance.

Bleaching is a third alternative. It tends to be less expensive, but good results can be more difficult to achieve because it is hard to control just how much lighter a tooth may become. Discuss these alternatives with your dentist.

105 **Dear Dr. Wilcox: I am a sixteen-year-old boy who has bleeding gums. My dentist suggested that I buy an oral antiseptic called Amosan for rinsing my mouth after eating, and an expensive toothbrush. I have followed his suggestions and so far there is no change.**
When the gums bleed easily, it generally means that they are not healthy. It takes time, care, and effort to restore them to health.

Your dentist has given you two good suggestions, but you should see him again because you also need instructions on the best way to use the toothbrush to stimulate the gums back to health. Briefly, this includes using a *soft* (not firm-bristled) toothbrush and brushing so that your stroke starts *on* the gum itself and then continues up or down the entire surface of the tooth. Some dentists also recommend you use a brush that has a little rubber tip on the handle, with which you gently massage the gums between the teeth.

106 **Dear Dr. Wilcox: I am an eighteen-year-old girl with a very embarrassing problem. I am too shy to talk about it to my dentist or doctor. My problem is bad breath. Please don't suggest I brush my teeth, use mouthwash, and floss my teeth. I've tried all of them, and they don't work for me. I dread going to school in the morning when I haven't eaten anything, because there is nothing to mask my mouth odor. Is there anything I can do?**
Halitosis, or bad breath, is a common problem. As you imply, the most frequent source of the odor is the mouth, and regular brushing and flossing can remove food particles that can cause the problem. I hope that even if it isn't eliminating your halitosis, you are still continuing to brush at least twice a day and floss regularly to prevent the buildup of plaque that, unless removed, can contribute to chronic gum problems or cavities.

If ineffective oral hygiene is not the problem, the source of your halitosis could still be your mouth. A chronic dental infection could be the cause. Other medical problems that can lead to halitosis include throat, sinus, or nasal infections or disease and certain lung problems. Rarely—and not without other symptoms of serious illness—liver disease, diabetes, or kidney failure can in specific situations cause unusual breath odors. Obviously, these latter causes are exceedingly unlikely in your case.

More common for your age group are certain habits that may lead to halitosis. Cigarette smoking is a leading cause of bad breath. Drinking alcohol and eating garlic are other common causes (garlic can be excreted by the lungs for more than twenty-four hours after it's been eaten).

Physicians and dentists deal with questions like yours all the time. They will be able to tell you if there *is* a problem—sometimes people think they have halitosis when their breath is actually normal. If halitosis is present, they can find its source and treat it accordingly.

Dear Dr. Wilcox: I get painful white sores in my mouth once in a while. What causes them, and what can I do about them?   **107**

Canker sores, or aphthous ulcers, were once thought to be caused by viruses, but the cause really isn't known. They tend to occur if you are run down, tired, under stress, or sick, or if you accidentally injure your mouth while brushing your teeth. Prevention means avoiding any of these conditions. Otherwise, they tend to come and go, usually lasting no more than five days, though in rare cases they can linger on for weeks.

Treatment is aimed at making them less sore. Taking acetaminophen (e.g., Tylenol) as directed on the label or rinsing your mouth with a warm saltwater solution (¼ tsp/1ml of salt in an 8 oz/250 ml glass of water) can give relief. If the pain is very severe, your doctor might suggest using an anesthetic (pain-relieving) gel called xylocaine. Some doctors also suggest rinsing your mouth four times daily with a solution made by mixing the contents of a capsule of tetracycline (an antibiotic for which a prescription is needed) with water. Another prescription medication that might provide relief is a steroid-containing cream such as Kenalog. Ask your doctor what might work best for you.

Dear Dr. Wilcox: I am wondering how I can stop my eyes from becoming more shortsighted. I've read in science magazines that there are three methods to help eyes: (a) wear a special kind of contact lens that   **108**

will eventually lead to normal vision; (b) acupuncture; (c) flatten the cornea so the vision becomes normal. Do any of these methods work? Do they help in preventing further damage to the eyes? What is shortsightedness? Is it the retina that is being damaged? I don't watch TV very much, but I study quite late every night. Is that a possible cause for my shortsightedness?

I am an active person, and my parents think that contact lenses may blind my eyes rather than repair them. They said that I might poke myself in the eye when trying to put them in, or a ball might hit my eyes and shatter the lens, or the lens may eventually adhere to my cornea. Is this true?

Myopia (shortsightedness or nearsightedness) occurs when the distance from the front to the back of the eyes is longer than it is in someone with normal vision. Because of this, when you sit at the back of a classroom and try to read the blackboard, the image on the blackboard focuses in front of (or "short" of) the retina (the lining in the back part of the eye), and things look clear only if they focus right on the retina. Properly fitting glasses or contact lenses allow the images to focus on the retina.

Basically, you tend to inherit the shape of your eyeballs from your parents, and myopia is more common in certain ethnic groups. The distance from the front to the back of the eye increases during adolescence and then stabilizes by the thirties. If you have a tendency toward shortsightedness, it will probably get a bit worse during these years.

Acupuncture will not correct myopia because it cannot change the shape of your eye. Wearing "special" hard contact lenses in an attempt to change the shape of your cornea (the clear membrane over the colored part of your eye) can temporarily allow images to focus in the right place, but once the lens is removed, the cornea gradually goes back to its old shape, and in minutes or hours you're as shortsighted as you were before.

The last procedure, called radial keratotomy, is an operation to change the shape of the cornea. The results are variable, and there are many associated problems, so it is recommended that this surgery be considered only as a last resort.

Contact lenses may be fine for you, but you should see an ophthalmologist to be sure. Your family doctor can help you find one. Contact lenses won't "repair" your eyes, nor will they "blind" them. They may even provide protection in certain types of accidents, and they might improve your vision more than eyeglasses would.

Dear Dr. Wilcox: I was told by my eye doctor that the lining of my eyelids is laden with flakes of mascara and/or eyeliner. Apparently, this is the cause of the stinging in my eyes after hours of reading, late nights, or any other strain. My doctor informed me that this is a common finding of ophthalmologists with women in North America due to the prevalent use of eye makeup. He advised me to use less mascara and to keep the eyeliner a safe distance from the lash line. He did not, however, seem to have a solution for removing the makeup that is already there.

109

Eye makeup can be a common cause of eye irritation. If the edges of the eyelids become irritated by flecks of makeup around the lashes, the condition is called blepharitis. If bits of makeup inflame the conjunctivae (the transparent membrane that lines the eye), the condition is called conjunctivitis, and the eye feels sore and may look red.

If blepharitis is the problem and you can see makeup on the inflamed lid margins amidst your lashes, you can try to gently remove it with a cotton swab moistened in warm water. But be careful not to cause more irritation by rubbing hard where makeup is really stuck on. Try gently, and if it doesn't come away, you can always try gently another time. Eventually, it will wear away on its own; you should be free of it in several months.

Flecks that have caused conjunctivitis are a different problem. Don't try to remove them. These bits actually become embedded *in* the membrane, but they too will gradually work their way out in a few months. Letting them do so is far safer than poking at them.

Dear Dr. Wilcox: I am usually quite a happy person, except that I am self-conscious about my nose. I think I would feel a lot better about myself if I could change its shape. Could you please tell me what the success rate is with rhinoplasty operations, and how could I go about finding a doctor who can perform one? Also, would this operation be covered by my health insurance?

110

A rhinoplasty, or operation to alter the appearance of the nose, varies in cost from place to place and surgeon to surgeon, but $1,000 to $4,500 is the usual range. If the operation is considered "medically necessary"—if, for example, the surgery is part of an operation to relieve difficulty with breathing through the nose—some health insurance programs will cover at least part of the cost.

Success rates, however, are more complicated to discuss. Medical success and cosmetic success are two separate issues. Medically, complications are rare. There is always a risk when a person undergoes a general anesthetic, but it is not greater for rhinoplasty than for other operations. Probability of cosmetic success, however, has to be evaluated for *each individual patient* by a surgeon who has taken the time to get to know you and your expectations as well as what type of skin you have and what will have to be done to change your nose.

Having realistic expectations is critical. Obviously, changing your nose won't solve your life problems or transform you into some attractive actor's double. Remember, too, that this surgery will change something you've grown up with, unlike, say, a facelift, which is meant to make people look more like they used to. With rhinoplasty, one has to adjust to a new appearance, which may take time.

Related to having realistic expectations is making sure the decision to have a rhinoplasty is not made during a time of crisis or upset. In general, this would exclude having the surgery done during a turbulent time of life when there are many unsolved problems, unless an obvious deformity exists and must be corrected. It also must be delayed until your face and bone structure have matured. Usually, you'd have to be *at least sixteen.*

How do you find a surgeon who will carefully evaluate your case (including your goals and expectations)? The best way to start is to ask your family doctor for a referral to a surgeon he or she knows and trusts.

111 **Dear Dr. Levine: I am a fourteen-year-old girl with a hearing handicap. My problem is that I don't have many friends. My sister is very popular in her school and has many friends. She gets so many phone calls and makes me so jealous because I can't hear. Nobody seems to feel sorry for me except myself. I'm even afraid I won't make any new friends this year**

because people are always teasing me because I talk funny.

My parents are telling me that I'm getting my hearing back soon—a bionic ear that will help restore hearing. But I don't want to have an operation—I'm even chicken to go for tests at the hospital.

I would expect that you're wrong that nobody feels sorry for you except yourself. I'm sure that your parents and sister are sympathetic to your plight. I know I am, and I'll bet most readers feel the same way.

It sounds callous to say so, but life goes on. Many people who have handicaps nowadays are saying they don't *want* sympathy but would rather have opportunities for maximizing their potential, for example getting education and jobs, being treated as real people.

You are still young and learning about yourself and how to cope with a very real problem. Of course you feel sorry for yourself! But you've got to develop all those interests and talents and strengths you do have. Many hospital hearing clinics and centers for the deaf have mental health professionals attached to them. You might speak to your parents about setting up an appointment with one of them.

Your sense of isolation and loneliness is temporary. With proper help and support you should do very well. And if that operation does become available, what have you got to lose?

112

Dear Dr. Levine: I am an eighteen-year-old boy, and I have a serious problem. I am a stutterer. No matter how hard I try, I can't stop. It is so embarrassing and frustrating to get stuck on a word in the middle of a conversation.

If I sense I am going to stutter on a word, I usually scramble to find another word to replace it. A lot of the time I just don't talk. Because of my cover-ups, my friends don't think it's a very serious problem, and they don't know the enormous effect it's having on me. I feel so helpless and angry.

I started stuttering when I was about thirteen. It wasn't very serious back then, but it's becoming worse and worse.

I find it mind-boggling that an eighteen-year-old who has a long-standing stuttering problem should not have been evaluated and treated years ago. Most hospitals have speech pathology departments and clinics. There are speech therapists in most communities who do therapeutic work with all kinds of speech disorders.

Stuttering is a complex disorder, combining psychological and organic difficulties. I don't want to pretend that it is always immediately cured; it often takes time. But it is almost always improved and controlled. I know many stutterers who have reached high levels of achievement in a wide variety of fields (including psychiatry!). You can do it too.

113 **Dear Dr. Wilcox: I am nineteen and have a cleft palate. I have had seven operations and had one just a year ago. I have never dated, but that doesn't bother me. When I do start dating, however, what should I say or do about my nose? I'm very shy about it (I am scared I will be hurt by comments, as I was with boys when I was younger). Please give me some suggestions.**

For those who are not familiar with cleft palate, it is basically caused by a failure of the bones that make up the roof of the mouth to fully join while the baby develops before birth. This gap in the bones can affect other facial structures, particularly the nose, but all of these problems can be corrected with surgery. Although cleft palate can be associated with certain genetic causes (in which case there are usually other malformations as well) or with the mother taking certain drugs during pregnancy (for example, diazepam [Valium] or sulfa antibiotics), most often it occurs without obvious cause. It affects one person in a thousand.

The hurtful remarks you heard when you were younger were made by kids who were ignorant, insensitive, and immature. Because of this past hurt you feel a bit wary. But you will find as you begin to date that your confidence will build and those old hurts will fade. You will also find that sharing experiences, thoughts, and problems will flow naturally as you get to know and care for someone.

You won't need or want to say anything about the surgery when you first meet someone, any more than you would give your date a list of the most significant events in your life. Having seven operations before the age of nineteen certainly would be significant in anyone's life, but this fact will emerge naturally in the course of the many hours one spends getting to know someone else, just as the many other details of your life will.

Dear Dr. Wilcox: I am a seventeen-year-old girl. I have
a problem that is getting worse and worse and is affecting me emotionally as well as physically. For many
years I have been getting headaches (ranging from
mild to very severe) and inexplicable pains (mostly
in my legs and forearms), and they are getting worse
and more frequent.

114

I am beginning to get other side effects as well—
slight weight gain, variations in mood (either depressed or anxious and tense), occasional dizziness,
nausea, and increasing difficulty in concentrating.

Doctors have told me my problem is "change in
metabolism," "nervous stress," etc. I have not been
to see a doctor for a few years now and am skeptical
about doing so. I want to know what I can do.

Diagnosing such problems requires a doctor's examination
and, if necessary, blood tests. Trying to arrive at a diagnosis based on your letter wouldn't be fair or accurate. Ask
your friends or family to recommend a doctor they trust and
make an appointment to discuss your problems thoroughly.

It's certainly possible that stress is a factor, but without
more information, one can't say for sure. Stress is very powerful; it can make any symptom, even the pain of a broken
leg, seem worse. It can also make us focus on symptoms we
might otherwise ignore.

Studies have shown that everyone has a "reportable
symptom" (a vague ache, a mild pain, a funny feeling, etc.)
at least once every three to five days. Generally, people choose
to ignore these; the symptoms go away, don't recur, and are
forgotten. But if the person is under stress, he or she may
focus more on the symptom and feel the need to seek help.
Stress can, then, influence choices we make, needs we feel,
and perceptions of our well-being.

It can be very frustrating to have symptoms that cannot
be, or have not been, medically explained. Often, in these
cases, a physician can offer reassurance but still not be able
to say what the problem is. Instead, he or she may only be
able to tell the patient what the problem *isn't*.

The fact is that some problems cannot be easily diagnosed and labeled; accepting this, knowing that the problem has been thoroughly investigated, and receiving a
complete explanation from the doctor can ease your mind.
But if your feelings of distress continue, they should be

pursued, perhaps best with a counselor trained in dealing with such problems.

Discuss your fears and discomforts again with a doctor you trust.

115   **Dear Dr. Wilcox: I am a fourteen-year-old male who has been going through very tough times these past few months. I have felt a burning sensation in my stomach and near my heart. It could be heartburn, but why has it been going on for so long? I've tried liquid and tablet antacids. Nothing. Only relief for a few days. I can't live with pain in my stomach for another seventy years. My dad has had a stomach problem almost all his life. Is it hereditary? Please give me a quick solution that will stop or ease the pain in my abdomen now! I cannot live like this.**

Pain is your body's way of letting you know something may be wrong. Although we all have minor aches and pains for a day or two that we ignore, when pain persists it should *not* be ignored. See your doctor soon to find out what is wrong and be treated to get rid of the problem.

A burning sensation where your ribs come together in the front is usually caused by irritation of the stomach or esophagus (the tube that carries the food from your throat to your stomach). Burning can also occur when the duodenum (the part of the small bowel into which the stomach passes the food for further digestion) is irritated. The partial relief you get with antacids is a clue that the pain is coming from one of these three areas, because irritation of the esophagus, stomach, and duodenum can be eased by decreasing the amount of acid present (that's what antacids do). Although irritation can cause this kind of burning, ulceration—sort of an extreme form of irritation—can too.

Until you can see your doctor, there are some simple things you can do that may help decrease the burning. Avoid caffeine (cola, chocolate, coffee, and tea), don't take aspirin, and if you smoke or drink alcohol, *stop now.*

Make an appointment with your doctor soon; he or she may also give you some tips on how to take your antacids for maximum benefit until you can be seen.

116   **Dear Dr. Wilcox: Recently I found out I have a prolapsed mitral valve. The doctor said I wouldn't need to have surgery or take medication. I have heard that**

some women with a heart condition are not advised to have children. Is this true? I would very much like to have children when I'm older.
Recent studies have indicated that mitral valve prolapse (or MVP) may be present in 6 to 18 percent of healthy young women. In the vast majority of cases it causes no symptoms and requires no treatment, except that anyone with MVP should inform her dentist, so that she can be given antibiotics prior to any dental work. (Whenever heart valves don't move smoothly, they can be more likely to catch the bacteria that can get into the bloodstream during dental procedures.)

The mitral valve is made up of leaflets that divide the left atrium, or top chamber of the heart, from the left ventricle, or bottom chamber of the heart. Like the rest of the heart valves, it helps keep the blood flowing in one direction. In MVP, one or more of the mitral leaflets dips a tiny bit toward the back when the heart contracts (beats).

Heart conditions that cause complications in pregnancy are *very* different from MVP, so don't worry. Women with these problems may have any of a variety of serious cardiovascular lesions. Those most at risk have cardiac diseases that make them ill and unable to carry out normal daily activities.

Dear Dr. Wilcox: I'm healthy and physically in good shape (except for being about 4 lb/2 kg overweight). The problem is, almost every time I get up suddenly from a sitting or lying down position, I feel very dizzy and my vision goes black. In a few seconds it goes away and I'm okay. Could you tell me what's wrong? **117**
An elaborate series of internal reflexes allows one's cardiovascular system to adapt to changes in position and to maintain one's blood pressure so that there is always an adequate blood flow to the brain and vital organs. However, when one quickly jumps out of bed, for example, there can be a slight delay in this adaptation, so that until all those reflexes do their job, there is slightly less blood flow to the brain, and one feels momentarily faint.

It is worth mentioning the problem to your doctor, particularly if it is a new problem or is getting worse. He or she may check your blood pressure with you lying, sitting, and/or standing and may do a blood test to make sure that a problem such as anemia isn't aggravating the situation.

118 **Dear Dr. Wilcox: I am a chronic hiccuper, but I find I have been hiccuping more often in the portable classrooms than in the regular school classrooms. I am wondering if there is something wrong with me. My sister feels there might be something wrong with my diaphragm, or I might be reacting to the chemicals in the portables.**

The medical term for hiccup is singultus, and it is a symptom virtually everyone has experienced at some time. Although there are many causes of hiccups, being in a portable classroom is *not* one of them.

A hiccup is caused by a sudden spasm of the diaphragm. The characteristic sound is produced by closure of the vocal chords as air is breathed in. When one gets a bout of the hiccups, they usually occur two or three per minute.

The most common causes of hiccups include excessive tobacco smoking, laughing too hard, excessive alcohol intake, accidental air swallowing, and stress. Home remedies are generally based on diverting one's attention from the hiccups. Sipping ice water, slowing and counting breaths, and distracting conversation are some that may work. Breathing carbon dioxide has a more scientific basis as a cure; having the hiccuper cover his or her nose and mouth with a paper bag and breathe into it for three to five minutes is the home version of this remedy.

There can, however, be medical reasons for persistent hiccups. In these cases, hiccups usually would occur during both sleep and waking hours, and there would be other symptoms as well.

Although a medical cause is not common in your age group, your problem has persisted for a long time and is obviously bothering you. Although you now have a general idea of what causes hiccups, your doctor can discuss your problem further.

119 **Dear Dr. Wilcox: I have a very large Adam's apple that sticks out from my neck. It is often uncomfortable when I wear certain shirts and difficult when I shave. I was wondering if there are any ways I can have this changed and what methods would be used.**

The Adam's apple is actually part of the larynx, or voice box, and is called the thyroid cartilage. At puberty it increases in size, especially in males, and therefore contributes to the enlargement of the larynx and the deepening of the voice that occurs so prominently in boys during the teen years.

The thyroid cartilage is more noticeable in men than in women and often is especially noticeable in tall, thin males.

There are, however, many other possible explanations for a lump that can occur in the region of the thyroid cartilage and can be mistaken for a large Adam's apple. The list is very long and includes cysts that are present at birth but only become obvious during adolescence, lymph nodes that enlarge when illness is present, and even the thyroid gland itself.

Your physician can easily determine whether your Adam's apple is large or one of these other masses is present. If it is the Adam's apple, it may become less obvious as you become older and heavier (there really is no other treatment). If it is one of the other causes, the treatment will depend upon the specific problem.

Dear Dr. Wilcox: I'm a thirteen-year-old girl. I have recently learned I have a mild case of scoliosis. I am worried about having to wear a brace. Would you please tell me what kind of exercise I should do?

120

In scoliosis, which occurs primarily in females, the spine curves away from the midline of the back, and some of the vertebrae (the small bones that make up the spine) are rotated rather than being aligned one on top of the next like a carefully built tower of blocks.

It's best if structural scoliosis can be detected early so that any needed treatment can be started to prevent a worsening of the curve. Often parents bring their daughter to a doctor because they notice that one shoulder is higher than the other or one shoulder blade is more prominent than the other. For diagnosis, X-rays are essential to confirm the degree of curve and rotation present.

There are two types of scoliosis, structural and postural. Postural scoliosis disappears when the person lies down, and X-rays show no structural changes. It is treated by general exercises to improve posture or by correcting any other factors that may be affecting posture.

In structural scoliosis, however, treatment varies depending on the degree of curvature. If it is very slight, the doctor may want only to monitor it to make sure it does not increase. Otherwise, braces can be worn, and many who wear them find their physical activities are only slightly limited. As well, if the curvature is less than 30 degrees, a system of electrical stimulation during sleep can be effective. Other techniques are also available. Exercises are best used for maintaining and improving flexibility of the spine. Appropriate exercises can be outlined by your doctor.

Only your doctor can know your individual case and answer your specific concerns. Scoliosis is a common and very treatable problem. Discuss your particular questions with your doctor; he or she knows you best.

121 **Dear Dr. Wilcox: Two summers ago I had mononucleosis. I suffered with the discomfort for two weeks in bed, and at that time I had no idea of what mono was, so I just obeyed my doctor.**

Now I am planning to get married as soon as my fiancé and I reach our scholastic goals. He is very concerned about what happened to me in the past and has made me feel very uncomfortable by telling me that I still have the virus inside me. I am now very worried because I want to have children someday. Will having mono affect my ability to bear children? Can it cause any type of problem (i.e., sexually or in childbirth)?

Viruses are the most common cause of infections in humans and are responsible for the colds and flu we all experience. Mononucleosis is caused by a virus called the Epstein-Barr (EB) virus. About half of all students entering a university have antibodies to this virus in their blood, which means they've been exposed to "mono" at some point. Most, however, will report never having had symptoms of it.

In adolescence, symptoms of mononucleosis will develop (if they are going to) three to seven weeks after exposure. After three to five days of vague symptoms (mild fever, headache, fatigue), the more classic symptoms of marked sore throat, fever, and swollen glands occur. The diagnosis is confirmed by blood tests. The treatment for an uncomplicated case is usually just having the patient rest until he or she feels better; activity won't make mono worse, but while ill with it, people are generally tired and don't have the energy to do much. If the spleen becomes enlarged, it is important to avoid sports or excessive exercise that could injure it and cause it to bleed. By examining you, your doctor can tell if your spleen is enlarged. Once it returns to normal size, all activities are permitted.

Only *rarely* do patients develop what is called the chronic EB virus syndrome, in which symptoms of the initial infection can come and go over a period of many months. This condition can be diagnosed by means of blood tests.

As with most viral infections, mono is passed from one person to another, but, interestingly, it is uncommon for roommates, siblings, and spouses of patients with mono to develop it too. Rarely do patients have any idea from whom they contracted the illness; it is most often transmitted by someone who, at that moment, had no symptoms.

I wonder if your boyfriend has confused mono with some other disease, because his concerns don't fit the situation. Perhaps you should discuss it with him again and then clarify any further questions with your doctor. Mono will have no effect on you sexually or on your ability to have children. As with many other viruses (for example, German measles), there does seem to be a risk of passing the virus to the fetus if a woman has the active viral infection while pregnant. Obviously, this is not an issue in your case.

Dear Dr. Wilcox: I have had a small lump under my arm for about four years. When touched, it hurts. I went to my doctor four years ago, and he said it was nothing. I went again about two months ago, and this time he said it was just a gland and not to worry. Doctor or no doctor, I just don't seem to trust his words. He really did no thorough examination. Is there anyplace I can go to find out exactly if cancer is present? Is it also possible for a gland to form a bump and hurt for a period of over four years?

122

Lymph nodes are sometimes referred to as "glands." They are small oval structures that occur in groups in different parts of the body. They are part of the body's defense system against disease. The lymph nodes filter out the material produced by infection and inflammation. Also among their complicated duties are breaking down the filtered noxious substances, producing special infection- and inflammation-fighting cells called lymphocytes, and helping to produce antibodies that fight infection and illness.

When the body is under siege by anything—from flu to cancer—the lymph nodes do their job and enlarge. If the nodes involved are near the surface, you may be able to feel them beneath the skin. Areas where enlarged nodes may be most easily felt include the neck, the underarms, and the groin. After years of fighting infection, or after a particularly severe bout, some nodes may stay slightly enlarged. Usually these nodes are very small, are rubbery or soft, and can be moved around a bit. They can at times be tender.

A hard node, one that enlarges for no apparent reason,

one that enlarges steadily over a short or long period of time, or one that feels as though it is stuck to the structures beneath it should always be checked out by a doctor, since such nodes could be signs of cancer or other serious disease.

Nodes aren't the only cause of lumps in the underarms. Cysts, infected ingrown hairs, and collections of fat called lipomas are just a few other possibilities.

To evaluate what seems like an enlarged lymph node in the underarm, a doctor may check the other areas where lymph nodes can be felt to see if there are any other enlarged nodes. He or she may also check your abdomen to see if your liver and spleen are normal size. If the evaluation reveals abnormalities of concern, your doctor may do some blood tests or X-rays and may reexamine you later.

The fact that you've had a "lump" for four years without noticing any change is very reassuring. If you aren't comfortable with the examination you received, you can go back to your doctor to discuss it with him. You could also seek a second opinion from another doctor.

123 **Dear Dr. Wilcox: I'm twelve years old, and two years ago I got bronchitis and was hospitalized. Ever since then I keep getting it at least once every two months. Antibiotics don't seem to help. To me it's very serious because I want to be a lifeguard. My life is shattered over this. Is there anything else that would help? My doctor said no.**
There are too many details missing from your letter for me to be able to give you specific advice, but I can try to help define the problem.

First of all, bronchitis can mean different things to different people. By formal definition, bronchitis means inflammation of one or more bronchi (the main tubes in the lungs). Acute bronchitis usually means the inflammation is caused by some kind of infection, and it may be treated with antibiotics, drugs that kill bacteria. The symptoms of acute bronchitis can include fever, cough, and chest discomfort.

Chronic bronchitis is a name sometimes given to a condition in which the recurrent irritation or inflammation of the bronchi leads to damage that results in ongoing lung problems. It is a disease primarily of people over the age of forty-five. Smoking is the major cause. Exposure to certain industrial chemicals can also contribute to it. It is hardly likely that any of this could be going on in your case.

The other most common way in which the term bronchitis is used is in reference to the inflammatory changes that accompany asthma. In asthma, though, the most prominent change in the bronchi is spasm or temporary narrowing that leads to coughing, wheezing, and shortness of breath. Although infections can trigger this response, attacks in some people may be initiated by breathing cold air, pollution, exercise, allergies, or stress. Sometimes the trigger can't be found. There are, fortunately, a variety of medications available that can prevent the inflammatory changes that accompany spasm or relieve spasm once it occurs.

There are also, of course, unusual and rare lung problems that can cause chronic cough or symptoms similar to bronchitis.

You need to sit down with your doctor to discuss your own case. Are you having a series of infections? Is there a chronic problem? Is there wheezing? What treatments have been used and what alternatives are there? Do you need to see a specialist, in this case a respirologist? And is there any reason to think you can't still be a lifeguard? In most cases the answer would be "no" and your lifestyle shouldn't be affected.

Dear Dr. Wilcox: I'm a fourteen-year-old female and am of normal weight for my height. For quite some time I've noticed that my fingers are always cold. They feel like icicles. I've tried dressing warmly, and that helps keep my body warm but not my fingers (or toes). The house temperature is always warm. **124**

This, like so many problems, isn't easy to address because I don't know enough details. But I will at least give you some general facts about the causes of cold hands and feet.

In most cases, the condition is idiopathic—that is, it just happens, it isn't serious, and we don't know the cause. Stress *may* play a role; almost everyone has experienced cold, clammy hands when upset over something, such as a final exam.

Acrocyanosis is a condition that results in chronically cold, often mottled or blue/purple hands and feet. The cause is unknown, it's not dangerous, and it is most common in young women. I'm glad you mention that your weight is normal: acrocyanosis is particularly common among women with anorexia nervosa, the eating disorder in which patients starve themselves. Most people who have acrocyanosis, however, do *not* have anorexia.

One condition that can cause cold fingers and toes and

should be investigated by a doctor is Raynaud's disease. It can be associated with other medical problems, and treatment may be needed. Again, it is most common among young women. In this condition, one or more fingers turn white when exposed to cold. The affected fingers then turn blue and become painful. Finally, as the area rewarms, the blue is replaced by a brilliant red. Classically, the whole process takes from fifteen to sixty minutes until the fingers look normal again.

There are a few unusual circulation problems that can cause temperature change, numbness, or tingling in *one* arm (not both). Checking your pulse while you are in different positions can help a doctor make sure this is not an issue.

What can you do about your cold hands? By dressing warmly and protecting your hands from the cold, you are doing everything you should. If your hands cause you no discomfort, just carry on and don't worry about them.

125 **Dear Dr. Wilcox: For about the past month I have noticed a slight discharge from my breasts. At first it was thin, like watery milk, but now it's thicker and there's less of it. I've never had intercourse, and my periods are fairly regular. There are no lumps, and since it's in both breasts I don't think it's cancer.**

Because discharge from the breast may represent a significant medical problem, you should make an appointment to see your doctor soon.

What you describe sounds like galactorrhea, or secretion of milk when a woman is not breast-feeding a baby. The discharge may be white, yellow, clear, or even greenish, and it may be from one or, more usually, both nipples.

Excess production of the hormone prolactin by the pituitary gland is the ultimate cause of galactorrhea. The key is to find out why this excess prolactin is being produced. The most serious reason is the presence of a growth called an adenoma in the pituitary. (It can and should be readily treated.)

More common and less serious causes include physical stimulation of the breast that sets off prolactin production: excessive nipple stimulation during lovemaking, chest wall scars with disrupted nerves, and even infection of the area by herpes zoster (the virus that causes chicken pox and shingles, not genital herpes) can be such "mechanical" causes.

Other causes of increased prolactin secretion include a

wide variety of drugs, thyroid problems, physical injury, certain anesthetics, and surgery. Some experts also say that severe psychological stress can affect the hypothalamus gland, which can then cause the pituitary to produce excess prolactin.

A discharge from the breasts called colostrum also occurs from the fourth month of pregnancy on; obviously, this is not an issue in your case. If discharge only comes from one breast, this too must be investigated; a growth in the breast could be the source.

Dear Dr. Wilcox: For over two years I've had lumps in my breasts. They are quite large now, and sometimes I feel sharp pains. I'm scared I might have cancer, but I haven't anybody I can confide in, especially my family.

How can I find out for sure? I can't go to my family doctor and would like to remain anonymous if I go elsewhere, although I don't know where.

126

There are many causes of lumps in the breast. First of all, remember that normal breasts rarely feel completely smooth because of their structure: they are composed of fat, tiny glands, ducts, and fibrous bands that divide the breast into lobules.

Because the components of the breast respond to the hormones of the menstrual cycle, the breasts may be especially lumpy and even sore before one's menstrual period. By examining your breasts regularly after each period and by checking with a physician, you learn the normal architecture of your own breasts. Of all cases of breast cancer, only two per thousand occur in women under the age of twenty-five. There are, however, noncancerous breast lumps or masses that occur more frequently than this in the teens; these include cysts (small collections of fluid) and growths called fibradenomas (rubbery growths).

Cysts can be drained with a tiny needle, although they also may disappear after one's period. For this reason, many doctors will simply ask you to return for a recheck five to seven days after your period starts. If a growth does not contain fluid and does not go away, it should be removed by minor surgery.

If you feel a lump in your breast, it must be checked by a physician. He or she can tell you if it is significant and also make sure you are examining your breasts properly. Your school nurse may be able to help you find a physician.

127

Dear Dr. Wilcox: My mother died of breast cancer a number of years ago. Will I get it too? I really just want to know the statistics. I'm seventeen, and everyone ignores my question.

Having a relative with breast cancer does *not* mean you will also develop it. It simply means that your risk of breast cancer is greater than it would be if no one in your family had breast cancer.

Six of every one hundred women will develop breast cancer at some time in their lives, the vast majority over age forty. If a woman has a sister with breast cancer, her risk triples; if her mother had the disease, her risk is about 1.9 times that of the average woman.

Other factors that seem to increase risk include having had no babies, having had a first baby after age twenty-five, having fewer than six children (that's most of us!), having never breast-fed, and, possibly, eating a high-fat diet.

Women who examine their own breasts for lumps have a significantly lower risk of dying from breast cancer than do women who never check, probably because they find problems early in a treatable stage. Interestingly, women who are more likely to examine their own breasts include those who have lost a close relative to cancer. Your doctor can teach you to examine your breasts or can give you a pamphlet illustrating the technique. The American Cancer Society also has pamphlets. You can get the address from the phone book.

128

Dear Dr. Wilcox: I have an embarrassing case of gynecomastia. The breast development started at around age fourteen. Although it is minor, I've always felt self-conscious about it, and it has kept me from participating in certain sports (swimming, basketball), even dating.

Gynecomastia is the medical term for enlargement of male breasts. Most boys probably have some gynecomastia during adolescence, due to a temporary, self-correcting hormone imbalance. It feels like a little movable disc of tissue with distinct borders right under the areola (the dark skin that surrounds the nipple) and can be a bit sore when pressed. In a small percentage of cases the change is pronounced enough for a boy to notice it and seek medical advice.

When breast enlargement increases or persists (as yours has), it is especially important to see a doctor, since significant medical problems can be the cause. These can be diagnosed by physical examination and appropriate blood and urine tests. Your doctor can also arrange for you to speak to a plastic surgeon if you wish to consider surgical correction of the gynecomastia (after several years, the likelihood of its spontaneous correction has diminished). Generally, regardless of the cause of the gynecomastia, surgery can give you a normal male chest.

Dear Dr. Wilcox: About two years ago I noticed a curve to the left in my penis. Since then this curvature has increased, and it's really beginning to depress me. I just want to know what might have caused this to happen to me and if it can be helped. I am too embarrassed to turn to my parents or friends at this point. **129**

There is a condition that causes progressive curvature of the shaft of the penis, known by a variety of names including Peyronie's disease, plastic induration of the penis, and penile fibrosis. It is not a common condition but could be causing your problem. It is caused by the development of plaques of thick scarlike tissue within the left or right side of the penis.

Why these layers of tissue develop is not known, but treatment is available. You should see a urologist, a specialist in problems of the body's genitourinary system. Medications are available that can decrease the fibrous layers that cause the penis to curve. If these don't bring relief, surgery can correct the problem. Your family doctor can recommend a urologist.

Dear Dr. Wilcox: I have a problem that is making me very insecure and emotionally unstable. I am a young male in fairly good physical condition. But my problem is that my genital organs (penis and testicles) have not reached maturity, in spite of the fact that I have experienced some kind of puberty. I feel that this isn't a common problem, and that if I tell someone, they might laugh at me. **130**

Should I tell my family doctor? Are there physicians who specialize in this kind of problem? Is there any hope that something can be done for me? Why did this happen to me?

Often when people are worried about their bodies or health, they feel alone with their concerns and are afraid to ask for help or reassurance. When the concern is particularly personal, as yours is, the fear of being the only one with such a problem can be even greater. The point is that you aren't alone with these concerns and your problem is far from rare.

Lack or loss of full genital development is called hypogonadism, and you could use this term when you discuss your concerns with your family doctor. Yes, you should tell your doctor; he or she could then, if necessary, arrange for you to see an endocrinologist, the type of specialist who deals with these and other hormone problems.

It sounds as though you are worried about the "maturity" rather than the size of your penis and testicles. As you undoubtedly know, the size of the normal mature penis varies greatly from one male to the next, as does the age at which full maturity is reached. (See 32.)

Hypogonadism is very different from a simple variation in size or timing of development. The penis and testicles do not appear mature, and because of associated hormone problems the person often notices diminished beard growth and lack of pubic and axillary (underarm) hair, as well as other possible symptoms.

The list of causes is long, and only through careful discussion, physical examination, and special blood, urine, and other tests can a firm diagnosis of the cause be made. Treatment will depend upon the cause. See your doctor soon.

131 **Dear Dr. Wilcox: About two years ago, I read an article that suggested that males should feel their scrotum and testes, checking for tumors or any other changes. Since then I have been checking regularly. About six months ago I noticed that a lump had started to develop. For a while I have been just standing by, figuring it was normal. Now it has grown and is almost the same size as my testes.**

You are right that males should gently examine their scrotum and testes regularly, feeling for lumps or changes, just as girls and women should examine their breasts once a month. Early detection of disease is important. Although cancer of the testes is most common in men in their twenties and thirties, it is not rare in teenagers.

Most males will never find a lump or change, but many will and, like you, will be surprised and perhaps frightened. Although tumors are what we are most concerned about identifying, there are many other causes of lumps inside the scrotum (enlarged veins, collections of fluid, and hernias are just a few of the other causes of lumps).

Testicular exam is important because cancer of the testes is one of the most common malignancies that affects young men, and it can be readily treated. *You need to see a doctor to have a diagnosis made so that treatment, if necessary, can be arranged. It is important to make an appointment soon.*

What can be felt while examining the normal scrotum and testes? Each testis is a firm oval of tissue about 1.6 by 1 by 1 in (4 by 2.5 by 2.5 cm) when mature; the left testis is capped by a small crescent-shaped duct called the epididymis, an elongated portion of which continues down the back of the testis. These structures are suspended by the spermatic cord, which ultimately attaches inside the abdomen after running through a tiny canal where the scrotum attaches to the body. If exposed to cold, muscles in the cord contract and pull the testes up toward the protective warmth of the body. When exposed to higher temperatures (a hot bath, warm weather), the muscles relax, and the testes are carried lower in the scrotum. This response is necessary because sperm are most effectively produced at a constant temperature several degrees lower than the general body temperature. *(See 33.)*

Dear Dr. Wilcox: Stubborn hemorrhoids have been with me for almost three years. They tend to disappear and reappear at different times. I have seen a doctor and have followed her directions.

132

What is the long-term danger of hemorrhoids? They don't bother me very much, although occasionally they bleed. If I have weak veins (which I'm sure I do), could the hemorrhoids just be a form of varicose veins and not a sign that my diet is low in fiber? Hemorrhoids are dilated veins in the rectum. Varicose is just another word meaning dilated, so, yes, you could call these varicose veins.

Internal hemorrhoids occur well inside the rectum; their most common symptom is bleeding associated with bowel movements. If they become quite large, however, they can prolapse, or protrude, through the anus and are then visible.

External hemorrhoids, caused by the dilation of rectal veins located closer to the anal opening, are often symptomless, although they can cause itching and irritation. If a blood clot forms in an external hemorrhoid, there may be pain, but the situation is not dangerous.

Possible long-term complications of internal hemorrhoids include anemia from chronic blood loss, infection, ulceration of the hemorrhoid and then scarring when it heals, and, as mentioned, thrombosis or clotting in the vein. However, these are not common, especially if one avoids constipation and other situations that can make the hemorrhoids worse.

Some people do have "weaker" veins than others, but constipation can cause people to strain when defecating, and this increased pressure causes the veins to dilate further. Eating fresh fruits and vegetables, whole-grain products, and bran as well as drinking plenty of water (some people say eight glasses a day) helps prevent constipation. Pregnancy, prolonged standing, and straining to lift heavy objects also increase pressure within the veins and can aggravate the hemorrhoids.

When hemorrhoids bleed or become painful, ointments or suppositories can be prescribed. The key "treatment," however, is avoiding the straining that can make them worse.

133 **Dear Dr. Wilcox: Lately my anus has been uncontrollably itchy. I haven't said anything about it to anyone because I'm too embarrassed and because I believed it would go away in time.**
I hope it will help you to know that you are not the only person with this problem and, indeed, it even has a special medical name: pruritis ani.

What can cause pruritis ani? It can be associated with hemorrhoids, fissures (cracks) in the anus, and problems in the rectum, such as an inflammation called proctitis. It can also be caused by skin problems, including allergic reactions to toilet paper, chronic itchy skin conditions that also occur elsewhere on the body, or infections/infestations such as pinworms or candida (yeast). If any of these are the cause, specific treatment aimed at their eradication will eliminate the itch.

Things you can try on your own no matter what the cause include gentle cleansing of the area with wet soft cotton instead of toilet paper, bathing the area twice a day, making sure the area is *completely dry* before putting on cotton (not nylon) underpants, and avoiding overwashing with soaps and antiseptics.

If you scratch in your sleep, you can even wear gloves to

bed so as not to undo all your good daytime efforts. If the problem persists, see your doctor. A steroid cream may decrease the irritation, but it must only be used for a short time in small amounts (long term, it can damage the skin).

Dear Dr. Wilcox: I am thirteen and have a terrible problem. For a while I've been constipated, and sometimes I go a week without having a bowel movement. When I do have one, it is very painful and afterward it starts to bleed. For a while the problem stopped, and my bowel movements were frequent (every day). Lately, however, it has come back. I am too embarrassed to talk to anyone about this, but I'm scared.

134

Constipation is very common. North Americans consume a diet that is notoriously low in fiber, the component of food that helps the bowels work well. High-fiber foods include whole-grain breads and cereals, whole-wheat bread, oatmeal, bran cereal, beans, peas and lentils, and raw fruits and vegetables. We need three to five servings of breads and/or cereals a day, and four to five servings of fruits and/or vegetables a day, to help maintain a healthy diet. (We also need other foods; *see 39.*)

Unfortunately, many people go days or even months without coming close to the proper intake of the bread/cereal and fruit/vegetable groups. This is especially true of people who eat only fast or processed foods. Besides increasing your fiber intake, you should be drinking the equivalent of eight glasses of water a day. Some people find that having a whole-grain snack (for example, a bowl of cereal) at bedtime followed by two glasses of water can relieve constipation. Regular exercise also helps. If you don't exercise regularly, start.

If these suggestions don't clear up your problem in a few weeks—and that includes eliminating the bleeding—you should then see your doctor. The hard stools you pass probably result in little internal tears and scrapes that bleed.

Dear Dr. Wilcox: I am a teenage boy with a very embarrassing problem. When I urinate I have two streams. I do not like to use the urinal, so I have to sit on the toilet. Could you tell me what is causing this and what I can do about it? I don't want to see our family doctor, as she is a female.

135

You describe what can be an important problem for which you may need to seek medical care. If you are uncomfortable

with your present doctor, get the name of a physician a friend
or relative trusts and make an appointment. You ultimately
may need to see a urologist, a specialist trained to deal with
urinary problems.

The tube that leads from your bladder and extends down
to your penis, carrying the urine from the bladder to the
outside, is called the urethra. If anything internal partially
obstructs the urethra, the urine comes out in a weak stream,
sometimes dribbling, sometimes in two streams, and often
requiring the patient to sit down to urinate because the
stream isn't strong enough to reach the urinal if the person
urinates while standing.

Causes of urethral obstruction include scarring inside the
urethra, growths, and structural abnormalities that can be
present at birth. *All* can be corrected. Infection and increased stress on the rest of the urinary system, including
the kidneys, can be complications of *some* of these causes.
The potential damage from these possible complications
makes it all the more important that you see a physician soon.

136 **Dear Dr. Wilcox: When I go to the washroom in public, I can't urinate. I freeze up. If I'm alone, there is
no problem. It's just when people are there. It really
scares me, because I have to hold it and come back
another time. I read that the prostate gland has
something to do with this.**
First of all, rest assured that a prostate problem is *not* causing your difficulty. Second, I hope it will help to know that
you are not the only person with this type of problem and
that help certainly is available.

The prostate is a gland about the size of a chestnut that
lies beneath the bladder. It is present only in males. It surrounds the first inch of the urethra, the tube inside the penis
through which urine and semen leave the body. The prostate produces fluid that becomes part of the semen, the liquid that contains the sperm that are ejaculated during male
orgasm. As men get older, an increasing enlargement of the
prostate often leads to pressure on the urethra. The resulting compression can interfere with urination, leading to such
symptoms as difficulty starting or stopping urination, or
production of a dribbling urinary stream.

When a symptom occurs only in a very specific setting, it
often means that stress or anxiety is contributing to that
problem. Examples might be diarrhea that occurs only be-

fore taking exams, headaches that come on only when your least favorite aunt comes for dinner, or difficulty urinating when in a public washroom.

If it is only an occasional symptom and doesn't bother you, you can just learn to live with it. However, if it is making you uncomfortable and interfering with your daily life— as yours seems to be doing—you may choose to get help. Your family doctor can help you find a professional who could help you learn to decrease the stress you feel when confronted with a situation that upsets you, perhaps using techniques that include autorelaxation. Make an appointment so that you can get the help you want.

Dear Dr. Wilcox: I have been a constant bed wetter for as long as I can remember. Last year I went to my doctor, and he checked my bladder and urinary system. He couldn't find anything wrong. He then suggested restricting my liquid consumption after six P.M., which didn't work. After this my mother tried waking me up several times during the night to go to the washroom. This worked, temporarily.

137

My brothers often blackmail me by saying they will tell my friends unless I do and act as they say. None of my friends knows, but I would not be able to face them if they did. Whenever I sleep over, I remain awake until I'm sure I won't have any accidents. What can I do to stop it?

Nocturnal enuresis, or bed-wetting, can be a frustrating problem, but it can be cured. Interestingly, it often clears up within six months after the first doctor visit, regardless of the treatment used. In your case that didn't happen, but at least you made the first step in getting help. Although your doctor's first suggestion didn't work, you, your doctor, and your family can, with teamwork, try other techniques that may help. One is an alarm system that awakens you if the bed is slightly wet and enables you to get up to go to the bathroom. This works well if the problem is that you sleep so deeply you don't usually awaken in time. After a while you learn to awaken in time.

Another technique is called "drybed training." It involves receiving rewards for staying dry, using the alarm (as described), being awakened frequently at night to urinate, changing your own bed if it gets wet, and "positive imaging": you lie in bed, imagine needing to urinate and then getting up and going to the bathroom in time. There are also medications that in some cases may be helpful. Before trying any of these treatments, it may be useful for your doctor to send you to a urologist (urinary specialist) to make sure that nothing has been overlooked.

See your doctor again. Tell him what you've tried so far and how the problem is affecting you and your relationships in and outside the family. Don't give up. There is help.

138 **Dear Dr. Wilcox: I have recently become sexually active and feel that it is my responsibility to ensure against unwanted pregnancy by going on the birth control pill. (We have been using condoms until now.) My problem revolves around gynecological exams. I have heard some real horror stories that have made me put off going to a doctor. Knowing what to expect might help me prepare myself for the exam.**

To make sure your uterus (womb), ovaries, vagina, cervix, and surrounding tissues are healthy, the doctor does what is called an internal or pelvic exam. It takes only a few minutes, and although it may be a bit uncomfortable, it should *never* be painful.

Not knowing what to expect and hearing "horror" stories make the anticipation far worse than the exam itself. After they've had their first internal exam, patients often tell me how surprised they are about how little there is to the whole event.

There are a few things you can do to help. First, ask the doctor to explain what he or she is doing or is going to do as the exam proceeds. Second, try to relax the muscles in your legs; by doing this, you can also relax the muscles that surround the vagina, making the pelvic exam far less uncomfortable than if all your muscles were tense.

There are two parts to the exam. One is done with a speculum, a small plastic or metal instrument that allows the doctor to see the cervix and inside the vagina. The other part involves checking the size of the uterus and ovaries.

The speculum is gently inserted into the vagina. It may feel a bit cold, and there may be somewhat more pressure felt than when you insert a tampon. The speculum is a narrow tube that opens up like a duck's bill, pushing aside the walls of the vagina so that the doctor can see your cervix at the end of the vagina. Using a cotton swab or a small, light wooden spatula, the doctor will gently scrape the cervix to take a sample of cells to make sure there is no evidence of cancer of the cervix. This scraping is the Pap smear, and most women feel nothing when it is being done or report only a slight "pinchy" feeling.

The assessment of the uterus, ovaries, and surrounding tissues is done by hand. Wearing gloves, the doctor puts one hand on your lower abdomen and also puts a gloved finger inside the vagina. By gently pressing down on your abdomen and up toward your abdomen from inside, the doctor can feel the size and shape of the uterus and other structures. Again, this takes less than a minute and should cause a feeling of pressure *but no pain.*

Any female who has sexual intercourse should have a Pap smear and internal exam done regularly to make sure all is well. You'll find it isn't awful or painful, that it takes very little time and causes little discomfort. Remember it is vital for protecting your good health.

Dear Dr. Wilcox: I've heard about endometriosis. What is it?

139

The endometrium is the lining of the uterus and is the tissue that is shed during menstruation. After each period this lining builds up again. If you become pregnant, the fertilized egg implants in the uterus, and the lining is not shed.

Endometriosis is a condition in which tissue resembling the endometrium is found outside the uterus. The sites of these extrauterine islands of endometrium include the ovaries, the ligaments or fibrous bands attached to the uterus, and parts of the peritoneum (a thin lining that covers the uterus, bladder, and lower portions of the large bowel).

The classic symptom of endometriosis is pain during menstruation that gets progressively worse period after period. Other possible symptoms include pain during intercourse; constipation and pain during defecation, worse around the time of the period; and difficulty in becoming pregnant. Most patients with endometriosis are between the ages of twenty-five and forty-five, though it can also occur under the age of twenty. The severity of endometriosis is not necessarily reflected by the severity of the symptoms.

Gynecologists use history, physical exams, and ultrasound and/or laparoscopy to make the diagnosis. Laparoscopy, done under general anesthetic, involves looking into the area of the uterus by inserting a tiny "periscope" through a small incision just below the navel.

Endometriosis is treated to relieve pain or to help infertile patients become pregnant. A number of different treatments have been suggested, including a very new one using a laser to eliminate the misplaced endometrium. More standard treatments include prescribing hormone-containing pills (either the birth control pill or an "anti-estrogen" pill) to decrease its spread. For women who are infertile due to mild endometriosis, however, just waiting an extra year may result in pregnancy as often as does hormone therapy or surgery!

Because endometriosis may exist without any symptoms, there are women with this condition who never seek or require treatment. If you have symptoms that concern you, make an appointment to see your doctor.

140 **Dear Dr. Wilcox: I've noticed a large sore around my vaginal area. It's more like a large piece of extra skin that's hard and gets very sore. When I am sitting down it sometimes hurts quite a bit. I've stayed home from school once because it got so itchy. I haven't said anything to my mother or anyone else. I don't know what type of doctor to go to, either.**

Your family doctor is the appropriate person to see. If necessary, he or she can refer you to a gynecologist (a doctor who treats problems involving the female reproductive organs) or a dermatologist (skin specialist).

It isn't possible to tell you what the sore is without seeing you. There are, however, several common problems that could fit the description you give. Cysts, warts, and weakening of the vaginal walls leading to protrusion of other tissues are three possibilities.

Cysts can form when tiny fluid-secreting glands become blocked. These cysts can be very tender and if infected form painful abscesses that must be treated. In some cases they can exist in a chronic form for years.

Warts are caused by a virus, which can be passed from an infected person to someone else during sexual intercourse. These warts can be single or multiple, can be very large, and can feel irritated and sore. Several effective treatments are available, but accompanying vaginal infection (vaginitis) must also be treated if present. The birth control pill can alter the acidity of the vagina and in some women seems to promote the growth and recurrence of warts when the viral infection is present. *(See 141, 148.)*

Relaxation of the muscles in the vaginal area is usually a problem of older women whose tissues have been over-stretched during childbirth. When this occurs, the bladder, rectum, or bowel may cause a bulging in the vaginal area. Although far rarer during adolescence than cysts or warts, it can occur in cases of marked obesity, in a teenager who has had a baby, or in someone with abnormal connective tissue.

Dear Dr. Wilcox: I recently found out I have vaginitis. Is it harmful in any way? How can I get rid of it? **141**
Vaginitis is a very general term and simply means inflammation (irritation) of the vagina.

There are many different causes of vaginal irritation. Forgetting to remove a tampon after a period is over can cause marked irritation and vaginal discharge. Washing with heavily perfumed soaps or using certain bubble baths can sometimes cause irritation of the vulva (the area outside the vagina) and result in symptoms similar to those of vaginitis.

Infection, however, is the most common cause. The most common is monilia, also known as candidiasis or yeast. It is *not* a sexually transmitted disease (STD). It is normally present in the vaginas of many women, but yeast overgrowth can cause a great deal of irritation. There are many treatments available that can be prescribed by your doctor. *(See 143.)*

There are quite a number of other infections, and treatment depends on which you have. One very important one is gonorrhea, which is transmitted by sexual contact. If not treated, this STD can cause pelvic inflammatory disease (PID), a very serious infection in the internal pelvic organs that can cause infertility. If you *think* someone you've had sex with may have had gonorrhea, you must see a doctor. *(See 145.)*

You don't say how you found out you had vaginitis. If it wasn't diagnosed by a doctor or nurse, you should see one.

Dear Dr. Wilcox: Ever since I have been having sex with my boyfriend (the past year), I have had a discharge with a rather offensive odor. I thought it was something to do with my period, but it wasn't. What causes this? What can I do besides showering twice a day? **142**
The vagina normally produces secretions as a way of cleansing itself, and therefore every woman normally has some clear or white mucusy discharge. But when a discharge causes itching or irritation or has an unusual or offensive odor, infection is usually the cause.

Because you are sexually active, you may have a sexually transmitted disease (STD), which is the new designation for what used to be called venereal disease (VD). Infections in this group are passed from one person to another by sexual contact. The list of STDs is fairly long and includes gonorrhea, syphilis, genital herpes, chlamydia, and venereal warts. Each is caused by a specific type of bacteria or virus, and the treatment, of course, varies with the cause. Risk of contracting STD increases with the more sexual partners one has. The risk decreases with fewer partners. The use of condoms provides some protection.

It is imperative that you seek medical help, since some infections—especially gonorrhea and chlamydia—can cause deep internal infection and scarring of the tubes that lead from the ovaries to the uterus, which can lead to infertility.

See your family doctor or, if you prefer, call your local department of public health to find out the location of the nearest STD or VD clinic. Be sure to mention that you have a sexual partner. Depending on what sort of infection you have, he too may need to take medication so that you don't keep passing the infection back and forth.

143 **Dear Dr. Wilcox: Could you please tell me something about the STD yeast, especially the symptoms and the danger of having it if not treated?**

Yeast, or candidiasis, is one of the most common causes of vaginitis in women during their years of menstruation. It is not dangerous and should not be grouped with the classic STDs.

STD stands for "sexually transmitted disease" and is the newer designation for diseases that are passed from one person to the next by sexual contact. Venereal disease, or VD, was the label previously used for these diseases, such as gonorrhea or syphilis.

Although yeast may be passed sexually, that is not considered its primary method of transmission. The parasite *Candida albicans* is normally present in the vagina in 30 to 50 percent of all women. When it is present in balance with the other microorganisms that make up the normal flora of the vagina, there usually are no symptoms. If, however, this balance is disturbed for some reason and the yeast proliferates, a woman may experience, especially around the time of her period, the vaginal irritation, itchiness, and abundant discharge—often thick and white—that are characteristic of yeast infection. Her sexual partner may experience irritation of the skin of the penis. To alleviate the discomfort and get things back in balance, antiyeast medications are prescribed.

Common causes of an imbalance in the vaginal microorganisms that can lead to an overgrowth of yeast include antibiotics that may as a side effect eliminate some vaginal bacteria, hormones in the birth control pill, and anything that decreases the acidity of the vagina. In cases where *Candida* was not previously present in the vagina but "infection" occurs, the exact way in which the yeast was transmitted is rarely easily discoverable.

The yeast itself does not pose a danger. What can be dangerous, however, is to think you have yeast, not bother to see a doctor, and then have it turn out that something more serious—an STD such as gonorrhea, for example—is causing your symptoms. Frequent, severe yeast infections can also be a sign of other health problems. Have a doctor check if there is any question of infection.

Dear Dr. Wilcox: I am a twenty-year-old woman and am afraid of catching AIDS. I recently learned from a television show that a person can catch AIDS from heterosexual contact—specifically "exchange of body fluids," including kissing mouth-to-mouth.

144

I am not sexually active in terms of having intercourse. What are the chances I will catch AIDS from kissing or necking with a guy?

First, let's start with a few facts. AIDS (acquired immune deficiency syndrome) is not a common disease. It is "caught" in only two ways—by having intimate sexual contact with someone who has AIDS or by getting AIDS-contaminated blood into your blood system (for example, by sharing a heroin needle with an infected person).

People at greatest risk are those involved in male homosexual relationships that include anal intercourse. Also at great risk are people who use IV (intravenous) drugs, because of the possibility of being infected by a contaminated needle.

There is no evidence that anyone has ever contracted AIDS just by kissing—casually or otherwise—someone who has the disease. But because researchers have detected the virus that causes AIDS in the saliva of a few patients who were severely ill with AIDS, it has been suggested that it is reasonable for people with the AIDS virus to refrain from "trading" saliva with their sexual partners because it *might* be infective.

Research by epidemiologists (scientists who study the spread of disease) suggests clearly that the risk of a healthy heterosexual person catching AIDS from another healthy heterosexual person by just kissing is virtually nil, and by having intercourse is small. But using condoms during intercourse can further decrease even this risk.

You can get further information by contacting your local public health department, which will have books and pamphlets about AIDS and how to minimize risk of getting it, and you will find their major recommendation is for condom use during sexual intercourse.

145 **Dear Dr. Wilcox: A guy I slept with says I have gonorrhea. I feel fine and have no vaginal discharge. Is it true it can just go away on its own? What should I do?**

Gonorrhea is a sexually transmitted disease and is, therefore, passed from one person to another by sexual intercourse or by other intimate genital contact. It is extremely widespread, with an estimated 2 million new cases each year in North America alone and more than 100 million new cases worldwide.

One of the reasons that it has reached such near-epidemic proportions is that up to 80 percent of women and 40 percent of men who have the infection have absolutely *no symptoms* and may thereby pass on the disease without knowing it. When a person is diagnosed as having gonorrhea, it is important that anyone who has had sexual contact with that person be notified so that he or she can see a doctor. The absence of symptoms does *not* guarantee the absence of infection.

Unfortunately, untreated gonorrhea doesn't just "go away." It can spread to the deep, internal parts of the reproductive system (and in women may cause internal scarring that can lead to infertility) and can also cause one to become generally or "systemically" ill. Treatment with antibiotics prescribed by a doctor is, obviously, very important.

146 **Dear Dr. Wilcox: Please tell me what the danger is of having an infection of the vagina called chlamydia. What is it, anyway?**

Chlamydia trachomatis is a small microorganism often considered halfway between a virus and a bacteria. If untreated, chlamydia can cause a woman to become infertile (unable to get pregnant) by causing scarring from infection of the internal reproductive organs.

Chlamydia is as common as gonorrhea; one-third of all women who go to VD (STD) clinics have this infection. It can cause a vaginal discharge, but sometimes a doctor may suspect its presence only because the cervix (the end of the uterus that protrudes into the far end of the vagina) looks red and irritated.

One gets chlamydia by having sexual intercourse with someone who has the infection. A man may catch it from a partner, not develop symptoms, and then unwittingly pass it on to another woman. Some men, however, experience burning when they urinate if the infection is present.

If you have chlamydia, it must be treated. Your sexual partner(s) should also be treated, or you risk catching it again. Tetracycline pills, taken four times per day for at least five to seven days, can cure the infection.

Dear Dr. Wilcox: A friend of mine told me that vaginitis can be caused by things like *Trichomonas* and *Gardnerella*. What are these, what are the symptoms, and how do you get these infections?

147

Trichomonas is a microorganism that can cause vaginitis (the infection is called trichomoniasis). *Gardnerella* may also be a cause of vaginitis, but currently it is felt that it is more likely a type of bacteria that can normally be present in the vagina.

Trichomonas is a tiny organism that under the microscope looks like a little pear with a long tail. It is an extremely common cause of vaginitis and produces a heavy, foul-smelling, sometimes frothy discharge that irritates the vulva (the area outside the vagina). Intercourse may be painful, and urination may cause a burning sensation when this infection is present. Trichomoniasis is usually transmitted from one person to the other by sexual intercourse.

Up to 20 percent of women may have *Gardnerella* present in the vagina, and most will have no signs of infection. It is thought, however, that *Gardnerella* can be responsible for the symptoms of so-called nonspecific vaginitis or bacterial vaginosis (mild itchiness and a watery, gray-white discharge with a strong "fishy" odor). If *Gardnerella* is found when a vaginal discharge is tested, it is treated as an infection.

Neither trichomoniasis nor bacterial vaginosis is serious, but the symptoms can be annoying and unpleasant. Both can be eliminated by taking a medication called metronidazole (these pills must be prescribed by a doctor). Avoid all alcohol for two days after taking this medication; the interaction between alcohol and metronidazole can cause severe nausea. To prevent reinfection and the risk of spreading it to others, your sexual partner should also be treated. Your risk of contracting these or any infection that can be sexually transmitted increases with the number of sexual partners you have.

148 **Dear Dr. Wilcox: I am a sixteen-year-old boy. I have many shiny bumps around the bottom of the head of my penis. My friend says they could be warts, the kind you get from having sex with a girl who has them on her genitals. I've never had sex. Could they be warts? If not, what are they? And also, what would warts look like?**

Venereal (genital) warts are caused by a papilloma (or wart-causing) virus and are transmitted by sexual contact. The warts themselves usually look like little cauliflowers and are *not* smooth and shiny, so you probably do not have warts.

Because exposure to certain strains of this virus can increase a woman's chance of developing cancer of the cervix later on, any female who has had genital warts should be sure to see her doctor every year for a Pap smear and vaginal exam.

The warts in males or females are easily eliminated by various treatments, the most common of which involves painting the wart with a medication called podophyllin that makes the wart slowly shrink and disappear. Podophyllin should never be used on warts *inside* the vagina. Special freezing, called cryotherapy, is another treatment; it must be used carefully to avoid scarring. Some research using an antiviral chemical called interferon shows it might eventually be a useful treatment.

But what about your problem? One possibility is a condition called molluscum contagiosum, which is also caused by a virus. These little dome-shaped bumps are smooth and may occur in little clusters. They too can be treated with cryotherapy or can be scraped off (curetted) by a doctor.

A more likely diagnosis, however, is a normal condition called "pink pearly penile papules." These are tiny bumps that occur as a ring around the corona (or the bottom of the head of the penis) as you describe. Approximately 15 percent of all adolescent males will have these. They are not a disease and need no treatment.

Dear Dr. Wilcox: My ex-boyfriend just told me I have herpes. (He was the last person I slept with, and that was four months ago.) Well, I freaked out. I've heard a lot of stories. I hear there's no cure. Please tell me everything about it. **149**

To tell you everything about herpes genitalis would take far more space than is available, but I'll do what I can.

First of all, view your boyfriend's comments with some skepticism. He can't make a long-distance diagnosis.

Herpes is one of the most common viruses in the world. Herpes type II is the cause of the genital infection that has been reported on so much recently. It should be seen as an annoying affliction but not a dangerous or dreadful one. The infection is passed by intimate contact with an infected area. Because the virus is not sturdy, it dies very quickly outside of the human body. This means you cannot catch genital herpes from toilet seats, pools, etc.

It is possible to spread the infection from an infected site on your body to another area by touching the sores, then immediately touching your eye, for example. (Eye infections are rare, but serious.) But again, you'd have to transport the virus very quickly for this to happen. Simply washing your hands after touching the infected area eliminates this problem.

Half of the people who have genital herpes have either no obvious symptoms or very mild ones. The classical sequence of events is the occurrence of tiny red pimples that quickly turn into very painful blisters that finally break and look like little red craters or ulcers on the genitals. They heal completely in days or weeks. Because the virus stays on the nerve endings even after the sores are gone, the sores may recur if the activity of the virus flares. The chances of passing the infection on are greatest when the sores are present, and sexual intercourse should definitely be avoided at that time. (Remember: a *single* ulcer that is *not* particularly painful can be a sign of syphilis, a very serious sexually transmitted disease that requires prompt medical attention.)

There is currently no cure for the herpes virus. There is a cream that *may* make the sores clear up more quickly the first time they appear. A pill called acyclovir appears to suppress reoccurrences, but (a) it is not widely available, (b) it does not get rid of the virus, and (c) its long-term safety is unproven.

Although in adults the infection is not dangerous, it can be devastating to a baby delivered through the vagina at the time of active infection. If tests show the infection is active around the time of delivery, the baby can be safely delivered by caesarean.

Your doctor can tell you more and, if there are any sores, could take a swab to see if they are herpes. He or she will, regardless, see you for your important yearly Pap smear. You can also get helpful and up-to-date information by calling your city's VD (STD) hotline (in your phone book).

150

Dear Dr. Wilcox: I am ashamed to say I think I have what is commonly referred to as "crabs." The part that shames me is I don't know how I can tell. I feel no vaginal itching, which I should, according to books, and see no evidence of bugs when I examine myself.

I have just lost a boyfriend because of this problem and am sick about it. I know it couldn't have been him giving them to me because he was generally concerned and tried to talk to me about it.

The first time it happened he went to the store and got lotion, and I put it on, I took a shower, and that was it. Two weeks later he cornered me again and notified me he had them again and that it was over since I didn't care about my body and his.

Pediculosis pubis, or "crabs," usually causes severe itching in the pubic area, and it is this pruritis (itching) that usually leads people to seek medical help. One might also notice: (a) tiny gray-white specks on some of the pubic hair (these are the eggs laid by the lice), (b) tiny blue-black dots on the skin resulting from the insects' bites, or (c) the presence of 1/16-in- (1- to 2-mm-) long, gray-white lice. A magnifying glass may be required to see any of these three signs.

As you can see, this doesn't fit well with the situation described in your letter. It might also be useful for you to know that although pubic lice are commonly passed from one person to another via close physical contact (such as intercourse), they can also be transmitted by shared towels, bedding, or clothing. As part of an effective treatment, therefore, towels, underwear, and bedding must be laundered in hot water in addition to the person's using a local treatment (a special cream or shampoo) on the pubic area itself. The local treatment must be used properly, and exact instructions are best given by one's doctor.

To check if there is any reason to think you have or may have had pubic lice, see a physician. Your request for help is not an unusual one, and he or she will be very willing to answer your questions.

SIX:

Sex and Sexuality

*The results of self abuse [masturbation] are di-
sastrous. It destroys mental power and memory,
it blotches the complexion, dulls the eye, takes
away the strength and may even cause insan-
ity. It is a habit most difficult to overcome, and
may not only last for years, but in its tendency
may be transmitted to one's children.*
      Mrs. Mary Wood-Allen,
What a Young Woman Ought to Know *(1898)*

*I*s it true that sex makes the world go round? You might
think so from the sheer volume of media attention de-
voted to the topic; from the universal popularity of sexual fantasizing, dreaming, and yearning; and from the
hundreds of letters our readers send us concerning sexual
matters.

Issues that were taboo only a few years ago are now common topics of discussion. Sexual behavior has changed in
recent years; our society is now more permissive, and teenagers are experimenting at an earlier age. But this greater
freedom is not without its problems. Partly due to pressure
from television and popular magazines, some young people
have felt compelled to engage in sexual behavior before they
really wanted to. There are too many pregnant teenage girls,
too many teenagers contracting sexually transmitted diseases, and too many people hurt by unthinking or exploi-
tive sexual partners.

Sexuality is a most wonderful part of the human experience, but like anything else it can be abused. There should
be no rush, no external pressure. Sex should be treated like
a sexual partner; lovingly. Enjoy it—but only when you're
ready, and the moment is right.

151 **Dear Dr. Levine: I am a fourteen-year-old girl.
Everyone says I look a lot older. When I walk down
a street or when I'm in a car a guy may honk his**

horn, say "hi," or wave. This really scares me; I feel as if I want to kill him. I am so afraid that guy may hurt me. I've tried to ignore them, but I am too afraid of running into them someday. And as a result, I am afraid of guys as boyfriends. What should I do? I've never been asked out yet.

You are in good company. Many girls and young women have been complaining over the past few years about being viewed as "meat" by men who whistle, leer, suggest, or touch. Most of these men are harmless, or even cowardly if you meet their glance (I'm not suggesting that you do this). Of course, one never knows which one will turn out to be dangerous. Some of the oglers are good-humored and will respond with laughter to a good putdown or a smile.

The best response, however, I have been told, is no response—that is, no eye contact, no answer, no hanging around. Do not give them the time of day. Your fear of guys should diminish as you have some experiences with them as more than just "mashers" with rude or lewd jokes. My prediction is that you will be just fine.

Dear Dr. Wilcox: I am a seventeen-year-old female. Recently I got into a lot of trouble with my mother because my boyfriend gave me a hickey on the neck. My mom said she thought this was disgusting and claimed that hickeys are dangerous since they may cause cancer. Is there any truth to this?

152

Hickeys do not cause cancer, nor does any type of bruising. Your mother is probably trying to tell you, in a roundabout way, that she is concerned about you and your boyfriend and how sexually active you may be. If you can discuss these concerns, it might be helpful.

Dear Dr. Levine: I am a seventeen-year-old girl with a problem. I haven't kissed many guys, but each time I have, I felt like throwing up. Recently I've been dating a guy I really care about. I dream of situations where he would kiss me, but when I'm alone with him and he puts his arm around me, I feel as if there are knots in my stomach. He hasn't kissed me yet, but I'm worried about my reaction. Am I abnormal? Lately I feel so nervous I can't eat anything.

153

First of all, if by abnormal you mean that the majority of girls your age don't feel that way, then you are "abnormal"—by your definition only. If you mean by abnormal sick or crazy, then you are not abnormal—by my definition. In other words, you are a young woman who has some conflicting feelings around your relationship with guys—but you are not disturbed.

I can't tell you the specific reasons for your reactions to physical contact. They may have to do with some unpleasant past experience, lack of confidence in yourself, or some unconscious fears having to do with sexuality. If kissing continues to "sicken you," or you can't convince yourself that an arm around you is not necessarily an unpleasant act or an attack, then you might be interested in speaking to a counselor at a drop-in center or adolescent clinic in your area.

154 **Dear Dr. Wilcox: I know that it's normal for a guy to have a wet dream occasionally. However, I seem to be having them on a regular basis, sometimes four or five times a month and sometimes on two nights in a row. Please tell me if my problem is abnormal.**
What you describe is perfectly normal. Most boys first experience wet dreams, or nocturnal emissions, twelve to eighteen months after the penis and testicles have begun to grow and mature. The frequency with which these emissions occur normally varies greatly from one person to the next. The testicles are continuously producing sperm, and the emissions, which are often but not always accompaniments of sexual dreams, provide a normal way for it to be released.

155 **Dear Dr. Levine: I am eighteen years old and have been masturbating now for three years. I would like to know the side effects, setbacks, and harm I have been doing, and whether or not it is normal for a girl my age. Is it stress related? What is driving me to continue?**
You are a healthy individual, and masturbating is not going to change that fact. If there are any readers who don't know what masturbating is, it refers to an individual sexually stimulating himself or herself.

It is an extremely common activity during adolescence, but it can serve as a form of sexual outlet at almost any age. There is no "harm," no "setbacks" or "side effects." Is it stress related? The answer to that is a qualified yes. By that I mean that some people find masturbating to orgasm an effective way to reduce tension. (It certainly can relieve sexual tension.)

Anything can be overdone by individuals who have some problems, but it is not masturbating that is the major issue in these cases. The only side effect that occurs commonly is undue guilt in people who feel that they are weird or sick or bad. They are none of the above.

Dear Dr. Wilcox: I am a ninteen-year-old male who has a problem with masturbation. I have been doing it since I was fourteen and cannot stop. It has become something I need and causes me to feel very insecure about myself. I worry about being with a girl for the first time. I may not be able to have sex with her if this keeps up, and I wonder if I'll survive sexually.

156

I feel I am slowly deteriorating. I've done it so much that I have large swollen thickened lumps under each nipple that cause extreme embarrassment if I am seen without a shirt on. I have also had sores on my penis.

I am worried and insecure. Please, please help; how can I quit?

Masturbation is a normal part of one's sexuality. It is especially common during adolescence, when it is usually a major outlet for sexual feelings. Virtually all adolescent males and many females masturbate. Despite the old wives' tales, it is a harmless practice. It will *not* cause pimples, sterility, warts, or hair on your palms, or make you crazy, blind, or a less adequate lover in later life.

It's difficult to see a connection between the lumps you describe and masturbation. The sores could result from masturbating with something that irritates the genitals, or causes excessive friction; simple manual (hand) masturbation generally cannot cause any physical problems.

In your situation, the main concern is the deep distress and insecurity you are experiencing. Although I can reassure you that masturbation is not abnormal, and although it doesn't sound as though it is such a compulsive activity that it is interfering with your daily life, your worry and concern are affecting your happiness and self-confidence.

Your doctor can help you or refer you to someone who can discuss your concerns with you and help you rebuild your self-confidence. Make an appointment soon.

157

Dear Dr. Levine: My boyfriend and I plan on getting married in about two years. I am, I guess, a little old-fashioned in my ways: I still believe in being a virgin until I get married.

My boyfriend seems so understanding and says he can wait for that special day, but it seems too good to be true, and at times I feel I am depriving him of a natural, healthy thing in life. He is not a virgin, and I was scared that, because he had made love before, in time he may get bored with me.

I love him very much and vice versa. I don't want to lose him over something like sex. What do you suggest? The feelings are present, but the morals seem to overpower them.

You and your boyfriend seem to have made a clear choice about this issue, and you are in agreement with each other. You love each other, you share a similar moral code—what is the problem?

Your boyfriend hasn't given you any evidence of being deprived; he doesn't sound bored; he sounds like he loves you and respects your mutual decision. I don't have strong feelings that your sense of morality is absolutely right for all people. But it is certainly right for you. Best of luck to both of you.

158

Dear Dr. Levine: I am a fifteen-year-old girl. My problem is, I'm going out with a guy who's older than I am. He wants me to have sex with him. I don't feel I'm ready to go that far yet. If I say no to him, I might lose him, and if I say yes, I might regret it later. What should I do? How can I tell him my answer?

Your letter is short and clear, and it tells the whole story. At the risk of oversimplifying, my answer is short and clear too: don't do it. You are young and, more important, you don't feel ready. Too many kids are pressured into having sexual intercourse before they are emotionally ready or mature enough. Yes, you might lose your boyfriend, but if that's what is going to determine whether he stays with you, the relationship is not going to last anyway.

You'll have plenty of time to ease into sexual activities when you feel truly relaxed about them and strongly desirous of them. There is no need to rush, and certainly not to feel pushed into behavior that might have serious consequences.

Dear Dr. Wilcox: I am sixteen years old. I have been **159**
having a petting relationship with this fifteen-year-
old boy for the past two months. We have not had
intercourse. The reason is because I'm very scared
and so is he. I really enjoy being with him. He says
that he enjoys it too. I don't like him more than as a
personal friend. I wouldn't want him to be my boyfriend. We have a lot in common. We both like to
laugh, make jokes, go out dancing, etc. He told me
that he respects me too much to be my boyfriend
and I agree. He is really mature for his age.

The problem is I just don't know if I'm doing the
right thing. I don't think that he is using me because
he doesn't act like he is. I really enjoy being with
him in all ways. Do you think that I should continue?

The doubts you have about the way this relationship is
evolving come through loud and clear in your letter, and
because of this you have actually answered your own question. The uncertainty you feel is real and reflects how uncomfortable you are with the current situation; don't ignore
it. The sexual aspects just don't fit or seem "right" to you.

You have no doubts about liking him as a personal friend
or enjoying his laughter and having nonsexual interests. A
good friendship is the first step toward developing a close,
happy relationship. Developing good communication and
shared interests are the aspects to emphasize and work on.

Dear Dr. Wilcox: I am in love with a boy who says he **160**
loves me. Almost every time I go to his house, he
wants to go to bed with me. When I say no, he gets
mad, and this really upsets me.

I don't go to the same school as he does, and his
friend tells me he is just using me and that he really
likes another girl. When I ask him if it's true, he says
no, they're just trying to upset me. I don't know whom
to believe.

It takes a great deal of time and effort to develop a mature
relationship. Your letter indicates that you have many doubts
about this relationship, and it sounds as though you don't
know this boy very well at all. From your description of the
situation, you are smart to question just what is going on
and what you should do about it.

Seeing him at his house is putting far too much pressure

on you both and may lead you to a sexual encounter that is inappropriate for your age and for the relationship. Stop seeing him there, but if you want to get to know him better and build up your understanding and enjoyment of each other, spend time together with groups of friends and at organized activities such as parties, movies, or dances. If he objects and only wants to see your alone at his house or yours, he is not interested in getting to know you, nor does he respect your feelings, and the relationship should then be ended.

161 **Dear Dr. Levine: I am a seventeen-year-old with a big problem. I can't seem to say no to guys. It started about three months ago. I hadn't gone out with a guy in over a year, and when an older guy asked me out I felt obligated to have sex with him. He never asked me out again, but numerous others have, and I just can't seem to say "stop." (I did go on the Pill for safety's sake.)**

I agree with you that you have a big problem. You don't once say in your letter that you enjoy sex, that it is something *you* want. It is only described in terms of what the guy happens to want or need. And these guys sound as if they are not close to you and not particularly caring.

Why do you feel "obligated"? This has to do with your feelings about boys in general and also with your lack of respect for yourself.

Going on the Pill has some advantages if you are going to persist in this activity. But the Pill is not in itself going to solve anything. You are setting yourself up for destructive relationships and personal unhappiness. I suggest that you get some help soon. Speak to a counselor at an adolescent clinic or to your school social worker or guidance counselor.

162 **Dear Dr. Wilcox: I am getting married. How can a man find out if his girl is a virgin?**

He would ask her, and because they have a secure relationship based on clear communication, trust, and mutual respect, they would be able to discuss such issues in comfort. (Physical "proof," by the way, is unreliable. *See 163.*)

Have you gone with your fiancée for any premarriage counseling? Your doctor or minister/religious leader could help you find an appropriate setting for you. Research has shown that premarriage classes do help couples get to know each other better so that they can solve the inevitable problems that arise when two people are learning to be a couple. You should consider how many of the qualities listed in the first paragraph are characteristic of your relationship.

Your question does, unfortunately, imply a lack of trust and respect. Working to build a strong and secure relationship with your fiancée is essential if your marriage is to succeed. And investing the time now—working with your fiancée and perhaps involving the professionals mentioned previously—would be well worth the effort.

Dear Dr. Wilcox: I will soon be sexually active with my boyfriend. The only problem with this is that he thinks I am a virgin. If he discovers I am not, it could mean the end of our relationship. When we first have intercourse, will he know? Should I tell him now and not take the chance? **163**
Although everyone has his or her own thoughts about when sex is appropriate in a relationship, many people feel that sex is an expression of deep feeling of one person for another and that that feeling is part of a mature, trusting relationship. Trust, security, and understanding do not sound like they are very strong in your relationship. Should you be considering including sex as part of it?

But in regard to your question about the physical signs of virginity, the answer is that there is no absolute way for one to know if a woman has or has not had intercourse previously.

Although some women may experience a small amount of bleeding the first time they have intercourse, many women do not. The degree of bleeding depends on how much of a ring of tissue (called the hymen) there is near the vaginal opening.

The amount of hymen present varies from woman to woman. If it is thick, it may tear with first intercourse; if it is not, there may be no tissue torn and no resultant bleeding—in other words, no "sign" that this was the "first time."

In rare cases the hymen entirely blocks the vaginal opening, a situation that can be easily corrected with surgery. If you have had a period, you know the hymen does not normally block the vaginal opening completely.

Dear Dr. Wilcox: I have had sex once and found it to be slightly painful. I would like to know how many times it's going to hurt. I hate the pain and bleeding. **164**
The pain you experienced was caused by the tearing of your hymen. The degree to which this ring of tissue is present

varies greatly form one female to the next. If it is prominent, there may be quite noticeable pain and bleeding during first-time intercourse. If very little tissue is present, there
may be no bleeding or pain at all. *(See 163.)*

If there is hymen tissue present, discomfort during first
intercourse is greatly minimized by gentle stretching of the
vaginal opening during foreplay (or "petting"), by ensuring
that the vagina is moist and well lubricated before attempting intercourse, and by having intercourse itself in a gentle
and unhurried way. There isn't a magic number of times
after which intercourse is always comfortable, but keeping
these factors in mind should minimize discomfort; ignoring
them will increase it.

Dyspareunia is the medical term for persistently painful
intercourse. Common causes of dyspareunia in your age
group include: (a) attempting intercourse before the woman
is sufficiently aroused (in response to arousal the vagina becomes lubricated with extra secretions that make intercourse more comfortable), and (b) the presence of vaginal
infections (vaginitis). There are many causes of vaginitis *(see
141, 143, 147)*. You should see a doctor if intercourse continues to be painful.

165

**Dear Dr. Levine: Several months ago I made love for
the first time. It turned out to be a terrible experience, and I've been emotionally upset since that time.
I've talked to my friends, but they just don't seem to
understand what I'm going through. I'm frightened
that I'll never be able to trust anyone ever again. Do
you think I should seek professional help, or is this
a normal reaction?**

I would not recommend professional guidance to anyone if
their sole complaint was that their first sexual experience
was a failure, or even terrible. Our initiation into sexual intercourse is often so full of expectations, pressure, fear, and
notions picked up from media hype that it is hard to imagine it can ever be a wonderful experience. To these pressures we can add the specific personalities of the lovers and
how they get along, respect each other, display sensitivities,
kindness, trust, and maturity.

From the little you say in your letter, it sounds as if you
are talking about not only a failed sexual experience but
a breach of trust. However, I can't comment on that since
I just don't know enough about you or the experience
you had.

If the feelings you are describing do not abate, if none of

your friends or family can understand or be of any help, or if you find it extremely difficult to go out with anyone—then it would be a good idea to speak to a professional.

Dear Dr. Levine: I've been going out with this guy for nearly two years. I'm seventeen, he's twenty-three. Here's the situation. "Hans" and I start kissing and petting, which I like. But Hans always wants sex. I hate sex. I thought I'd learn to like it in time, but I just hate it more each time. I feel empty and hollow, even though I know Hans tries to make it good for me. I've talked to a few close girlfriends about sex, and none of them can honestly say she likes it. I think no girls like sex. They just say they do to turn a guy on.

166

    I'm not scared of getting pregnant; I'm on the Pill.

    How can I learn to enjoy sex? Hans and I are getting married someday, so I have to learn how to like that horrible thing.

While it may seem simple on the surface, yours is a very complicated letter. It is *not* only a matter of enjoying or not enjoying the act of sexual intercourse. You are seventeen, and presumably you and Hans have been having sex for at least a few months. I agree with you that many seventeen-year-old girls who are sexually active do *not* enjoy the act itself as much as the holding, caressing, and loving. Perhaps you were pressured into having sex before you were emotionally ready. Maybe you have some mixed feelings about Hans. Or could it be that you have some moral questions about having sex at such an early age?

    I don't think there is anything "wrong" with you. If you don't enjoy intercourse but like the necking and petting, why not restrict yourself (for now) to the latter? Would Hans go along with this? It sounds like he wouldn't go for this too readily. What makes you so committed, at your age, to marrying Hans? Shouldn't you experience dates and romance with more than one young man during these maturing years?

    As it is, I'd be hard pressed to say that you have a sexual problem. If in a year or more you feel the same way about sex, I would be more inclined to recommend that you see a sex therapist or psychotherapist. But definitely not now.

Dear Dr. Wilcox: I would like to know what it is like for a girl to have an orgasm. I am too shy to ask anyone else about this.

167

Orgasm is defined as the culmination, or peak, of sexual excitement. For women, this involves an intense awareness of stimulation to the genitals and a throbbing sensation that is actually a series of muscle contractions of the outer portion of the vagina; these contractions occur over a period of seconds but sometimes can be prolonged by continued stimulation. Muscles in the uterus and rectum also contract. After the throbbing or contractions stop, there is often a feeling of marked relaxation and release.

The muscle contractions help rid the pelvic organs of extra blood that has come into the area during sexual arousal. If arousal has been extreme but orgasm has not occurred, there may be a deep ache in the pelvis that gradually resolves as the extra blood that has "congested" in the organs slowly leaves the area and re-enters the general circulation.

You might want to read more about sexuality. There are many good books on the subject available through your local library or bookstores, or you could get pamphlets from your department of public health.

168 **Dear Drs. Wilcox and Levine: Is there anything physical or mental that can be done to prevent erections that occur at the wrong times? It is embarrassing.**

During adolescence boys frequently experience spontaneous erections. Although erection of the penis most commonly occurs with sexual arousal, spontaneous erections occur suddenly and unexpectedly. They are completely normal and healthy, although, as you say, they can occur at inopportune times. As you get older, they will happen less and less often. Many boys and men find that having a full bladder stimulates an erection (this probably contributes to awakening in the morning with an erection) or that the friction of tight clothing can do the same. Eliminating these two factors might *slightly* decrease the number of spontaneous erections you have.

There is really nothing you can do to *stop* them. Just remember that every boy in your age group is in the same boat and that these erections will occur less often as you get older. What you are describing is normal, common, pleasurable (albeit at times embarrassing), and totally healthy. Enjoy!

169 **Dear Dr. Wilcox: I am a sixteen-year-old male and have matured fairly well physically. My problem is erection. What exactly occurs during erection? Is the penis always supposed to be upright and pointing**

upwards? When I have an erection, my penis does enlarge, but it doesn't point straight up. Am I normal? What's wrong with me?

The penis contains layers of very spongy tissue that, during erection, expands and becomes firm as the blood supply to the penis increases with sexual stimulation. Spontaneous erections (without sexual stimulation) also occur; they are more frequent during the teen years than during adulthood. *(See 168.)*

What occurs during an erection? The arteries that bring blood to the penis dilate (expand), and a large quantity of blood rushes into the spaces of the spongy tissue. As these spaces expand, they compress the veins that usually carry the blood away from the penis and back to the body. When this happens, the pressure within the spongy tissue increases, it becomes firm and expands, and the penis becomes erect.

The word "erect" may be a bit misleading. By erect, we mean that the penis stands away from the body, not that it has to point straight up. In fact, how much it stands away from the body varies greatly from person to person.

The erection ends when the arteries constrict, or get smaller, forcing the blood into the veins and thereby out of the penis. When more blood leaves the penis than enters, the penis becomes flaccid (soft) again.

It sounds, then, like you are experiencing normal erections. Don't worry.

Dear Dr. Wilcox: I am an eighteen-year-old male, and my girlfriend and I have been going together for eight months and are deeply in love. Last month we decided we were mature enough to make love. The first two times were great. But the last few times we've tried to make love I could not sustain an erection. This problem only occurs during sexual intercourse. I can sustain an erection at other times. Could you explain why this problem didn't occur the first two times and what may be the cause of it?

170

Most men experience episodes in their lives when they have temporary difficulty maintaining erections in specific situations. Generally, these problems resolve on their own and are caused by anxieties the man may not be able to identify. Some experts say that, because these episodes are not uncommon and are transitory, one doesn't need to seek professional help unless the difficulty persists for several

months or more. One problem with this advice is that each
"failure" may make you more anxious about the next encounter, and this anxiety can further interfere with maintaining the erection.

Stress-related erectile difficulties are particularly common
in young men who have only recently begun to have sexual
intercourse and in men with new partners or in stressful
life situations. (There are also medical causes, but they are
much more common in older men and in these cases the
erectile problems would not be limited to specific situations.)

Alcohol, however, can greatly interfere with maintaining
an erection in any man. A drink may make one less inhib-
ited, but it affects the nervous system so that the ability to
have successful intercourse and reach orgasm can be impaired.

Why are you having problems now? The possible anxieties that could be affecting you are endless. Common concerns include worries about whether or not intercourse is
appropriate to the relationship and what it means to each
of you; concerns about being able to please one's partner;
anxieties about possible pregnancy; problems at work; in-
terpersonal problems; and religious or moral conflicts. This
is far from a full list, and not knowing you I can't say which,
if any, are applicable to you.

If the problem persists, you might allow yourself a chance
to relax and not attempt intercourse for a while but simply
enjoy each other physically in ways that feel less anxiety-
producing. If your concerns persist, counseling certainly is
available; your family doctor or the counseling services of a
good general hospital could direct you.

171 **Dear Dr. Wilcox: I have been married for a number
of years, and my problem is premature ejaculation.
This happens continually. During intercourse I have
thought about other things (hockey, etc.), but it did
not help.**

**If there is anything you can suggest that may help,
please let me know. My marriage is at a very low
point now.**

One of the simplest definitions of premature ejaculation is
a man's inability to voluntarily delay ejaculation. (Ejaculation is the expulsion of semen from the penis during a male's
orgasm or sexual climax.)

Premature ejaculation is one of the most common male

sexual problems. It can be a long-term problem that occurs with minimal sexual stimulation regardless of partner or situation, it may be an isolated event (often with a new partner), it may be a temporary problem experienced by newly sexually active males, or it can be a symptom of a problem in a relationship. In *extremely* rare cases it may have a medical cause, such as infection/inflammation of the prostate gland or problems with the nervous system.

Fortunately, effective treatment is available. It consists partly of teaching the patient to become aware of the sensations, or aura, that occur just before orgasm. The patient and his partner then practice stopping stimulation just when the aura is reached, then resting and resuming stimulation, repeating this sequence several times in a row. The male concentrates on the erotic or sexual feelings he is experiencing and avoids distracting thoughts. Although the instructions and steps to this "relearning" of sexual response are too lengthy to be detailed here, a sexual therapist can review these with you (and your wife) as well as explore whether or not there are any specific factors contributing to your problem. Your family doctor or the psychiatry department at your local hospital can refer you to a sexual counselor. If you live in an area where there are no counselors nearby, you should still see your family doctor. Literature is also available that would enable him or her to begin to help you. Make an appointment soon.

Dear Dr. Wilcox: I have heard that you can't get pregnant the first time you have sex. Is this true? **172**
No, it *isn't* true. Pregnancy results when a sperm fertilizes an egg. Because ovulation can occur at *any* point in a woman's menstrual cycle (although it *tends* to occur midway between the beginning of one period and the start of the next), there is *no* "safe" time to have intercourse.

Dear Dr. Wilcox: I am thirteen years old, and although I think about it, I've never had sex. I've had my period and I've missed a couple. I'm scared. **173**
Reading between the lines of your letter, it sounds as though you are afraid you might be pregnant. Don't be. If you have *never* had a sexual encounter with a boy that included contact between his penis and your vaginal area, then you cannot be pregnant.

Pregnancy can, however, occur without sexual intercourse. It can result from close genital contact between a male and female if the male ejaculates (expels) semen *near* the vagina, because the sperm contained in the semen can swim through the vaginal secretions to the vagina. (During true sexual intercourse, the semen is generally ejaculated inside the vagina.)

Many girls find their periods are irregular at first. This is because the very complex hormone system that regulates the menstrual cycle is not yet mature. Most girls find their cycles become regular after two years of having periods. For some, however, it can take much longer. *(See 17–19.)*

174 **Dear Dr. Wilcox: I am sixteen years old (female). I'm afraid I have gotten myself into more trouble than I can handle. My most recent and most serious problem is that I just couldn't say no to my boyfriend. Now I fear that I may be pregnant. I need help but do not know where to go.**

An unplanned pregnancy is an extremely stressful event. You will need expert counseling and support. If you can contact a birth control clinic, the staff will either help you or refer you to someone for help. To find such a clinic, look in the phone book under Birth Control or Planned Parenthood. If you live in a small town, you may have to use the phone book of the nearest large city. You could also contact your family doctor or school nurse; both should be familiar with the resources in your community.

You will need to have a pregnancy test to see if you *are* pregnant, and this can be arranged by whomever you contact for help. A urine test for pregnancy can often give you the answer when your period is only ten days late; if the test comes back negative (not pregnant), it is wise to repeat the test a week or so later. A blood test is available that can diagnose your pregnancy even earlier than the urine test. *(See 175.)*

If it turns out that you are *not* pregnant, you will still have established contact with professionals who can discuss with you the various methods of birth control available and can help you choose an appropriate method if you are going to continue to be sexually active.

175 **Dear Dr. Wilcox: How can you find out if you are pregnant?**

A doctor can do a simple urine test to diagnose pregnancy. During pregnancy, the amount of hormone called human chorionic gonadotropin (HCG) increases. By the time one's period is ten days to two weeks late, the level of this hormone is usually high enough to make the pregnancy test positive. Some newer urine tests can supposedly diagnose pregnancy even sooner than this.

In special circumstances where it is important to know if a woman is pregnant before the time the urine test becomes positive, the blood level of HCG can be measured. It will be elevated even when the level is not yet high enough to make the urine test positive.

Drugstores do sell pregnancy tests, but these don't eliminate the need to see a doctor. If a woman has a positive drugstore test, she will still need to see a doctor for medical care. If it's negative, she still needs to check with a doctor to see why the period is late. Medical help is very important in both cases.

If you have had sexual intercourse or intimate sexual contact (contact between the penis and the vaginal area) and your period is late, you could indeed be pregnant. You should see a doctor as soon as possible.

Dear Dr. Wilcox: My fiancé and I both want kids and want to know what kind of tests are done to determine our chances of having a baby. **176**

I hope you are looking a bit into the future when you ask about fertility, since marriage requires a great deal of work, especially in the early years, to make it strong and secure. Until you are ready to become a parent, you will need to use a method of birth control that is reliable and meets your needs. Your physician can help you choose one.

Tests regarding fertility (the ability to conceive) are generally not done in advance. If you and your fiancé are both healthy, you have no more risk of infertility than any other couple. Approximately one couple in nine has some difficulty with conceiving. Tests to investigate infertility are started after a couple has been having intercourse without using any form of birth control for a year and the woman still has not conceived.

After a complete medical exam, including history, has been done for both husband and wife, the next test is often an analysis of the man's semen to check the number and condition of sperm. Although estimates vary, in 40 percent of cases there is a problem with the man's fertility, in 50 percent a problem with the woman's, and in 10 percent the cause cannot be found.

A variety of specialized tests are used to determine the cause as clearly as possible. Treatment depends on the specific cause.

177 **Dear Dr. Wilcox: I am an eighteen-year-old female wondering why I have not been able to become pregnant (not that I want a baby right now). I lost my virginity almost a year ago. I was with different guys all the time, neither of us using anything. I've been seeing one guy now for about six months. We don't use anything. I haven't thought of going on the Pill because I'm scared of the side effects. Every weekend we make love and I haven't missed my period yet. I'm beginning to think I'm infertile and won't be able to bear children in the future. This scares me because I want children. I know I'm taking chances and I have been lucky. But please give me advice.**

You are right: you have been lucky. Probably the worst way in the world to test one's fertility is to have an unplanned and unwanted pregnancy. In a sense, you've been playing Russian roulette for the past year and have somehow managed to avoid a pregnancy.

There are several factors that may have helped you *not* become pregnant. Most couples who are trying for a pregnancy have intercourse more often during the woman's most fertile days of her month, those halfway between the beginning of one period and the (expected) beginning of the next. If you've been having intercourse only on weekends, you (fortunately) may not have been hitting the fertile days.

How frequently you have intercourse also affects your chances of becoming pregnant. In general, 25 percent of women will be pregnant the first month of unprotected intercourse, 63 percent in six months, 75 percent in nine months, and 80 percent in one year. However, in one study, 83 percent of women became pregnant within six months if they had intercourse four or more times per week, whereas only 16 percent became pregnant if they had intercourse once per week.

Those two factors, timing and frequency of intercourse, may have played a role in your not becoming pregnant, although no one can say for sure. Regardless, however, you shouldn't press your "luck." You should see a doctor soon to choose the type of contraception (birth control) that is best for you.

You should also know that although there are many different causes of infertility and most of them are inborn (present at birth), the major cause of infertility in young women is sexually transmitted infection, such as gonorrhea and chlamydia, that leads to internal scarring. The choices you make now can help prevent it from being a problem for you. Women most at risk of catching gonorrhea are those who have had sex with a number of different men. Condoms can, however, be an effective barrier. *(See 145, 146.)*

Dear Dr. Levine: My problem is with my parents. Before I met my boyfriend, I used to talk to my mother about sex. She used to say that I should wait until I was married, and I agreed. Now that I have had sex, I don't know how to tell her—or if I should at all. She might get mad, and my father will probably think I sleep with every guy. Could you give me advice as to how to tell her, so I can get some birth control? My boyfriend uses something, but I would feel safer if I did too. **178**

You don't tell me how old you are. If you are only fourteen, I would frankly be more concerned. I would wonder if you are having sex for reasons other than love, about your going on the Pill at too young an age, and indeed if you could control your sexual ardor for a while.

If you are eighteen, I'd still want to know if you're really comfortable with what you are doing, but you'd obviously be in a better position to make judgments about birth control.

While it certainly would be different at each age, if you are going to be sexually active, then you must be protected. I would hope that you could discuss this with your mother at *any* age. *(See 184.)*

Dear Dr. Wilcox: My boyfriend and I feel that we are ready and plan to make love very soon. What are the chances of pregnancy if we use the condom only? **179**

The statistics regarding "failure rates" for different methods of birth control are usually given as the number of pregnancies that will occur among 100 women using that method for one year.

For condom use the figure ranges, depending on the study, from a high of 36 (36/100) to a low of around 10. An "average" rate would be around 15–20, but if condoms are used with contraceptive cream, foam, or jelly (all are available without a prescription), the rate is solidly down to 15 or less.

A low failure rate depends on proper usage to prevent breakage. The end of the condom should not be pulled tightly down onto the tip of the penis; leaving an inch or so of empty condom at the tip will help prevent splitting of the condom and can also "catch" the ejaculated semen, decreasing the chances of its being forced down the sides and out the end of the condom at the base of the penis. Adequate lubrication, either with the woman's own vaginal secretion or with a water-soluble jelly like K-Y Jelly (never use petroleum jelly; it may dissolve the condom) will also help prevent breakage. Because the tiny drops of fluid that may appear at the tip of the penis during arousal may contain sperm, there should be no genital-genital contact unless the condom is in place. Finally, soon after ejaculation, while the erection is still present, the man should hold the condom firmly at the base of the penis and withdraw from the vagina; this will help prevent any spillage of semen from the condom.

The pluses of using condoms include ease of purchase (they can be bought at any drugstore without a prescription), lack of side effects, and the fact that they can be an effective barrier to sexually transmitted infection. The minuses include less than 100 percent protection from pregnancy and, some people would say, less spontaneity (putting the condom on interrupts lovemaking).

There are many good books and pamphlets available on contraception. You can get them from your doctor, a birth control clinic, or a Planned Parenthood office.

180 **Dear Dr. Wilcox: I would like to try the rhythm method of birth control. When is the safest time to make love? I am twenty, married, and my period has been regular for the past ten months. If I do become pregnant, my husband and I don't mind.**

The rhythm method—having intercourse only during "safe" parts of the menstrual cycle—is *not* an effective form of birth control and should not be relied upon exclusively. Up to half the women attempting to use rhythm for contraception will become pregnant within one year. The problem is that one can only *estimate* a woman's fertile time, and many things—particularly stress—can change the time of ovulation.

To get a rough idea of your fertile time, the time to avoid intercourse, review your calendar for the past year or so and figure out how many days there are in your cycle, counting from the first day of bleeding of one period (Day 1) until the first day of the next. Find the number of days in the longest cycle and the number in the shortest. From the larger number, subtract 11. From the smaller number, subtract 18. For example, if the longest cycle is 30 days, then $30 - 11 = 19$; if the shortest cycle is 25 days, then $25 - 18 = 7$. The resulting numbers give the days of your cycle between which you are most vulnerable to pregnancy and should avoid intercourse. In the example given, this would be Day 7 through Day 19.

Body changes also occur that can indicate ovulation is near. If any of these changes are noted at a time outside your mathematically predicted fertile period, you should abstain from sex for a week. (Since the changes may start several days before ovulation, and sperm can survive up to four days after intercourse, you need a week of abstinence to be safe. The problem, of course, is that if you have intercourse one day and note the changes the next, it is already too late, and pregnancy may result.)

One change is that mucus secreted by the cervix increases as the time of ovulation nears. During the first days after menstruation there will be only mild moistness at the vaginal opening. As ovulation approaches, the mucus increases in amount and becomes thicker and stickier. At ovulation there is a great deal of mucus, which has the consistency of raw egg white.

Another change is in basal body temperature (BBT), which you check by thermometer before you get out of bed in the morning (five minutes under your tongue). Just *before* ovulation *some* women note a slight *decrease* in temperature; *all* women will note an *increase* at ovulation. Keeping a chart for a number of months will help you figure out your pattern.

The last change may be the most difficult to judge: your cervix becomes softer and sits higher in the vagina about the time of ovulation. By inserting your forefinger into your vagina, you should be able to feel your cervix at the far end of your vagina. Unlike the soft walls of the vagina, it has the same consistency as the tip of your nose.

Using rhythm is neither easy nor very reliable. If you followed each and every recommendation *perfectly*, some claim your pregnancy risk would be only 10 percent, but few will do so. For most women, especially teenagers, trying to use rhythm is like flipping a coin—half will get pregnant.

181

Dear Dr. Wilcox: I see my boyfriend only a couple of times a month *at most* since he goes to a university out of town. How effective is the diaphragm, and are there any dangers? What does it look like? Is it uncomfortable?

The diaphragm is a circle of rubber that comes in a size range similar to the circumference of large and small coffee cups. No more than two hours before intercourse, 1 tbsp (15 ml) of contraceptive foam, cream, or jelly is put on it (and often also smeared around its rim), and it is then inserted into the vagina. It tucks under the pubic bone in front and is secured at the inner end of the vagina by having its rim under the cervix. Although in most women it slips into place as easily as a tampon, you have to make sure it covers the cervix; otherwise, it won't provide a wall to the sperm, and pregnancy could result.

The contraceptive foam (or jelly or cream) is used to kill any sperm that wander by the barrier. It is also recommended that, as an added precaution, an applicatorful of the foam, jelly, or cream also be inserted into the vagina just prior to intercourse. The diaphragm is left in place for another six to eight hours to ensure that the sperm have been blocked and killed. If it is properly in place, neither you nor your partner will notice its presence.

It is *critical,* however, that the diaphragm never be left in the vagina more than twenty-four hours, and it is best to remove it six to eight hours after intercourse. Leaving it in too long has been associated with toxic shock syndrome, a very rare but potentially lethal infection. *(See 24.)* Some researchers feel that women who use diaphragms may have a slightly increased chance of developing urinary tract infections.

With a properly fitted diaphragm (yes, you have to see a doctor) that is used correctly, the failure rate is 10 to 15 percent. Most failures occur because people skip using it from time to time, forget to put the cream or jelly in, or don't go back to be refitted, even when they discover that the diaphragm doesn't fit properly and shifts, particularly with orgasm. (It also must be refitted if you gain or lose 10 lb/5kg or have a baby in the interim.) It should be rechecked yearly by your doctor.

For a very conscientious patient—and particularly one who has intercourse infrequently and at predictable times—the diaphragm can be quite effective. If you couple its use with rhythm *(see 180),* it could be virtually 100 percent effective.

Dear Dr. Wilcox: I heard you can buy some stuff in the drugstore that looks like whipped cream and that will keep you from getting pregnant. Is this true?

182

Contraceptive foam, jelly, or cream can be purchased in a drugstore without a prescription. It is usually in the section near the pharmacist where condoms and pregnancy test kits are also shelved.

Inserted into the vagina prior to intercourse (never *more* than thirty minutes before having sex; it can lose its effectiveness), it prevents pregnancy by killing the sperm that are deposited in the vagina during sex. Unfortunately, it doesn't do this very effectively, and 38 to 40 percent of women using this method may become pregnant.

Most failures seem to result from not putting the foam, jelly, or cream in place prior to genital-genital contact (even foreplay, if there is touch between the penis and vaginal area, since the drops of lubricating fluid the penis produces may contain sperm); from not using it "just this once"; or, when using contraceptive suppositories (which are related to foam), not waiting for the suppository to dissolve prior to starting intercourse. Studies of very highly motivated couples who use it every single time and don't have intercourse more than a couple of times per week indicate that these contraceptives would have a much lower failure rate if used properly.

Dear Dr. Wilcox: My boyfriend, while aware that I am on the Pill, is still afraid of my becoming pregnant, and he hesitates to ejaculate while he is still inside me. I feel that this detracts from the pleasure we both experience. I have talked over the problem with him several times. It is not that he does not want to make love to me, it is simply this fear.

183

What are the chances of my becoming pregnant while using the Pill? I take it correctly, have never missed a day, and was thoroughly examined by a gynecologist before going on it.

"Low-dose" birth control pills containing a combination of estrogen and progesterone can be a very effective form of contraception when taken carefully and prescribed appropriately. "Low-dose" means they have 35 mcg of estrogen or less—*not* that they are low in effectiveness. Although figures vary slightly from study to study, the failure rate is generally quoted as *less than 1 percent.* In other words, the birth control pill is *more than 99 percent* effective. (The effectiveness of the infrequently prescribed progestin-only pill—it has no estrogen—is less than this.) The only method of birth control that is 100 percent effective is complete avoidance of sexual intercourse and of all genital-genital contact.

Most of the failures that occur with the Pill are the result of women taking it irregularly. But there is also concern that other medications taken by a patient on the Pill can impair its effectiveness. Among these are drugs for the treatment of epilepsy and tuberculosis, and antibiotics such as ampicillin and tetracycline. However, even if the rate of failure is doubled or tripled, it is still very low compared to that of other forms of birth control. All questions about possible interactions between the Pill and other medications should be directed to one's physician.

Your boyfriend withdrawing prior to ejaculation is adding little further protection to the greater than 99 percent effectiveness you have from the Pill. Because sperm can be present in tiny amounts of fluid that emerge from the penis during arousal and before ejaculation, withdrawal alone is a particularly ineffective method of contraception.

184   **Dear Dr. Wilcox: As I will be eighteen in a month, I feel that I should be responsible for my actions. Where and how do teenagers like me get birth control pills? Does one need a prescription? Would my request be confidential?**

Yes, birth control pills *must* be prescribed by a physician, and they will be prescribed only after he or she has evaluated your health status by examining you physically and taking your and your family's full medical histories to make sure there are no medical reasons that would make the Pill inappropriate for you and your contraceptive needs. Many experts feel that the Pill, when prescribed in this way, is one of the best and most effective birth control methods available.

For help regarding contraception, there are a number of resources available. All contacts would be kept confidential. Your family doctor might be the best person to see since he or she knows your medical background. Also, many communities list a birth control hotline and the address of birth control clinics in the phone book, under the heading Birth Control. Or you could call the Planned Parenthood office nearest you or your community's public health department for further direction.

Dear Dr. Wilcox: I am healthy and nineteen. I would like to go on the Pill, but I have friends who say it causes cancer, heart attacks, and strokes. Is this true? Is the Pill going to kill me?

185

No. If you are a healthy, sexually active nonsmoker under age twenty-four who uses *no* birth control, you are twelve times more likely to die than if you *were* on the Pill. Even smokers under twenty-four are safer on the Pill than they are using no contraception (the Pill cuts their risk of death in half).

As far as cancer is concerned, again, *no*, it is not true. Today's birth control actually seems to provide protection against cancer of the ovaries and endometrium (lining of the uterus) and has no influence on cancer of the cervix or breast. As for heart attacks and strokes, the *old* stories about the *old* pills—the ones that contained 50 mcg of estrogen or more—did raise real concerns. But newer studies on the pills that have 35 mcg of estrogen or less provide a clearer view of today's situation.

The risk for women on the Pill of having heart attacks or strokes is increased but is still small for *nonsmokers under age thirty-five.* For example, if you take the Pill, you have a three times greater chance of having a stroke than if you were not on the Pill. What does this mean in real numbers? That one in *thirty thousand* Pill users may have a stroke! The risk is greatest among Pill users who smoke *and* are over age thirty-five. Therefore, doctors prefer their Pill users to be nonsmokers and anyone who smokes *and* is thirty-five (some say thirty or under) simply should not be prescribed the Pill.

There is some concern that the Pill may lower the level of HDL (a type of fat that *decreases* the risk of heart attack) in the blood. Since the higher the HDL you have, the lower your risk of heart attacks, the worry is that by lowering HDL, the Pill may increase the risk of heart attacks or strokes. However, this possible effect is very small; drinking alcohol, smoking, being overweight, and eating fried rather than broiled meat each has a greater effect on HDL than does the Pill.

High blood cholesterol itself is a risk factor for heart attack and stroke; therefore, women with high blood cholesterol should probably not take the Pill, since it seems unwise to add even the smallest further risk to someone who may already be more vulnerable than average to the occurrence of these problems.

On the positive side, the Pill is not only a very effective means of birth control but also provides a number of fringe benefits: it can decrease cramps and menstrual flow, decrease breast cysts, decrease the incidence of infections of the uterus and pelvis (so-called pelvic inflammatory disease), and help acne.

186 **Dear Dr. Wilcox: When should a woman absolutely not take the Pill for health reasons?**
In medical jargon, you are asking for a list of "absolute contraindications" to the birth control pill. Although the list may vary slightly according to source, here are some general guidelines.

No woman should be prescribed the Pill if she has had a heart attack, stroke, or other event involving a blood clot; if she has a poorly functioning liver or a liver tumor; if she has a tumor whose growth will be stimulated by Pill; if she has vaginal bleeding of unknown cause; or if she may be pregnant.

Other strong though not absolute contraindications include severe migraine, high blood cholesterol, high blood pressure, gall bladder problems, diabetes, breast-feeding, having a broken leg (a leg in a cast is more prone to blood clots), "fibroids" (enlargements of the muscle of the uterus), and being a smoker age thirty or over.

Recent major studies recommend that all women stop the Pill at thirty-five, although other experts feel healthy women can continue it to forty or so.

187 **Dear Dr. Wilcox: A friend of mine went off the Pill because she was so nauseated she couldn't stand it. Does this happen a lot?**
Nausea, and even vomiting, are not rare problems with the Pill, but they can be avoided. First of all, use a birth control pill with 35 mcg of estrogen or less: this side effect is less common with these than with the 50 mcg pills used years ago. (Generally, no one should take the 50 mcg pills anyway.)

If you are on this newer and lower-dose pill, try taking it at bedtime. If you experience any nausea, you'll sleep right through it.

188 **Dear Dr. Wilcox: Why isn't the "morning-after" pill more widely used? It seems a lot easier than taking a pill every day.**
A morning-after pill may sound like a simple, easy way to prevent pregnancy, but it isn't. Morning-after pills contain

a very high level of the hormones progesterone and/or estrogen. Such high levels apparently prevent pregnancy by altering the lining of the uterus (so the egg cannot implant and develop there), by affecting the hormones released by the ovaries so a favorable environment for a pregnancy is not created, and also by changing the quality of the mucus produced by the cervix (the part of the uterus at the innermost end of the vagina).

To be effective, the pills must be started within seventy-two hours of a *single* act of unprotected intercourse. Failure rates vary with what combination is used, but for those most commonly prescribed, the rate is 1.5 to 5 percent (at least ninety-five out of one hundred women will *not* become pregnant).

The morning-after pill, however, should be seen only as an *emergency* measure. There are a number of risks associated with its use. First, 10 percent of any pregnancies that occur will be ectopic. This means the egg implants outside the uterus, which may lead to fatal internal bleeding and which must be treated surgically. Secondly, if taken when the woman is already pregnant, it may harm the fetus. There is also some concern about the effects of exposures to high hormone levels, and using it over and over is not considered a good idea. Other side effects that are more uncomfortable than dangerous include headache, nausea and/or vomiting, and breast pain.

Dear Dr. Wilcox: What is an IUD? I have seen it mentioned in books along with other methods of birth control but have never known what it was. **189**
The initials IUD stand for IntraUterine Device.

An IUD is a small sticklike object, about 2 in (5 cm) long. Some are made of plastic, some contain copper, and some contain one of the female hormones called progesterone.

A doctor puts the IUD into the uterus through the small opening in the cervix (the end of the uterus that projects into the innermost part of the vagina). This is most easily done during menstruation. Some cramping can occur. Once inside, the IUD seems to work by preventing the egg from implanting in the uterus, so that even if it is fertilized, the egg can't attach itself to the lining of the uterus and a pregnancy can't develop. It may also have other effects that prevent pregnancy. It can be left in place from one to three years or more, depending on the type, before it must be removed and a new one put in.

The failure rate for the IUD is 1 to 5 percent during the first year it's in place; the rate decreases thereafter.

Possible side effects of IUDs include pain, increased bleeding with periods, perforation of the uterus by the device, and unintended pregnancy (the uterus may even expel the device, leaving the woman unprotected). But most important, use of the IUD increases the risk of a very serious infection called pelvic inflammatory disease. This infection may lead to infertility.

Recent studies show that for women who have never had babies, the IUD can double the risk of becoming infertile. The risk is greater with the plastic devices and less with copper-containing devices. The risk also decreases if the woman has only one sexual partner. Because of the infertility risk, it is felt that the IUD should not be the first-choice birth control method for women who have not yet had children. In women who have had at least one child and have only one sexual partner, however, the copper IUDs do not appear to increase the risk of infertility.

At the present time, because of the threat of numerous lawsuits connected with the effects of IUDs (not because the medical risks have increased), manufacturers have withdrawn most IUDs from the market in the United States. These devices are still available in most parts of the world, and many women travel from the United States to Canadian clinics in order to obtain this kind of birth control.

190 **Dear Dr. Levine: Whenever I see a boy I like or am attracted to, I have these little urges. I think about him and what he would do in all sorts of situations. Sometimes I wonder what it would be like if he made love to me. Afterward I feel guilty for having such thoughts. Is this normal for a sixteen-year-old girl, or am I perverted?**

Your thoughts and urges are common; they are not abnormal or perverted. Some sixteen-year-old girls (and boys) are constantly preoccupied with sexual and romantic thoughts. Others couldn't care less at that stage. Your level of awareness and interest are not at all unusual, and you need feel no guilt whatsoever. They are healthy and happy thoughts. Just enjoy them.

191 **Dear Dr. Levine: I am a seventeen-year-old male who has fetishes. I find it frustrating, since I feel it is very**

degrading to become sexually excited over such silly objects as high-heeled shoes.

Fortunately, I am attracted to women in more healthy ways too. However, this is still a nagging problem. What causes people to have fetishes, and how can this problem be solved?

A fetish is an unusual preoccupation with and erotic attraction to a particular inanimate object (in this case, high-heeled shoes) or to an unusual part of the body (the foot, for example).

Some psychoanalysts feel that the preferred object is a device to ward off anxiety; others feel that the fetish prevents the usual sexual experience, which may be particularly frightening to the individual. They say that it keeps the fetishist from having to deal with his feeling toward the opposite sex (anger, fear, hatred, etc.). Some behavior therapists put it down to a conditioned response to some earlier experience; for example, a shoe may have been seen at the time of sexual arousal some time ago. Finally, the object is seen by some as symbolizing an entirely different experience but on an unconscious level.

If you are highly motivated to eradicate this sexual preference, various forms of psychotherapy may be attempted. As a first step, however, I would speak to an experienced psychotherapist to get his or her opinion and perhaps referral to a behavior modification program. If the fetish doesn't bother you very much, however, you could just decide to do nothing.

Dear Dr. Levine: I am an eighteen-year-old male, and I really don't know how to say this, but here goes. I want to wear diapers. You see, as a child I was a constant bed wetter. Specialists confirmed that there was no physical disorder, assured Mom and me that I was not unique, and said to be patient and that I would outgrow the problem in my own time.

Well, to make a long story short, my wetting became worse, and when I was about eight, my mom, totally frustrated (me too), decided to diaper me to save on the extra laundry. She literally diapered me and changed me every single morning. Gradually, my protests became weaker and weaker. At eleven I was still in diapers and loved it!

192

Sexual arousal has taken over (Mom several times masturbated me through my cloth diaper). Now, at eighteen, I only wet the bed about twice a month at most. But I find myself totally addicted to cloth diapers.

Since I now live on my own, I have complete privacy and play out my diaper fetish on a regular basis. Sexual arousal has become dependent on wearing diapers. Believe it or not, I have found a few female companions who have gone along with my fantasy.

I try to rationalize my behavior by believing it's nobody else's business, but sometimes I think I'm weird. I don't know if you have an explanation, but I had to tell somebody.

I wish that I could give you a clear-cut answer to your concerns. The fact is, your brief but very revealing history tells me some highly relevant things about your preoccupations. And your view of what has happened in the past to affect the future is probably quite correct.

You *do* have a "diaper fetish," that is, sexual stimulation and gratification from inanimate apparel. It obviously has to do with your past experiences with your mother and your unique history with diapers and bed-wetting.

But where we go from here is problematic, and this is a complicated and debatable area. What I might advise might be diametrically opposed to what another professional like me might say.

If this fetish of yours is not giving you or anyone else any problems; if you are not suffering shame, guilt, anxiety, or depression; if you are not hindered in your sexual and social relationships; if you are carrying on your schooling or job, and you can live with yourself quite happily, then you should do nothing.

If, on the other hand, you are finding this fetish getting in the way of your everyday functioning, or your relationships, then you should seek psychotherapeutic relief.

I've long since given up finding some people "weird" (your term) because of peculiar sexual fantasies. Very little surprises me anymore. Just when I think I've heard it all, somebody presents me with something entirely new and bizarre. As long as *nobody* is hurt or humiliated or offended, the state—and psychiatry—have no role in the bedrooms of the nation.

Dear Dr. Levine: I am an eighteen-year-old male. **193**
When I entered high school three years ago, my gym
teacher told us that we must wear a jockstrap for all
gym classes. Naturally, everybody obeyed the teacher.
Although most of my classmates appeared to treat
this as a big joke, for reasons unknown to me it became a matter of considerable trauma in my case.

In fact, it bothered me so much that I started to
fantasize (when in bed at night) about putting on my
jockstrap for gym classes. Eventually, this led me to
masturbate while thinking about wearing a jockstrap.

This has been going on for three years, and I can't
seem to shake the problem. I don't think I am homosexual, because I have no desire to be sexually
involved with other males. In fact, I have a girlfriend
and it is only a matter of time until we sleep together.

Can you tell me why I am so obsessed with this
jockstrap thing and if I am likely to get over it? I
should tell you that I dropped out of high school last
year. I think my hang-up was probably the main reason, but I'm not sure.

As readers know, I tend to be rather relaxed and tolerant
about private sexual fantasies and even acts, as long as there
is no detrimental effect on that individual or anyone else.
But once someone is made to feel uncomfortable by his or
her own sexual thoughts and preoccupations, or others involved are bothered or hurt, I am a lot less relaxed.

The main issue is that *you* see it as a problem and it has
become something of an obsession, so much so that it is
severely interfering with your life (you quit school). This tells
me that some sessions with a psychotherapist would be of
considerable benefit to you. Not only would you learn about
the derivation of these concerns, but you could well learn to
deal with the problem, lessen it, or eradicate it. Ask your
family doctor, minister, or school social worker or guidance
counselor to recommend a psychotherapist.

Dear Dr. Levine: I am a fifteen-year-old boy, and up **194**
to about two months ago I was completely heterosexual. But at that time I began to have trouble get-

ting excited by girls. I thought it would just pass, but it's getting worse. A few weeks ago I met a girl whom I sort of fell in love with, but I don't get sexually aroused by her. The worst part is that I'm afraid of becoming attracted to males instead, and it's bothered me so much that I almost believe that I am. I'm not a "femme" and I never have been; the worst thing that could happen in my life would be to turn gay. I'm embarrassed to mention this to any of my friends or family. It's like I don't know what I am. Please help me.

There is very little in what you have written that makes me suspect you are gay. The fact that you can't get aroused with a girl to whom you are attracted may be related to many factors having nothing to do with sexual orientation. For example, nervousness, fear, discomfort, or pressure on you to "perform" may equally account for your temporary impotence. Your concerns about being gay might even account for your difficulties; our brains play a large role in our sexual activities.

You are relatively young, and the progression of the next few years will answer your question for you quite decisively. I agree that discussing this with your friends or family at this stage might invite emotional and insensitive responses that would not be helpful.

195 Dear Dr. Levine: I am an eighteen-year-old male who is going through what I consider a mental hell. For many years I have been confused about my sexuality. I seem to have a strong attraction to the same sex. A few months ago I told a close female friend of mine because I had to tell someone and needed advice. This girl is a few years older than I, and we are very close. I trust her very much, but I wonder about her advice, which was to just wait and eventually I would know—or if I did not wish to wait I should have sexual experiences with both sexes to know for sure. When I asked her if I should seek professional help, she answered emphatically *no!* As I am a virgin, I don't wish to have my first time as an experiment, or really any other time. Anyway, I don't think I could bear it with a female as I have had several nightmares about having sex with females and I hated the experience.

What do you suggest I do? I need some good advice as I have been letting my grades drop and my relationship with my family has been getting progressively worse.

I certainly don't look upon psychotherapy as a cure-all, but in this instance I have to disagree with your female friend. I assume she is advising you against professional help because she has heard horror stories to the effect, for example, that some psychiatrists consider homosexual patients to be disturbed. Or perhaps she feels that seeing a psychotherapist is a sign of weakness.

In your situation, in which you have become withdrawn and unhappy, your confusion over your sexual orientation has affected your general psychological state. My own feeling is that, gay or straight, you should talk to an objective professional who can help you sort out your confusion. Whichever direction you end up going, it will certainly be better than living in a state of paralysis.

Dear Dr. Levine: I am a seventeen-year-old male. My cousin, whom I see about once every six months, was down to visit last month. Unfortunately, what happened is something I would like to forget.

My cousin is male. Whenever he visits, we have always slept in the same room, in fact in the same bed. Nothing was ever thought of it since we both date girls. Not getting into the intimate details, what happened that night is something I have only read about in books. I don't think I have homosexual tendencies, but I am afraid to tell anyone.

196

Let me try to reassure you. You are not the first, and certainly won't be the last, to experiment in your teenage years with sexual activity with a close person of the same sex. You are concerned, I guess, because of the implications of homosexual tendencies.

If you were homosexual, chances are you would already know, and the incident would probably not have upset you in the manner that it obviously did. To be certain that somebody is gay, his (or her) desires, erotic preferences, masturbatory fantasies, etc., would have to be uniformly along the same sex lines.

Because I know next to nothing about you, and even less about your cousin, it is difficult for me to say much more about your orientation and this experience in your young life. On the face of it, however, I doubt that you are gay.

197 **Dear Dr. Levine: I am a twenty-year-old male who is lonely and concerned. I have admitted to myself (after a lot of debating and thinking) that I am homosexual. Now that I know where I stand sexually, I don't know how I can have a relationship with someone. I have made some contacts but none that was really substantial.**

All my friends are straight. Many have asked me why I don't have a girlfriend. I never answer the question completely. Recently I have told only my closest friends and found their support.

Whenever I see someone I would like to meet, I become excited, nervous, and/or scared. Questions start running through my head, such as, "Is he gay? Could he like me? What if he isn't gay? Will I make a fool of myself by coming on to him?" Afterward I end up losing the chance of finding out or meeting him because of fear.

I'm afraid that one day I'll do something drastic and then regret it later. Please advise me on what I should do to find someone I could get to know as a friend or more than just a friend.

Usually by the age of twenty a person has a clear idea if he or she is homosexual or heterosexual. The question about one's sexual orientation is complex, involving dreams, fantasies, desires, and experiences. Let's assume, however, that you are what you say: homosexual.

Most large cities now have a number of services, resources, or meeting places that serve the homosexual community. Some are listed in the phone book and are designated as the (city) Homophile Assocation or Gay (something) Service, for example.

I don't want to minimize your problems, because we all know it isn't easy for gay people, surrounded as they are by a predominantly heterosexual and often hostile population. But some of your problems and questions are those often posed to me by twenty-year-old straight young men and women. Don't make this problem your sole reason for living. There are other interests, relationships, experiences, and needs that have to be fulfilled simultaneously and that will enrich your romantic life rather than detract from it. By concentrating on them, you will meet new people and prevent an obsessional quality from coming to your quest.

Dear Dr. Levine: For five years I have had homosexual feelings, but I always imagined that they would disappear. It never used to bother me that much, but now I feel like it's weighing me down. I hate the thought of homosexuality and I do not wish to ever take part in such a relationship. I used to pray to God and ask Him to change me. He never did. Besides losing faith, I am now losing my self-respect and happiness. I have loving friends and a great family, but I would never share my feelings with them for fear I would lose all love and respect. Lately I have felt nothing but hatred and scorn for myself, and I feel depressed when I realize I face a life without knowing true love with any person. I feel angry and sickened. Please help me if you can.

198

I feel for you. I obviously can't on the basis of your letter say with certainty that your sexual orientation is exclusively homosexual. But at your age you probably have a good idea of where your interests and erotic preferences lie.

You may know that homosexuality is not by definition a psychiatric disorder. If its manifestations are accepted by the individual, he or she can live a fairly satisfactory life. Many homosexuals are in prominent positions in society and in all professions and walks of life. Many are married and have children. Most are still "in the closet," or secretive about their sex lives, in order to avoid exposure and social rejection. With all the talk of tolerance and acceptance, homosexuality is still looked upon with derision and opprobrium by many. If an individual cannot or will not accept that orientation, it can cause him (or her) considerable psychological pain, which seems to be your situation at present.

Your attitudes may modify over time. Be that as it may, I would suggest that you speak to a psychotherapist at this point. You are going through a private hell right now and need guidance and support. Some communities, for example, have organizations for homosexual young people that offer counseling and groups. There are also gay Christian congregations. However, I don't think that you're ready for

that. Your family doctor could suggest the name of a good
psychotherapist.

199

**Dear Dr. Levine: I am a twenty-year-old college stu-
dent. One of my neighbors, an eighteen-year-old guy
I have known for many years, recently entrusted me
with the fact that he is gay. He was, in fact, quite
well informed about the subject, but he wanted to
voice his thoughts to someone he could trust. Unfortunately, I don't feel qualified to provide the proper
advice about dealing with parents and friends.**

**What can I do for him, and should I keep on lend-
ing an ear? As for the community services that could
be of assistance to him, he doesn't wish to use them
for fear that he'll be told he's sick and that he can
be cured. He truly knows about his sexual preference. Yet he's so mixed up and fearful of that lifestyle.**

You are more qualified than you think to help this young
man. You listened, you didn't condemn or reject him, you
didn't laugh at or ridicule him, and you are willing to continue talking to him and to help him. This alone puts you,
unfortunately, in a minority position. It is not that you are
"encouraging" homosexuality—far from it. You are giving
him a chance to express his confusion, sadness, and frustration in a trusting atmosphere, which is an unusual experience for many homosexuals.

Going to a local gay counseling agency or homophile as-
sociation is *not* going to get your friend labeled as sick. This
particular approach works for some, not for others. I don't
know what other information he wants from you. Mainly, I
think he wants to overcome his fears and deal with his confusion and guilt. It is a tough row to hoe. Usually by the age
of eighteen a male will know what his sexual orientation is,
but this is not a hard and fast rule. I think that you would
be ill advised to assist him in finding sexual partners or
lovers. Your major role is as an older friend, supporter, and
confidant.

200

**Dear Dr. Levine: I think I'm a lesbian. I've made this
assumption based only on desires and dreams (I have
studied Freud and psychoanalysis). Freud's theories
describe me directly as homosexual. I find this a little hard to accept, mostly because I live in a very**

small town where homosexuality is not a fad, it's
downright rejected. I'm afraid that if I am queer I'll
become an outcast. Being only fourteen, I have had
no sexual experiences, so I don't know what I am.
It's not the sort of thing you can try on for size. So
please tell me if there are any other ways of knowing. I don't want to hurt anybody, including myself.

I can't tell you, on the basis of your letter, whether you are
gay or heterosexual. You are young and inexperienced, and
your "dreams and desires," on which you base your as-
sumptions, can change markedly in the course of the next
few years or even months. To say that you have "studied
Freud" is only to tell me of your seriousness—and your confusion. For one thing, it would take extraordinary effort on
your part to master Freud at your young age, and for another, a little knowledge is, in fact, a dangerous thing. Furthermore, Freud's knowledge of lesbianism—at the turn of
the century—was woefully inadequate.

Time will tell. You will know by your relationships with
males and females, your fantasies, your erotic attractions,
your romantic attachments, and yes, your desires and
dreams. You will also learn by experience, but at the age of
fourteen, there is surely no rush.

Your town, by the way, is no different from many other
communities that dislike or reject homosexuality. Just make
sure that it is not your need to define yourself as unique
and different from your neighbors that is the impetus to
call yourself lesbian. There are other ways of rebelling.

If you do eventually turn out to be lesbian in your orientation, and it "feels right" to you, you will most likely find
"coming out of the closet" extremely difficult in your town.

**Dear Dr. Levine: I am a fifteen-year-old female who
is convinced that, because of a childhood of incest,
child molestation, rape, early puberty, and plain old
nature, I have homosexual tendencies. This is hard
for me to handle because the psychological effects
of my past have been weighing on me as has my parents' strong belief that all that has happened is my
fault and also that lesbianism is the second worst
thing in the world next to "looking for somebody to
rape you."**

**I am really having a hell of a time dealing with this
attraction to women because I feel like I am betray-**

201

ing the people I try to care about. But at the same time, I don't have any feelings for men and I don't wish to.

Are my feelings wrong, and if not, how should I deal with them?

At a very young age, you have already been through a variety of destructive experiences. Unfortunately, the "victim" (in this case, you) is often blamed for the terrible transgressions of others. Who these "others" are you don't tell us. Why your parents attribute fault to you is a complicated question, but it obviously serves to hurt you further and to render you powerless. It is a no-win situation.

As far as your possible homosexual tendencies are concerned, it would not be useful for me to agree or disagree at this point. We don't yet know the specific causes of homosexual orientation, but it does not seem to be necessarily related to terrible experiences at the hands of close members of the opposite sex. It makes sense to us that this would be the cause, but in fact this is a factor in only a small percentage of instances.

You probably have good reason to be angry at a man or men, given your past experiences. But we can't jump from that to saying that they caused your sexual preferences. Show your parents your letter and this response; open their eyes to the pain you have suffered. Some counseling sessions may be useful for all of you. *(See 291.)*

202 Dear Dr. Levine: I am a fourteen-year-old girl, and I have a best friend, Jennifer. Jen and I are very close for best friends. We love each other very much and I admit we do a bit more than a kiss on the cheek.

Before we met each other, we liked boys. I have absolutely no sexual attraction to any other woman, and as far as I know, neither does Jennifer. But somehow we have very strong feelings for each other, and sure, we're still interested in boys.

I don't know whether or not to call myself bisexual. What do you think?

I would doubt very much that you are anything but a normal young woman, developing intimate relationships, exploring her sexuality, experimenting, and being attracted to the opposite sex. Your relationship with Jennifer is merely a part of that complex process. I wouldn't discourage it; it will run its course, and you will have learned a lot about her, about caring, about sex, and about yourself.

It does not at all mean you're homosexual, nor will the relationship with Jennifer lead you down that path. Young girls often develop exceedingly close relationships with each other, as part of their growing awareness and maturity. Enjoy each other, but spend time with other kids, go out with boys, and experience *all* kinds of friendships.

Dear Dr. Levine: I am an eighteen-year-old girl and very confused. You see, I don't know whether I am normal or bisexual. I know for sure I'm not gay because I am very attracted to guys. I've had these weird feelings about women for about as long as I can remember and in the past have kept them deep inside. But as I get older I realize that these feelings could ruin my whole life. I don't want to be gay or bisexual; I just want to be me. All I really ever wanted was to be loved, wanted, and needed by someone, maybe anyone.

Being bisexual is totally against my religion, and I would be kicked out of my church and family if they ever found out. I am very ashamed of myself and wish to be just a normal teenager with normal sexual urges.

The thing that is blocking my thinking is an incident that happened last summer. This girl and I became good friends and one day she invited me to her apartment. We drank a little and joked a little and then she leaned down and kissed me full on the mouth. I felt a bit aroused but pulled away and cursed myself for enjoying it. The girl and I don't talk anymore, and we don't even see each other.

Is this feeling toward the same sex a phase, and will I become normal, or am I really different?

First, let me tell you that yours is a very well written, sensitive letter. The whole subject of bisexuality is actually very complicated, and there are few absolute conclusions we can make. I know very little about you, but I would be willing to wager that you are heterosexual. Nothing you have said suggests to me that you are homosexual.

Now, as far as bisexuality is concerned, I even doubt that you are genuinely that. The fact that you feel very warm

203

toward women and that you had one really quite innocuous experience says nothing about you having a bisexual orientation. Many women can empathize with your feelings, and that one experience can be explained in many ways (exploration, curiosity, attractiveness, wine, advances by her) other than bisexuality.

If you in fact are bisexual, there is no reason why you have to be worried about exposure or humiliation. Nobody has to know, if you don't want it revealed. I am not one of those who urge "coming out of the closet" as being *the* open and honest way; it can prove to be highly self-destructive. It works for some, but not for others.

You might wish to spend one or two sessions with an experienced counselor—*not* because you have any serious problem but merely to clarify your confusion and ease your doubts.

204 **Dear Dr. Levine: My problem is that I am a female in a male body. I have known this since I was five years old. I am now nineteen. It is not an easy subject to discuss because most people have no idea how I feel. Sometimes I dress in women's clothes and it feels so right. When I take them off, I become depressed and feel cheated and cry. I want to be a woman so badly.**

I read any material available about transsexuals and sex-change operations, but such articles are usually vague or outdated. I am not a transvestite, as most people would assume. I am not turned on by women's clothing. The simple fact is I want a sex change. Could you please tell me to whom I can write to find out about procedures and costs?

I'm sure that as a result of this answer, I am going to get a barrage of critical letters for encouraging this person to get a sex-change operation and, by so doing, leading other young people down the path of iniquity.

I do not know if you are a transsexual, which is a clear-cut psychological/medical "condition" that must be explored and investigated before a definitive recommendation and plan of action are instituted. Transsexualism refers to a situation in which an individual is physically of one sex but feels like the opposite sex in every thought, fantasy, and dream. The causes are complex, but in a certain percentage of cases, after an exhaustive series of tests and interviews, a series of sex-change operations is undertaken. The process is long

and arduous, but for true transsexuals it "feels right."
Transsexualism, as you rightly point out, is different from
transvestism, and also from homosexuality.

Most major metropolitan cities have specialists who investigate and work with transsexuals. Your doctor can refer
you to the proper center nearby.

**Dear Dr. Levine: I am a nineteen-year-old male and
I think I am classified as a transvestite. I believe most
people think that a transvestite is someone they notice on the street who is wearing clothes of the opposite sex. But I have kept this dressing up to myself
as much as I can and do it strictly in privacy. I enjoy
it and admit that I get sexual pleasure out of it—and
nothing else. Am I sick or crazy? Will I ever be
able to get married? What do people think of transvestites?**

205

You are not sick or crazy. Transvestism is a "condition" in
which an individual gets sexual fulfillment from dressing
up in clothes of the opposite sex. One can talk about tolerance and liberalism and progressive thinking, but the truth
is that today there are certain harmless acts that can only
be performed in private, lest the individuals performing them
face the ridicule and rejection of society.

Certainly, dressing up in clothes of the opposite sex for
autoerotic purposes is one of those acts better left to the
privacy of the home, except in highly unusual circumstances, such as being in a particularly tolerant group sub-
culture where there are other tranvestites. Other than that,
the behavior is considered to be taboo. Transvestite organizations, however, recommend coming out of the closet.

I know transvestites who have married and maintained
successful lives. I know others who found the conflicts too
difficult to cope with (or their wives did) and have had to
seek professional guidance.

SEVEN:

Relationships

> *A young man with a thorough knowledge of physiology, phrenology and physiognomy, and who had properly studied his own organization would never "fall in love" with a girl mentally and temperamentally unsuited to himself.*
>
> S. R. Wells,
> Wedlock of the Right Relationship of the Sexes
> *(1869)*

*P*eople are social beings. Except for hermits and other antisocial individuals, we are all part of a complex network of relationships, some close, some distant; some good, some bad; some memorable, others quite forgettable.

We are all born into families; parents, siblings, uncles, aunts, cousins, grandparents affect us, impinge on us, influence our early lives. As we grow older, we get to choose our own relationships. Family members continue to play a big role throughout our lives, but friends now become increasingly important. Another type of relationship that dominates our entire existence at times (and has inspired volumes of poetry and prose) is bonded by romance and love.

All of these relationships form the fabric of our lives. They challenge us and enrich us. Nothing can spark as many diverse feelings, ranging from obligation to boredom, from compassion to white anger, and from utter misery to ecstatic pleasure. This is made abundantly clear from the letters we get, half of which mention other people as major players in the dramas described.

Good relationships are a vital part of our lives and as such should be nurtured, relished, and embraced. But if a relationship becomes destructive and cannot be improved, it should be severed and cast aside. Our goal is always to seek and create the former.

ROMANTIC RELATIONSHIPS

Dear Dr. Wilcox: Shortly we are having a Sadie Hawkins dance and there's this guy I like and I thought I might ask him to this dance. Only I'm shy! I can talk to guys and not feel strange, but I just can't seem to bring myself to ask them out. I'm afraid of being rejected.

206

Can you please give me some advice so that I don't feel this way, and help me to be prepared to ask this guy.

You are certainly not alone in your feelings. People generally do hope that others will respond to them in a positive way, but the most important thing to remember is that someone else's response to you does not decrease (or increase) your value as a person.

To have a relationship with another human being requires a willingness to take risks. The safest path would obviously be to never ask anyone to do anything because then there would be no risk of getting a negative response. But then there'd also be no chance to live any way but in total isolation. For that reason, we generally choose to accept the risks inherent in human relationships.

It can be hard to take a negative response, especially when one is just learning about male-female relationships and still feels very vulnerable. Try to remember that, regardless of positive or negative responses, you are still a valuable individual, that the risk-taking gets easier as one's self-confidence increases, and that virtually everyone has experienced the feelings you've described. The asking will gradually become easier and less threatening.

Dear Dr. Levine: I'm a nineteen-year-old male. Close friends tell me that I'm "so stable" and "so together." They also laud me for my "positive outlook on life." In the presence of friends I feel comfortable, and I guess I do project an unflappable image.

207

I've only had three dates in my life. The first two were about five years ago. Just recently I went on my third. Z and I were having a good time until she asked me for a slow dance. I started shaking (quite noticeably) during the dance. My nervousness proved

to be very disturbing (for both Z and myself). I felt like an imbecile for the rest of the evening. Z never said anything but I'm sure she must think I'm some type of degenerate.

I'd love to pursue a relationship with Z (she says she'd still like to see me again) but I'm scared (or more aptly, I scare myself). I feel so shallow; I can define what I can offer in a given relationship, yet I'm a klutz when it comes to being intimate.

I'm sure that if you showed Z your moving letter, she would respond with caring and concern.

Your fears get in the way and paralyze you. And just as with any fear or phobia (irrational fear), the ultimate test is to face the feared object. You *must* call Z and organize a date with her. You are not a klutz or a crazy. You are suffering from a lack of self-confidence that can be overcome by a good date with Z. Take a chance. I have confidence in you.

By the way, Z might have found your shaking attractive and disarming. Your vulnerabilities are, paradoxically, part of your strengths. You don't have to be cool or cocky or macho to be attractive to girls.

208 Dear Dr. Levine: I am a fourteen-year-old girl, and I have a problem I am sure is shared by many teenagers. I feel so rejected and unwanted. The guys I like never like me. They just never take a second look. Meanwhile, the guys I don't like drive me crazy bothering me. You're probably thinking I'm the quiet, shy kid in the class. Well, actually I am very popular and happy-go-lucky at school, with girls as well as guys. But no guys that I really like find me interesting. It's like I am putting on a happy front with them, but I'm very, very depressed when I see girls with their boyfriends and I'm alone.

I feel that I really need someone to show that I love them and they love me back. Please give me some advice on how to cope with my loneliness. I have a lot of friends and a large family but nobody really understands me. I'm very desperate. What are guys looking for?

I don't usually see this column as "Advice to the Lovelorn," but you, of course, know that the concerns you are express-

ing are extremely common. They are perhaps seen more frequently in young people who are shy, who are immature,
and who have poor relationships at home and elsewhere.
You, on the other hand, are just the opposite, by your own
admission. You are popular, accepted, and attractive. Friends
and family obviously like you.

It is not that I don't take your pain seriously; I do. There
is something special about an intimate, close, sharing, and
caring relationship. But there is a lot to be said for a close
family, many friends, and outside interests. At the (very
young) age of fourteen, you have plenty of time before you
think of committing yourself to one guy. You should enjoy
what you have rather than becoming preoccupied with what
you don't have.

To your last question my answer is: "Girls like you!" Just
be yourself, and guys will notice you. Meanwhile you can
afford to be patient and get involved in other interests—
friends, music, sports, hobbies, job, volunteer work, fitness
clubs, school, etc. This will make you a much more interesting and ultimately happier individual.

**Dear Dr. Levine: For three years, since I was thir-
teen, I've been dating girls (movies, etc.). On every
date something goes wrong. The first two were disas-
ters. I felt like shooting myself because I really liked
the girls. After that I began to feel awkward. I turned
to friends to do the talking for me. Now when I ask
girls out, the response is that they don't feel like it,
they're not ready, they have strict parents, or something in that line. I know I'm being rejected because
these girls go out with other guys.**

209

**I've lost girlfriends and been rejected so many times
that I feel like giving up. Now my marks at school
are going down. Is there any way for me to overcome
this down-on-myself feeling? Is there something
wrong with me?**

Once again, we have a writer who feels shy and awkward
with the opposite sex and then feels rejected. And this is a
vicious circle. Because the more this happens, the worse
you feel in general, and it begins affecting other parts of
your life.

What you are going through is natural, given your past
experiences. There is nothing wrong with you except for
a lack of self-confidence. And this will be largely overcome

when you prove to yourself that losing girlfriends is not an inevitable, built-in pattern of yours. Most of us have doubts about our own worth and feel depressed when we suffer consecutive losses. These, fortunately, are usually transient feelings.

Concentrate on yourself for a while; pursuing hobbies, sports, and other interests may help eliminate some of your insecurity—because that's what we're talking about. At some point you are going to have to take the bull by the horns and face what you're afraid of. When you feel yourself wavering, force yourself to hang in there.

210

Dear Dr. Levine: A few months ago I met a girl. It wasn't love at first sight, but close. After I was near her for two weeks, my feeling for her grew. Since then I have seen her around and talked to her for a few minutes at a time. It got to the point where I couldn't do anything without thinking of her. I decided to let her know how I felt about her, that I loved her. Since then she won't talk to me.

I can't call her at home because she once said she gets in trouble when friends keep calling her. All I want to do is talk to her. I've written her letters asking her to call me at any time, but to no avail. It's gotten to the point where I don't know what to do. I love this girl but have resigned myself to the fact that she does not love me. I would still, however, like to be her friend if she would give me the chance. I've tried all means I know of asking her, but she just won't reply. Please give me some advice.

It's always easier to give advice than to be enmeshed in unfulfilled romance, or as it used to be described, unrequited love. It's also easier to see things more clearly from outside the situation; you can't see the forest for all the trees.

From what you've said, I have no doubt that this girl (a) *knows* how you feel, (b) does *not* want to be your friend.

These are bitter pills to swallow, but you might as well face the truth and get on with your life. You have given her ample opportunity to reciprocate; she clearly doesn't want to. And you are making yourself miserable trying to break through an impenetrable barrier. The more you try, the more unhappy you will be.

You have to take hold of yourself. I know nothing about you except your total preoccupation with this girl. You've said nothing about your school, friends, interests, or activities, and *that* tells me that you have let this fantasied romance get completely out of hand. Is the rest of your life so miserable that she is the *only* reason to be alive? Frankly, I doubt it. You have to begin to pick up the pieces; get back to your friends and pleasurable pursuits. You'll meet other, even better girls as you go along.

Dear Dr. Wilcox: I am a sixteen-year-old girl who is deeply in love with a twenty-three-year-old guy. I've liked him ever since I met him ten years ago. I guess it started out as puppy love, but it's something more now.

211

The problem is that he was recently married. This has not stopped us from making passes at each other. His wife does not know about us, as far as I know, because she still talks to me. He has told me that he wishes he never got married, and I think the same.

The other problem is that they make a nice couple. I like her and I don't want to hurt either of them, but I want him and I'd do anything to get him.

You are confused because you know that mature love is not characterized by the game-playing and dishonesty that appear to be going on. You realize that mature love means that if someone you love makes a commitment, it is to be respected, and marriage is one of the most serious commitments we undertake. You know that you have no right to interfere with that commitment.

Dear Dr. Levine: I am a twenty-one-year-old female and very much in love with a thirty-nine-year-old man. I know there's quite a difference in our ages, but that isn't the problem. The problem is, he's married, with three children.

212

We live in different cities, and so we see each other only on weekends. Our time together is very special for us and it hurts tremendously when it is cut short for one reason or another.

We have been seeing each other for nine months and lately he has been coming out with expressions such as, "I don't think you would be able to put up with me if we were married." The other night he asked me specifically how I would handle certain situations if we married, and I really couldn't answer him

because I have never even let myself think about the possibility.

He means everything to me, but my head keeps telling me it will only hurt more and more the longer the relationship progresses. My heart, on the other hand, won't let me say those final goodbyes.

I don't have a magic answer for you. Obviously, in this day and age these situations occur, for better or worse. Marriages end, new relationships begin, families are "reconstituted." There is always pain and suffering involved. Some people feel that their major departures from convention are worth the inevitable problems; some don't. People have to decide for themselves.

In your situation, you seem to know all the implications of this relationship, its inherent difficulties, and the chances of its going anywhere. I don't know anything about your love, or the quality of his marital and family life, so I can't comment on the possibilities of his leaving his wife and children. I can say with certainty that there will be major upheaval if he does make that decision.

You are aware of all of this and also of the possibility that you will get hurt, but still you hang in there. It's love—illogical and, paradoxically, painful. You can't "say those final goodbyes"; in that case they will be said only when the relationship reaches a natural breaking point—you tire of each other, he proposes, you demand marriage, or . . . you can fill in other possibilities.

My guess is that it's only a matter of time, but that may be unfair to you both. You might want to have some counseling sessions in this period of emotional confusion.

213 Dear Dr. Levine: I hope you will help me. I am a sixteen-year-old girl. For the last couple of years I have found myself attracted to older men. I am not talking about men in their twenties or thirties. I am talking about men in their forties or sixties. My friends think I am crazy. They think I should like boys my own age, but I find those boys really immature. I just know I will end up married to someone old enough to be my father or grandfather. For years I have wanted to know if these feelings are wrong and why my friends don't feel the way I do about older men.

As an "older man," I could answer glibly that finally the youth of today have come to their senses and recognize true beauty, but that would be entirely facetious. There is an element of validity there, though, which means that there is no written rule that forces us to restrict our feelings of attraction to those of a certain age group. It is highly unusual, however, for girls your age to have these feelings for men so much older.

So, to make a simple, straightforward question very complex, I want to both reassure and caution you. The reassurance is along the lines of what I have just said, and I can cite many examples of young women who have married men much, much older than they are.

The cautionary note is to get you to examine your motives for these relatively uncommon feelings. I would ask you if by selecting men the age of your father, you are in fact searching for a substitute for a relationship that is becoming more distant between you and your dad.

Or is your attraction to these older men "protecting" you from dating younger guys, or from having to make a commitment, because these men are usually unavailable or not interested? These sound like somewhat cynical questions, but I have certainly seen examples of both.

Your feelings are not "wrong" or "bad" or "sick." They are interesting, and certainly worthy of some thought and consideration.

Dear Dr. Levine: I am a twenty-year-old female. My problem is that I am going steady with a seventeen-year-old who is very immature. We have been going out for nine months now and we have a lot of really good times together. He can be very kind and sometimes very romantic. However, other times he acts like a ten-year-old. I don't get upset and tell him to grow up, because I remind myself he is only seventeen and should be allowed to act like that. If I don't like his immaturity I could get someone else. How do you help someone grow up without hurting them? **214**

There are a number of possibilities here. One is that he won't change dramatically, that he will always act somewhat immature. Another is that you will "outgrow" him, that your needs will change and you'll lose interest. Still another is that he will mature and you'll live happily ever after. There are surely others that you can imagine, and it's obviously not something that anyone can predict with very much accuracy.

There is a clear discrepancy in your levels of maturity—in

addition to your age difference, girls tend to mature more rapidly than boys. You can gently give him advice if you feel that his behavior is ridiculous or embarrassing. But you are aware that this may offend him. It may also be unfair, since he may in fact be "acting his age."

If you are so intent on maintaining this commitment, I'm afraid you'll have to wait and see. Frankly, I think that you both owe it to yourselves and to each other to have relationships with others. That, by the way, will help him mature.

215

Dear Dr. Levine: I know everyone gets jealous once in a while, but I have a terrible jealous streak in me that's really ruining my life because I can't control it.

I've been going with my boyfriend for almost three years, and I love him dearly—he's my whole life. But I get jealous if he even looks at another girl. We broke up for three days recently. Because of this I was very depressed. I was taking handfuls of aspirins just to get through the day. I would have killed myself if I had the courage, but luckily I didn't.

The point is, if I can't learn to control my jealousy I will lose my boyfriend for good, and that will be the end of me as well. We are now back together, but I promised not to be so jealous anymore.

Jealousy—one of the truly destructive emotions. It is painful, it is debilitating, it is exhausting. We end up angry at the world and hating ourselves.

Obviously it stems from insecurity and lack of self-confidence. If we felt totally secure and comfortable with ourselves, and satisfied with our talents and accomplishments, we wouldn't need to begrudge others their attributes or successes.

But that's painting with a broad brush. Nowhere does the feeling of jealousy hit home more than in the sphere of romance, because our feelings of attractiveness, desirability, self-worth are at stake. Your jealousy may well arise from romantic insecurity. You may fear that your boyfriend will leave you for another, because you don't really believe that you have what it takes.

Another possibility is that you are blaming him for your own feelings. That is, not only do you possibly feel inadequate in his and your own eyes, but perhaps you are attracted to other males and can't face that possibility.

Well, this is conjecture on my part. You are right that jealousy can be very destructive. If you find that you can't control this emotion—which really underscores your feelings about yourself—you might well lose your lover. You are already contemplating suicide, which tells me that you should speak to a counselor or therapist without delay.

Dear Dr. Levine: I have been going out with this guy for seven months, but I want it to come to an end. There is another guy at school I like very much. But when I try to break it off with my boyfriend, he breaks down and cries. This makes me feel guilty. I would like to see him still, but not steadily. I don't want to hurt him. **216**

I wish that I could make this dilemma simple and painless for you, but I can't. The seemingly impossible situation in which you find yourself is just that—impossible. That is, you can't have it both ways. There are some situations that do not allow solutions that satisfy everyone, and this is one of them. Either your present boyfriend will suffer the pangs of rejection and you the pangs of guilt, or you will find yourself locked into a relationship that you no longer want.

At your stage of life you owe it to yourself and your boyfriend to experience other relationships. This means that you will have to withdraw from the intense nature of your union and endure the inevitable and (I hope) short-lived pain. If you don't do this, you will fairly soon feel resentful and make your young man "pay" for his demands on you.

As tough as it is, you will have to change the kind of relationship you have now. You will both be better off, and who knows what the future will bring? You may forget each other, or you may even reunite. Right now, however, your choice is clear.

Dear Dr. Wilcox: My boyfriend and I are seventeen. We want to get married. My mom says we're crazy, that it's not all that easy. What do you think? We've been going together for three years, and I've never dated anyone else but think I might want to. **217**

Marriage, as you know, is a major commitment. It takes a great deal of work to make a marriage successful. Divorce occurs in one of every three marriages. The statistics are even worse for people married during their teens: more than half of these marriages end in divorce. Learning to live together, to negotiate household task-sharing, and to manage finances are just a few of the many skills that must be developed during early years of marriage; unselfishness, ability to communicate, and knowing oneself are qualities one must also work on.

Emotional maturity takes time to develop. Give yourselves that time. Make sure you also give yourselves a chance to experience *other* relationships. If your relationship with your boyfriend is as strong as you feel it is, it will survive your (and his) dating other people. You are already feeling the rumblings inside that this relationship has become too intense too early. You need freedom for both of you to grow. Talk to your boyfriend about these concerns.

218

Dear Dr. Levine: I am twenty years old and have never had a girlfriend, for a reason that many people might see as strange. You see, I come from a poor family and through a variety of part-time jobs have supported myself through school. But this is just enough for me to get by on. I suppose if I worked more I could have more money, but then my schoolwork would suffer. I would like to take a girl out, but a simple dinner and movie would set me back about twenty-five dollars. I know this is the age of feminism, when a lot of women pay their own way, but I suppose I am old-fashioned, and if a woman paid her way on a date I would feel as though we were just going out as friends. I don't have anyone to borrow money from, nor do I want to be in debt.

I know there must be a lot of guys who are experiencing the same thing but are apprehensive about bringing it up for fear of sounding cheap. Any suggestions for young guys who want to date but are struggling just for public transit fare?

I could attempt to reassure you by saying that there are plenty of guys out there in your situation, that there are many young women who do not care about money, that you could be honest about your circumstances with girls who interest you, and that if a young lady is only interested in your money, then she is not worth your pursuit. And all of this is, in fact, valid.

But the truth is that it is tough to date when there is little or no extra income, and if you cannot date girls who would understand your predicament, you might have to postpone traditional dating. But that does not preclude having relationships with girls in various clubs, recreational activities, or interest groups. Many girls I know are as interested as you are in sharing the costs or doing things that are very inexpensive (like talking over coffee, for example).

You are articulate and intelligent, and I expect that your poverty-stricken state is a temporary one. It sounds like many girls would be pleased to be with you, money or no money. Just be sure that there *is* more to you than money, or its absence. It is the other things that really count in a relationship.

Dear Dr. Levine: I have recently overcome a problem involving a drug addiction; unfortunately I lost a very close and dear girlfriend over my problem. **219**

In the past I have enjoyed the company of friends in high school, but now I am finding it really hard to place my trust in new friends. (This year I moved to a community college.) I feel as if I'm a social outcast.

I have recently met a very special young lady who is everything I have been looking for in a mate. I have told her nothing of my past experiences for fear of turning her away; however, she senses I am holding something inside. I guess I would like to tell her, but I'm not really sure how to go about it. I am afraid if she found out what I was, it would change our whole relationship; but I feel she has the right to know everything.

I often find it interesting that young people who have come through a particularly difficult series of experiences often expect to feel and act as if nothing had happened, even immediately after the crisis. You've conquered a drug problem, you lost a girlfriend, you moved away—all involve major stresses. Go easy on yourself. You'll get back to friends and good relationships.

You now have a close female friend. You have to decide whether it's vital for her to know everything about you. The fact that you had a problem and managed to overcome it is impressive and tells us a lot about your strengths and perseverance. I guess if she leaves you on this account, then perhaps it wasn't meant to be.

Dear Dr. Levine: I am fifteen years old and I am going out with a guy who's in his senior year. My boyfriend **220**

plays bass in a rock band and thinks that if you're a member of a band you have to take drugs. Every night and day he is either stoned on drugs or drunk. He is always complaining he can't remember anything, and his eyesight is getting really bad. I really love this guy, but I don't like going with a stoned drunk.

My advice won't make you happy. There is no doubt in my mind that your boyfriend is being destructive to himself and to his relationship with you and perhaps even to his music career plans. Certainly the rock band scene is full of drugs, but I know of exceptional rockers who are straight and sober.

You or the band can give him an ultimatum: if it's booze and drugs, then it's not you. Sweet and simple. Whichever way he chooses, you are better off.

221 Dear Dr. Levine: My problem is that I'm only interested in a guy so long as I am unsure of him. When I meet a guy I like and decide to go after him, things are fine until I have him. Then, as things begin to get serious, I begin to panic, although I don't know about what, and I break off the relationship. This has happened several times.

You are describing a repetitive pattern of behavior, but you tell me little else about your life and past experiences. So what I have to say is largely conjectural, except insofar as what others with this pattern have taught us.

There are a number of possibilities: Perhaps you have difficulty with commitment, or emotional intimacy frightens you. Maybe you are fearful of guys discovering the "real you." Perhaps you fear eventual rejection. Or it might be much simpler: it may be that you haven't yet found the right guy, and this is how your mind and feelings tell you. Or is it that your parents' or some other important couple's marriage was difficult and you are worried about history repeating itself? Or maybe the chase and capture are all-important to convince you of your inherent attractiveness.

I could go on and on, but you get the picture. There are obviously a number of possible derivations of your pattern. If this continues and you are still stymied by reasons for it, or you can't seem to change, you might want to spend a few sessions with a psychotherapist.

222 Dear Dr. Levine: I am nineteen, and last year I met a wonderful man (twenty-one). We've been together ever since. Our problem is within me. He has talked of marriage and children. I think of a career (a six-year plan), maybe a couple of years travel, then, if he is here, I'd love to. I do feel love between us and could easily see myself with him years from now. The feelings I have for him are so strong it scares me.

Before we started dating, I had dated only two others, having just started to emerge from an ugly-duckling depression. I guess I feel like I haven't gone out with many people and feel tied to him. As my career gets under way, I have a better attitude on life, consequently less time and more friends. For the first time I really think I'm beautiful. Now the type of men I used to hope would merely look my way or speak to me are asking me out. Some I date as friends. I do want to casually date (not sleep with) these men.

What I'm really asking is, can a person who feels deep love for someone want to see other people too? Should they? I've got a good thing here, and I know it. I don't want to lose this dream. If I date others it's okay for him to, even if I lose him. It will be my fault. He hasn't got any hints I've dropped, but he once said he'd leave me forever if I dated someone else.

There are no hard and fast rules in this area. Some people marry after wide heterosexual experiences, while others marry their "childhood sweethearts" with little or no experience. The most common pattern is somewhere in between.

What you have to do is be true to yourself. That is, don't restrict yourself to him because of the way you are "supposed" to act. You are both young, and if you want new experiences, then you are entitled to them.

I am a believer in the ordained nature of relationships. If you date others and miss your boyfriend terribly, then you will have learned something very important to you both. If you do devote yourself solely to him at this point, you will continually wonder if you are missing something better. Better do it now.

FRIENDS

Dear Dr. Levine: I'm a seventeen-year-old girl who knows a terrific guy, who's sixteen. We go to the same

223

school and meet each other daily, just to talk. Whenever we're together, we laugh and have a really good
time. I enjoy his company immensely and am sure
the feeling is mutual. Occasionally he writes me letters and mails them to my house. We've never offi-
cially gone out, but whenever there's a school
function, he almost always asks me to go.

I treasure the wonderful relationship we have, but
I'm confused. How do I know whether he just wants
to be good, platonic friends, or if his intentions are
of a more serious, romantic nature? Since he's the
only male friend I've ever had, I've had no experience that would help me know how this guy cares
for me. Any suggestions?

I agree that your boyfriend is smitten with your charms;
but it may well be that he is even less experienced, more
confused and frightened than you are. You (as the older one)
may have to take the lead and ask him out on a date. Your
relationship sounds terrific and I don't think you'd be en-
dangering it. Good luck.

224 Dear Dr. Levine: In a boy-girl relationship, what determines whether the relationship is strictly that of
platonic friends or of a more intimate and romantic
nature? Since to become more romantically involved with someone, you first have to be good
friends, how can a girl know whether her relationship with a guy will stay that way or turn into something more serious? How do guys decide who they
want as "just friends" and who they prefer as a "girlfriend"?

Every now and then I get a question that poets and philos-
ophers have been wrestling with since time immemorial.
When is a relationship romantic or sexual or platonic? What
determines the nature of the bond?

There are no hard and fast rules. There are morals, which
vary from person to person. There are vibes, or "chemistry."
There is the right time, there is a state of readiness or desire. There are past experiences and future aspirations. There
are fantasies and dreams. There is group pressure and there
are expectations.

All these and more go into the "decision" to cross that
fine line you mention. Usually it is not that mechanical a
process. We choose our friends and lovers on the basis of

mutual attraction. It is only when there is a dilemma (should I or shouldn't I?) that we start weighing all the pros and cons.

I suppose you are asking the question out of more than academic interest. If you trust yourself, then be true to what you feel and want and to your system of values.

Dear Dr. Levine: I am an eighteen-year-old male. My biggest problem is that I can't communicate with men as well as I can with women. At school 90 percent of the people I talk to are female.

225

My two best friends are female, and we have been close since ninth grade. What bothers me most is that I was accused of being a homosexual because I don't try to get every girl into bed. I've had girlfriends and sexual relations but don't have the desire to take the "girls-most-likely-to" to bed. I now have dreams of beating and even wishing death to the guy who said what he said. It scares me to think such things, as I know it's not good for my head.

I don't know you well enough to say that you have absolutely no problems: I can't think of too many people I'd say that to, including myself. But there is nothing in your letter that gives me cause for concern about your emotional state. The fact that you prefer to talk to females may be due entirely to your sensitivity and emotional honesty, both of which seem to be present in interactions with females more than with males. Your violent fantasies and dreams are a far cry from reality and merely express your frustrations and anger. I read nothing in your letter to suggest to me that you are a homosexual. In other words, you sound fine. If you know people who are stupid enough to suggest otherwise, ignore them or drop them.

Dear Dr. Levine: For the past three years my best friend, "Susan," has been telling me stories about a group of friends I have never met or seen evidence of. Susan's stories have ranged from a boyfriend she supposedly dated for two years who lavished her with gifts (none of which I have ever seen), to parties and nights out with her friends.

226

I tried to believe those stories, but now her tales have become unbelievable. She has been saying that she is friends with prominent sports personalities who

are friends of her boyfriend. She says that she attends parties and games with them. All of this she supposedly does behind her mother's back. I'm sure the social life she describes as being her own is one a girl would dream about.

I really value our friendship, but I just cannot believe her stories and feel like a fool for pretending I do. I have tried to confront her with it, and she just insists that it's all true.

What can I do? Could her behavior signify a serious problem? (She is a good student and comes from a good home.) If she does have a problem, how can I help her?

I am going to assume that your suspiciousness is well founded, that Susan is indeed fabricating these stories. I have met a number of young people like her, who get so enmeshed in elaborate webs of fiction that they finally find it impossible to extricate themselves. Sometimes their worlds come crashing down when they are found out and confronted.

This isn't usually bizarre fantasy, nor is it delusion, the product of a psychotic mind; they know they are making up stories. It is, however, an indication of needs not being met, of intense wishes that their lives could somehow be better—more love, more excitement, more fame or fortune. Psychotherapy can often be helpful to these individuals.

Susan is fortunate that she has a friend as sensitive and as loyal as you are. Talking to her about your concerns has obviously not worked. Nor do you seem willing to "lay it on the line," which might jeopardize your friendship. If Susan is so entrenched that she will deny any fabrication, then you may just have to grin and bear it. Depending on your relationship with Susan's parents, you might want to discuss your concerns with them. If you can do this, they might be able to corroborate or refute your suspicions. Unfortunately, you can't be sure that Susan will accept any of your concerns in a positive light.

227 Dear Dr. Levine: My problem is with a really close friend of mine. Her mother died five months ago. Her parents were separated, and she took her mother's death very well.

The problem is, she told her boyfriend she wanted to be alone for a while. So he started hanging around

me. But we were already friends, and when she
wanted him back, he was ready. Only she then told
him not to talk to me. She thought we were more
than friends. She called him a liar, and they split up
as a result. They have now worked things out again,
and she said right off that he is not to phone me and
I'm not to phone him. He told me that last night.
She never tells me any of this.

She and I have been friends for six or seven years
now. We can really talk to each other, but now I feel
that our friendship is going down the drain because
of this guy. I'm afraid to confront her with this because I don't know what she'll do. I care for her too
much to ruin our (so-called) friendship. What do I
do? My mother says, just be there. How long will she
be this way?

People vary considerably in their reactions to the deaths of
their loved ones. You say that your girlfriend took her mother's death very well—I'm not so sure. It sounds like some of
her suspiciousness and the deterioration in your relationship can be at least in part attributed to her feelings about
her major loss.

I agree with your mother, but I would take it one step
further. I would talk to her as a close friend. Speak to her
warmly and supportively, telling her your feelings and setting the record straight. It isn't necessary to "confront" her;
rather, all this can be done in a loving and open manner.

Dear Dr. Levine: I am a sixteen-year-old girl. This
other girl and I have been good friends until now.
Something happened. She told me that she loved me.
I told her she was confused, but she would not accept that. She is certain she is gay.

228

A day or so later she told me to be understanding.
I was, but every time she brought it up I kept telling
her she was just confused. She said that I would not
accept her being gay. She's right. I still don't believe
she is, because people don't change overnight. She
was in love with this guy. I think he hurt her, and
now she thinks she can get comfort from the same
sex.

Anyway, our friendship is slowly deteriorating. We
no longer talk to each other; we seem to be avoiding

each other. I don't want to lose her as a friend. Maybe
I should terminate our friendship even though I don't
want to, but we aren't getting anywhere. I don't know
what to do.

I obviously can't tell you if your friend is gay. Some sixteen-
year-old girls (and boys) do know that they have strong homosexual urges; but some don't. The fact that your friend
had a close heterosexual relationship is not strong evidence
of either orientation. I would have to know a lot more about
her—her dreams, fantasies, feelings, erotic thoughts, relationships—before I would give any opinion.

But it is not doing your friendship—or either of you—any
good to continue to convey your concern or disapproval to
her. If she is valuable to you as a friend, why not be there if
she needs you but not come across as continually critical?
What if she *is* gay—or isn't? Frankly, if you can't manage to
be more tolerant of her seemingly new thoughts and behavior, your relationship will not last much longer anyway.

See 200–203.

229 Dear Dr. Levine: My friend and I have a big problem,
and we are not sure how to handle it. Two of our
friends (both girls) are becoming very close. At
sleepovers they practically fight people in order to
sleep beside each other. It started off with them just
holding hands, and now no one is sure how far it has
gone.

We are both really worried about them. We don't
want to see either of them get hurt. They are only
sixteen and seventeen. Is this a normal phase for girls
to go through at this age? They don't know that people have noticed their behavior. Do we tell them we
know? Do we tell them we care? Or should we just
let it pass as an adolescent phase?

I suggest that you maintain your friendship with them and
do not tell them about your breathless observations. They
may be having some sexual explorative play—that is not unusual. They may be extremely close friends—also not unusual. You both are obviously concerned, although you don't
state this explicitly, that this will develop into a full-blown
homosexual relationship. I can't judge from this vantage
point, but I suggest that neither can you. Furthermore, your
commenting on it, or even succeeding in ending that behavior, will not prevent homosexuality from developing.

I appreciate your obvious concern, but you would be better off enjoying your friendship with these girls.
See 200–203.

**Dear Dr. Levine: I can't take it any longer. I only have
one enemy at school and she is making my life miserable. Now she is turning other people against me.
One of my best friends hates me because of her. What
am I to do? When she bugs me, I don't show any
anger or frustration and I pretend that it doesn't
bother me, but it does. I hate it and I hate her.**

230

**I can't go to my school counselor because people
would find out and then I'd be doomed. I need your
help. I can't turn to anyone else. If I don't get some
help, I might do something drastic, and I don't want
to die.**

Your torment is obvious. Yours is not the first experience
I've heard about from young people who blame their problems on one particular antagonist at school or camp. There
is no doubt this can and does occur, but it is also common
that at least some of the time the power of the hated antagonist is grossly exaggerated. I'll accept your description of
the situation, but bear in mind that it may be more complex than it seems.

This girl who is so destructive and cruel obviously dislikes you for some reason. Perhaps she is jealous of your
looks or brains or popularity. But surely your real friends
see through her unpleasant and nasty words, because the
nastiness doesn't stop there. It tends to take over the whole
person and is quite transparent.

Your task is to get on with your life. There *must* be some
girls and guys there who don't fall for her miserable out-
pourings. You must have some interests and activities that
don't involve her. What about your relationships within your
family? Are there any redeeming features in your life? And
if not, is this situation *all* the responsibility of this girl?

You don't want to speak to a counselor at school for fear
of being found out. My reassuring you won't help, but I've
certainly seen many examples of total confidentiality, even
in high school. You might want to speak to a staff member
at a teen clinic or drop-in center. Or why not confide in your
parents? If all else fails, you might consider changing schools,
but this is not only a last resort, it is an admission of de-
feat, and giving a lot of power to someone who deserves none.
I am sure that you can make it where you are.

231 Dear Dr. Levine: I am a fifteen-year-old girl. My marks are average, and I have lots of friends. I get along well with my family and am allowed to do a lot of things.

The problem is that lately I have been getting into a lot of arguments with my friends. I haven't talked to two of them for two months. Just a few days ago I had two arguments. Pretty soon I won't have any friends left. What should I do? I've tried to talk it out with them, but that doesn't help.

I don't know enough about you to suggest a solution to your problem. We all at times can get irritable and snap at friends or family members. Often the specific argument has nothing to do with what is really going on.

That is, if we're depressed, or concerned about something that we are having difficulty dealing with, we sometimes pick on "scapegoats." Usually, it takes a while to figure out what is really bugging us.

Maybe your parents or friends could help you. Perhaps they've noticed changes in your behavior or can point out aspects of your personality of which you are unaware. And you should look at whether you've been unhappy recently and try to see what that's all about.

FAMILY

232 Dear Dr. Levine: I am a seventeen-year-old female with a fifteen-year-old brother. My problem is that I let him walk all over me. I am almost scared to confront him for fear of getting him mad at me. If I do get him mad at me, I get very upset, sometimes almost to the point of crying. I have a tendency to put myself down, making myself feel inferior to others, especially to him.

It used to be that he followed me around and idolized me. But somehow, when he became athletic, very talented, popular, and good-looking, I began to think he was better than me, and he probably sensed it.

He has a lot of problems communicating and has a very quick temper. That's probably because he is immature.

I don't know what to do anymore. He takes my things without asking me and then gets mad when I

tell him to stop. I am so tired of him taking advantage of me, yet I don't know how to stop it. When we go through a period of peace, it's great: we get along really well and I adore him so much.

Do yourself a favor: don't let him walk all over you.

If your relationship is so weak that confronting him about his abusive behavior will ruin the good times, then it isn't worth perpetuating. He *is* immature, and you are playing into his childish selfishness by tolerating his temper tantrums.

You are also playing into your own insecurity by actually encouraging him to continue. I would rather you risk his anger and his withdrawal from your relationship than continue to coddle his infantile ways. He will grow out of it, but you can help make this happen considerably sooner if you nip it in the bud—now.

Regardless of your brother, it's obvious you need to work on yourself, with a counselor at a drop-in center or adolescent clinic.

Finally, where are your parents in all of this; why aren't they helping you with this dilemma? I hope that you are able to confide in them and use their involvement.

Dear Dr. Levine: I'm an eighteen-year-old female and I have a younger brother who is fifteen. I am in a most awkward situation. My brother's behavior has drastically changed and is now so disgusting I can't stand it.

233

At home he has the gall to say the most disgusting and sexual things to me. I have confronted him with this many times and yet he makes me look like the idiot in front of my parents.

Having been a teaser myself (as a boy of fifteen), I think I can understand how he can say things that seem innocuous to others and yet are terribly meaningful—and disgusting!—to you. Or at least I can to some extent. The object of my teasing was much younger. You, on the other hand, are eighteen years of age.

Surely you can let the barbs and taunts of your kid brother (and I emphasize the word *kid*) just end in thin air. Why give him the time of day? He does it partly because it is titillating for him to torment and tease an older sister who conjures up sexual (and threatening) images in his fantasies. At some level he's both attracted to you and scared of you.

You have to give him the message that you are above his immature rantings. Ignore him, be aloof, pursue your own interests. Don't get sucked into his trap; don't descend to his level. Easier said than done? Sure. But I feel certain that you can do it.

234 **Dear Dr. Levine: I'm a fourteen-year-old female, and I have lost a lot of weight, so I'm finally getting my social life in order, except for one thing: my brother.**

My parents are divorced, and my brother is three years older than me and very protective—overprotective. He sits up and waits for me when I go out, and if I'm late he questions me. He is really very irritable. He is rude to my friends he doesn't like.

I'm in love with a friend of his who lives across the street. I might have had a chance with this guy, but my brother told him to leave me alone. He said this guy just uses girls and then gets rid of them. He is two years older than me and very polite. I'm kind of shy, so I can't go up and talk to this guy, and I do see him with this girl a lot. But my brother said he's just using her for sex, so I'm not worried about her. If he was just going to use me for the same thing, it should be my decision, not my big brother's.

I've tried telling my brother to butt out. He said he would but then goes and butts in again and tells me to forget about this guy. But I can't. I feel I'm really in love. I'm at my wits' end.

I assume that you and your brother are living with one of your parents. It's interesting to me that you haven't mentioned this in your letter. Is this a reflection of the nature of your relationship with him or her? Assuming that you can broach the subject with your parent(s), I urge you to do so. Obviously, you can't get your brother off your back on your own. He is most likely acting out of love, trying to protect you, but as a result you are feeling oppressed. I hope that either or both of your parents can help you out with this one; that's part of their function.

235 **Dear Dr. Levine: I am a sixteen-year-old boy who has a thirteen-year-old brother who is handicapped. I have adapted well to his handicap, but my friends at school tell jokes about him, and sometimes I find myself laughing at some of these jokes.**

One day I invited some friends over to my house

to watch some movies. One of them had a child in a wheelchair in it. All of a sudden my friends started telling "cripple" jokes about my little brother, and once again I found myself laughing, although deep inside I knew it was wrong. Just then my little brother came into the room on his crutches and realized we were laughing at him.

For two days my brother didn't talk to me. On the third day I found him on his bed out cold and my mom's bottle of sleeping pills empty on the floor. We rushed him to the hospital, where they pumped his stomach and he regained consciousness. I fear he will try to kill himself again. What should I do? And is it my fault? Please help me.

What a sad story. Your pain and guilt come through loud and clear. It would be easy for me to reassure you, but the fact is that what your friends did *was* cruel and must have hurt your brother grievously. That you joined in makes you feel terrible and remorseful, full of shame and humiliation. You are blaming yourself for your brother's reaction.

There is no excuse for cruel or sick jokes, or for any stories that make fun of people who are different from oneself racially, religiously, ethnically, intellectually, or physically. Yet you know as well as I that the world is full of these jokes, and the sad truth is that we *all* laugh sometimes.

We laugh to hide our discomfort, embarrassment, or anxiety. We laugh because, sadly, we all harbor some prejudices or stereotypes in our minds. We laugh because some of the jokes are genuinely funny.

But we don't laugh directly at your brother. He, personally, is not the butt of the perverse humor. Most of us have been butts of jokes. Sometimes they help us to laugh at ourselves.

You obviously have to apologize to your brother. (Your friends should too.) A suicide attempt is an extremely serious and ominous act. It may have been precipitated by what he heard when he entered the room, but there was suffering that he endured well before that. Your brother is unhappy and needs professional help. Show him your letter and this answer. Your support and love for him will be very helpful; he should know that he is lucky to have you as a brother.

Dear Dr. Levine: I feel like killing myself right now. I don't feel that I am of any importance in life. Why **236**

is it that the selfish people get the most respect? This occurs at home. I have two older sisters. One is very selfish. Everyone in the family recognizes this. I am the youngest and try to get along with both my sisters. I don't get respect from them. Sometimes I think it's because I am not selfish.

If I am away from home a lot (I have a job, along with school), my family gets on my back. So today I am doing the housework and my sister (who has done hardly anything) will not help, but no one will listen to my complaints. It's useless to argue, they say.

This seems unfair to me. I am very frustrated. I was taught that if you are a good Christian, people will love and respect you. I feel now that it must be the mean and selfish people who get the best out of life and never have to work. I am so disillusioned. My family says I am the difficult one. Why? What have I done? Look at my other sisters! What should I do?

You portray yourself as Cinderella, hard-working and persecuted—at school, at work, at home—always doing your duty and unappreciated.

I obviously can't discover from here who is right and who is wrong; what it is you do that makes them call you difficult; why your sisters are treated better than you—and on and on.

It sounds as if your family could use some counseling. Aside from rights and wrongs (there are usually good arguments on both sides), there is common decency and mutual respect that must be adhered to. If all your crying does is bring derision and laughter, things have reached a sorry state indeed. A family therapist could help you.

237 Dear Dr. Levine: I'm sixteen and really like a guy who is twenty-two. My feelings are reciprocated by him. One night when my father (he's my only parent and I'm an only child) was out, he came over. We went for a walk and talked for hours. When we got back, my father was there. The guy left. When my father found out how old the guy is, he didn't want me to get involved. We did anyway, and now I'm not allowed to see him or talk to him. We write to each other, and he phones me anyway. We both hate

sneaking around and wonder if there is anything that can be done. His parents say to play it cool, so to speak, but we need advice. Does age really matter?
This is a tough problem because it involves parental concerns, rights, and responsibilities, as well as yours. Your father obviously cares about you and is exercising his view of what his duty as a parent is. He wants to protect you.

You ask if age is really that crucial, if maturity and intellect can overcome a youthful age. The answer is a guarded yes; but that presumes you are that intelligent, mature individual who should make your father forget you are only sixteen years of age. I obviously can't judge that. To be frank, I have a strong feeling your dad is acting no different from the way most parents would in a similar situation.

But you are at an impasse now. It sounds like some compromises on both your parts are in order. It might be a good idea for both of you to sit down for a couple of sessions with a family worker at your local Family Service agency. Show your father your letter and this answer. It might help stimulate a dialogue between you.

I actually feel that both of you are right—and wrong. Your father can't cut you off completely from your boyfriend; this will only encourage sneaking around and resentment. But you shouldn't be making a commitment at your age to a much older guy. His parents are right. Play it cool.

Dear Dr. Levine: I'm nineteen and my girlfriend is sixteen. We've been going out for four years, and for all those years my parents and I have been arguing. My religion is different from hers, but that hasn't stopped me from seeing her. My parents laid down the law and said either I break up with her or I'll be thrown out of the house and disowned.

Her parents know me and think that our going out is fine, but my parents won't listen. They're not religious or anything, but they won't let me see who I want, even if I do love her. How can I still see her and have my parents accept it?
I frankly don't know what you should do. Parents often feel impassioned about their sons and daughters marrying out of their faith, and it will always be so. Sometimes they are right, sometimes they are wrong; sometimes their opposition helps, sometimes it hurts.

My concern is of a different kind. If you and your girl-

238

friend have been going steady for four years, this means that you were fifteen and she was twelve(!) years of age when this relationship began. Shouldn't you both experience and experiment a bit more before you even talk of permanent commitment? The conflict with your parents may be inevitable (it also may not be), but at least you will have more maturity and background to base your position on.

239 **Dear Dr. Levine: I am a twenty-year-old female, living with my parents. I wish to move out but am having many difficulties.**

Since getting my high school diploma three years ago I have been unemployed. I have tried my hardest to find work, only to find rejection (even after taking a basic job-readiness course). Without an income, paying my own rent is obviously out of the question.

It is imperative that I get away from my parents, especially my mother. Our ideas are so different that we continually clash. I have tried to change for them, but just as they have their beliefs, I have mine. I can't lash out at the object of my anger, so I end up hurting myself physically. The guilt and low self-esteem are overwhelming.

Last year I had several sessions with a psychiatrist (doctor's orders), and we both agree that I must get away from my possessive parents. By the way, my mother refused to let me go on with the sessions after hearing the verdict.

Yours is an unhappy situation and more complex than meets the eye. You are an unemployed twenty-year-old, which is unfortunately not an uncommon situation. That problem in itself is depressing and would beat lesser people than yourself. But you have another issue that is plaguing you—your unpleasant relationship with your mother and father. It is unfortunate that your mother is so adamant about your staying home, since a separation might go a long way toward improving the relationship.

There is no reason why you can't get some further counseling at a Family Service agency, at a hospital clinic, or with a psychiatrist or psychotherapist if your health insurance covers such treatment. Any or all of these would be helpful and wouldn't cost anything. You might also consider taking a skills training course or going back to school on student loans.

Dear Dr. Wilcox: I'm a sixteen-year-old girl, and my parents won't let me get my hair cut anymore. They want me to grow my hair. My bangs are really long. They get in my eyes. I'm starting to get split ends. I've been having my hair cut for many years now. I am now a junior. This is the time that I really have to look great. I will be graduating next year. Help! If I don't get a haircut, I'm going to do something that will hurt them. I feel ashamed going to school with my hair.

240

I can't help but feel there is some vital information missing from your letter because, at least on the surface, it doesn't make sense that you and your parents would be locked in a power struggle over a haircut.

When did this battle start, and what was going on at the time? Can you see anything that could have triggered their response? If the issue really is your hair, did you come home at some point with a cut they felt was too extreme in either color or style? Was the cost of the cuts getting to be an area of conflict? Do they associate your chosen style with behavior they find unacceptable? If you can find out why they are upset, maybe you and your parents can calmly discuss the issue and then come up with a mutually satisfactory plan to resolve it.

Or could the fight over your hair just be a symptom of other problems? As you try to assert yourself (which all people have to do as part of growing up), are you and your parents finding it hard to decide just how much independence you should have at this stage? Do they feel that they have some control over you if they can control your hair style? Are you paying for the problems created when your parents felt an older brother or sister was "too independent" or "got in with the wrong crowd"?

Obviously, I can only guess what lies behind this battle. What you need to do is find out what it's all about. You mentioned that if you don't get a haircut soon, you'll "do something to hurt them"; this certainly is one way to let them know how upset you are, but it is not productive and will only escalate the conflict. It also makes me wonder even more if a central problem in your family is that none of you communicate clearly or directly but instead fight about "things" (like haircuts) that keep all of you from letting the others know what your deeper concerns, fears, wants, and needs are.

If a poor communication pattern is deeply entrenched, counseling can sometimes help a family learn new and more effective ways of dealing with one another. Your family doctor or school guidance counselor could help you find an appropriate counselor.

241 **Dear Dr. Levine: I am a fourteen-year-old girl with a dream—to become a musician with my own band. I play the bass guitar and I write very good songs. At the same time I want to be a fashion designer. I am very creative when it comes to making music, writing songs, and creating new styles. My father is a respectable, understanding, and considerate man, but he doesn't think a musician is a very respectable person. I told him it's what I want to do with my life, but all he said is, "We'll discuss it when you've completed your education!" What should I do?**

This is one of the most difficult questions to answer because it involves second-guessing parents, which I am reluctant to do for a couple of reasons. One is that I don't know enough about you and your natural talents, your school performance, your friends, your family. Another is that I too am the father of young people who might prefer directions in life diametrically opposed to the ones I want for them.

Your father obviously wants what is best for you and fears that the choice of a career in popular music is risky and possibly even dangerous. He also knows that you are only (forgive me) fourteen and probably feels that you might change your mind between now and adulthood.

I guess I'm asking you to do two things. First, try to see your parents' side of this conflict (I would also urge them to try to see yours). Second, keep all options open. By all means keep up your music—study, practice, perform—but don't cut back on school, relationships, and other interests. Sure, it'll be tough and you'll be busy, but it will be worth it. You will be happy reaching your goal, whatever it turns out to be.

242 **Dear Dr. Levine: My mother, my brother, and I have a problem. Our father works from nine till nine and doesn't have much time to see us. The only time we get to see him is Friday and Saturday after six. Our mother spends all day preparing a beautiful meal for him so we can have supper together.**

He usually calls around four o'clock to say he will
be home for dinner at six-thirty and says what he
would like for dinner that night. He always ends up
at the local diner and doesn't show up till ten or
eleven. Meanwhile we are waiting for him.

Your letter makes me feel sorry for you. Your mother, your
brother, and you must feel a void in your father's absence,
and for him to call dutifully on those Friday and Saturday
nights, to build up your hopes and expectations only to dash
them again and again—well, that's cruel. Should you go
ahead and eat without him? If this is so regular an occurrence, then surely there is little point in waiting, is there?

Is there another side to the story? I take it that your father is a very hard-working man (I tally well over fifty-five
hours a week). Maybe that "diner" you mention (or is it a
pub?) gives your father a chance to relax with his friends
before coming home. I don't want to take him off the hook
for breaking promises, but what seems like a very straightforward type of situation is really quite complicated.

I don't know whether you've sat down as a family to discuss your mutual needs and feelings, but it sounds like such
a discussion is long overdue.

**Dear Dr. Levine: My parents love me a lot, almost
too much. They control my life as if I were only ten
(I'm sixteen), and I think I'll always be that age if I
don't do something soon. I have tried over and over
again to talk to them, to make them try to understand me, but it's no use. They won't listen.**

243

**I have been told that I'm very attractive, but there
is no use for me to start to like a guy and to get him
to like me, because I know I'll never be able to go
out with him. My parents first said I'd be able to go
out with a guy when I was sixteen. Now that I am,
they say eighteen—and who knows from there? I'm
not allowed out at night or anywhere alone with a
guy (even if he's just a friend). I am not even allowed
to stay after school and watch a volleyball game.**

**Why must my teenage years be like this? Aren't
these years supposed to be joyous and ones to remember?**

Ordinarily I defer to parents' wishes in this kind of circum-
stance. That is, parents have the right or privilege, ob-

viously, of calling the shots, of setting the ground rules for their kids' behavior. And there is a wide range of rules, as you well know.

But your situation does seem considerably more harsh than most I have encountered. Are your parents so unduly strict for religious or moral reasons? What are they afraid of? I ask that because it seems that their fear for your safety (purity, health, sexuality) is determining their relatively rigid approach. Unless, of course, you've given them cause for worry—but I tend to doubt that.

You say that you've tried to speak to them and this has fallen on deaf ears. You could show them my response to your letter. If you do, the message I want them to get is this: They obviously do have the power to enforce regulations at home, but their restrictions appear unreasonably tough. They might try relaxing their rules for a couple of months as an experiment and see what happens. They might see a much happier daughter at home, who will continue to do well elsewhere and not get into trouble (as they may fear).

Perhaps a close aunt or uncle can intercede, or your minister or principal—someone your parents and you trust and respect.

244 **Dear Dr. Levine: My four sisters and I are PKs (preacher's kids), and we have a real problem. Our father is excessively strict, and whenever we are punished it seems to become common knowledge. Father is the disciplinarian for the whole congregation, and any teenager who has caused a problem at home, at school, or in the community is sent to our house.**

Father decides on how severe—hand-spanking, paddle, cane, or belt. One employer in town sent one of his married employees for stealing from the cash drawer.

This is a problem, but I have a much deeper concern. I am eighteen. Seven months ago, Dad was quite sick for about eight weeks. I not only replaced him in the pulpit but also, under his direction, handled discipline. I really enjoyed it, and even thought about what would happen if he didn't get well. I even spanked my older sister. In all, I caned seven, spanked five, and used the belt on two. I still sin when I think of it. The other evening I answered the door

to a very attractive young woman and found myself wishing Dad was sick. Right now I am in jitters just thinking about it.

An unusual letter, describing a rather bizarre situation. Frankly, I am not at all surprised that you got some enjoyment from inflicting punishment, as you certainly have had years of training at the hands (and instruments) of your father. Taking his place enabled you to identify with your father (if you can't lick 'em, join 'em) and get some misdirected retribution in at the same time. I expect that you have some very mixed feelings about your dad.

There is also the curious relationship between sexuality and violence, which is unfortunately more common than many of us would like to believe. You are eighteen, and sexual issues loom large in your life.

Finally, all the punishment that you have received over the years may have convinced you that you are a "bad" person, so that doing wrong deeds may fit in with this view of yourself. Do you, in fact, see yourself as a sinner?

I am incredulous that no one in your father's congregation has reported him to the Children's Aid Society, the police, or other agencies that have anything to do with child abuse or inflicting pain on kids in *other* people's families. Obviously, the mothers and fathers in his church agree with the ethic of severe corporal punishment and with the idea of discipline being meted out by an external authority figure.

You may well decide at some point in your life to seek some form of counseling in order to enable you to understand your feelings about yourself, sexuality, morality, and your father.

Dear Dr. Levine: I'm a fourteen-year-old girl, and I can't stand my family anymore. It's not just that we don't get along. I feel that all of us will end up in an insane asylum before I'm twenty-five, when my parents will let me move out.

245

My two older brothers are very mean to me and sometimes hurt me. They say I'm fat and don't want to be associated with me. They put me on an exercise program and beat me up if I don't stick to it. Sometimes I feel like I hate my parents, but I really don't want to hurt them.

I want to know if it's possible for me to go to a

foster home. I come from a fairly well-off family. What will people think? How do I go about doing this? Is it wrong?

A very sad letter. Your family sounds like it is going through a rough time, and perhaps the brunt of the pressure is being applied to you. But I would doubt, with the hints of brutality, anger, and tension, that *anyone* is enjoying much of a happy life at home.

I assume that you've spoken to your parents about your unhappiness. If not, you must do so immediately. Even if they blame you, the fact that you need help may well get them to realize that they have problems too, and to seek proper help. If you can't do so, a close aunt or uncle or other adult whom your parents like and respect might be a good person to approach in order to "bare your soul."

If this doesn't work, you might consider speaking to your school guidance counselor or social worker, or you can go to a teen clinic at a hospital in your city.

246   **Dear Dr. Levine: I am a fifteen-year-old girl. When I was three years old my father walked out on us and hasn't been heard from since, except for some legal papers. I have his address and his phone number, and I was wondering if it would be really weird if I called him. I was thinking about calling him from a pay phone at school so my mother wouldn't say anything to me about it. I have talked with friends and they think it is perfectly normal for me to be curious.**

Your friends are quite correct: it is perfectly natural that someone abandoned at an early age should want to find out more about his or her past. I have heard all kinds of questions: Who is he (she, they)? Why did he leave? Was I the cause? What is he like? What is my background—race, creed, ethnic group, religion? Who am I really?

There are all kinds of fantasies that sometimes predate or accompany these questions, like vast riches or royalty or adventure. There is often a hope that life will change dramatically. But the bottom line is a search for identity, a sense of completeness.

I would urge you not to do anything precipitous. There might be occasional disappointment and pain or even rejection involved. You should discuss it with your mother and others first and give it a lot of thought. If your father walked out on you so many years ago and has made no effort to seek you out or to rekindle a father-daughter relationship, well, that speaks volumes about him, doesn't it?

Dear Dr. Levine: I am a seventeen-year-old girl and have a very serious problem. My father and I have a "not so good" relationship. I would like to be close to my father, but it seems everything I do makes our relationship slip further and further away. We talk about things all the time, and you'd think that would bring us closer, but it's the exact opposite.

247

My problem is, I can't talk to him about personal things. I try to prove to myself that I'm responsible enough to handle them, but in the end I prove myself wrong. I love my dad so much, and I do want to be close to him, but I don't know how. I've tried everything and now I'm desperate.

You sound as though you have a very good relationship with your father. You talk about all kinds of things together, and it's obvious that you care a great deal about each other. The problem you describe as "serious" is that for some reason you can't talk about very personal things with him.

I'm not sure what you mean by being "responsible enough to handle them." I assume you're referring to some sensitive issues, like sexuality. Some men do have difficulty in discussing these feeling-related issues with women in general, but particularly with their daughters. You will have to temper your desire for closeness with some idea of what is appropriate between you. It should certainly not be enough to make you desperate, unless you expect too much from him.

Dear Dr. Levine: I'm fourteen and have a big problem. My father is always telling me if I don't do better in school he'll hit me. I know he won't, but it still scares me. It's not as if I'm failing in school. And now he is forbidding me to watch TV, go to the movies with my friends, and talk on the phone. He's always saying he never had an opportunity at school.

248

You may think this is wrong, but I really hate him. Sometimes I wish he were dead. One time he started hitting me with a belt, and my mother had to stop him.

There are no counselors around where I am living to talk to. I have threatened to run away, but where

would I run? So all I can do now is hope he will change, which I know he won't. What can I do?

It sounds like your father wants to make sure that you get the education that he never got. His motives may be honorable, and he may even believe that he is acting out of genuine caring and concern for you, but he is losing the love and affection of his daughter.

His temper and threats appear to be making your life unbearable at home. He must be a very frustrated man, both with himself and with you. He probably thinks that you can do considerably better in school, or even that you are goofing off. (Are you?) Your mother appears to be caught in the middle, but clearly he is dominant when he goes on one of his tirades.

You say that there are no counselors in your town. Since I have the advantage of knowing where you live, I can tell you that in fact there are some. The Children's Aid Society and the Family Service agency have counselors who can be of service to your family. This *is* a family problem, not just yours and your father's. Your school has teachers and a guidance counselor in whom you could confide. Or you could speak to the social worker who is assigned to your school or its district. Your family doctor might also be of assistance—physicians often do short-term counseling of individuals and families.

With the help of your mother, you might consider showing your father both of our letters. It might get him to rethink his rather heavy-handed and even destructive approach. There is no excuse for his violence, and intervention is long overdue. Just remember that whatever approach is utilized, you will have to make some compromises as well.

249

Dear Dr. Levine: I am a fourteen-year-old boy with two sisters and one brother younger than me. I get along pretty well with them and my parents, but one thing bothers me. I have a strong physical attraction to my mom.

Is there anything wrong with me? Mom and Dad get along pretty well—no wonder, with Mom going topless a lot. I know she is doing this for Dad, because she never cooks supper with just her apron on when Dad is away on business trips. I don't want to

**say anything to my parents about this because I would
be interfering with their relationship.**

It is not unusual for a young adolescent to experience feelings of attraction for the opposite-sex parent. This is actually a reawakening of overwhelming feelings of love for that
person experienced a few years earlier.

The desires you describe have to do with idealization of
your mother, competition with your father for your mother's affection, a desire to "be like" your dad, and a "safe"
way to deal with your own sexual awareness and awakening.

Be that as it may, your mother's sense of propriety leaves
something to be desired. I can see her wanting to be as sen-
suous and sexual as possible with her husband, but to wear
only an apron while cooking with her kids around sounds
a mite silly, and unnecessarily provocative.

You are still young enough to find speaking to your mother
about this difficult, especially in light of your feelings for
her. Some young people in this situation might consider
saying something like, "Mom, I'd feel better if you'd cover
up," or "I'm really not comfortable with you walking around
undressed." If you can't do this, perhaps you could show
her your letter (and this response) as a way of opening up
the subject.

**Dear Dr. Levine: I'm a fourteen-year-old girl, and I've
been finding it harder to cope with my problems with
each passing day.**

250

**My parents have been separated for three months
now. At the beginning I found it hard to accept the
situation, but now I have taken the time to think
everything through and sort out my feelings, and I
feel and act a lot better.**

**I am now living with my mother and my seven-
teen-year-old brother. My mother is my problem. It
has been very hard on her because she never wanted
my father to leave in the first place. He is living with
my best friend's mother, which upset my mom even
more. I am still seeing my father every few weeks or
so. My mom doesn't mind me spending time with him,
but because of her own personal feelings toward him
she has been very short-tempered lately.**

She is seeing a counselor who deals with people

**who have trouble coping with being divorced or sep-
arated. She is getting better but is constantly jump-
ing on me for every little thing I do. She keeps telling
me to try to understand what she is going through.
She is making my life miserable.**

**I can always come to her if I am feeling down about
them splitting, but I'm just sick of the whole mess!
My brother isn't a help, either. The only ones who
help are my two close friends.**

**I just need to get away from everything and every-
body for a while but I have no place to go! Maybe I
should leave for good.**

Your letter is sad and poignant, and should be read by all
those families who are contemplating separation or divorce,
or who have gone through it, and by professionals working
in the field.

It speaks volumes about the inevitable suffering people go
through, and how one person's suffering can inadvertently,
but directly, affect another adversely. It is tough enough to
split up a union, but when there are kids involved there are
often tragic overtones. Sometimes there is a battle over cus-
tody, or money, or anything, and the kids are in the middle,
trying to maintain a balance and, as you say, "sort out (their)
feelings."

If you truly are having so much difficulty, you should talk
to both your parents about your feelings. Remember that it
has been only three months since the separation; these
wounds take *a lot* longer to heal. Discussing your feelings
with friends, aunts or uncles, etc., is often a help. If you
truly can't cope, then you should speak to a counselor at an
adolescent clinic or family agency. As time goes on, your
mother will get her bearings again, and you will learn to
cope with the loss of the family unit—with the ongoing love
of both your parents.

251 **Dear Dr. Levine: I am sixteen, and I am under a lot
of pressure. First, school is always on my mind because I'm failing two subjects. Second, I'm extremely tense and I am quite often depressed because
of problems at home. My parents have been separated for eleven years, and both are remarried.**

**My mother is wonderful, but my stepfather is a
creep. He and my mother were having marital problems, and he constantly blamed me. My real father,**

whom I see regularly, travels a lot, so my stepfather usually acts up while my father is away on business. My mother tries but usually ends up agreeing with my stepfather because she is trying "to keep the peace." My father has said he will take me out of here, but I wish to remain with my mother. But I can't take any more! I absolutely refuse to! Who are these people to make my life miserable?

Your unhappiness leaps out of your letter. You sound like you somehow "fell between the cracks" when your parents broke up. Your schoolwork is suffering, and your parents seem to have their own preoccupations. Unfortunately, this is a situation I see all too often.

First, I'd show them your letter and mine. They should learn just how unhappy you are. Perhaps they can be stimulated into action on your behalf—and theirs.

If this fails, I urge you to speak to an adult you trust—a relative, teacher, doctor. Maybe they can speak to your parents on your behalf. Or go to an adolescent clinic in your area: a staff member can help you get the attention and direction that you obviously need.

Dear Dr. Levine: This letter is from a mother, out of concern for her daughter. Last year we learned that our daughter had been skipping classes (her marks went down) as well as smoking at school and drinking socially with her friends. She does not have a boyfriend but belongs to a group of young people called the "drama crowd" for their interest in the theater.

252

We had a very serious talk, and she told us she had no major problem that was responsible for her actions. We asked her to be serious about school and to stop drinking and smoking. We now monitor her homework assignments.

Our daughter has a poor self-image right now. She attends church with us regularly, but she will not accept responsibility for her actions, instead always blaming someone else. This time, I am blamed. She claims I don't know who she is—that I am too "proper" and she can't make sexual jokes to me the way her friends do to their mothers. She claims she likes the people who hang around the "smoke hole"

**at school, and she doesn't think it fair that they be
stereotyped by parents and teacher.**

**It's very important to me to have a good relation-
ship with both my children (I did not have a good
relationship with my parents). My son and I are close;
my daughter is much like me.**

**I'm aware of the confusion, pressures, and fear
facing our youth, but how do I get her on the right
path without giving in to her moods and selfishness?**
You are obviously concerned for the welfare of your daughter and take your parenting role very seriously indeed. Your
daughter, on the other hand, perceives you as straight, con-
servative, and overly strict. I work with youth and I'm sympathetic to their concerns. But I'm also the father of three
of them, and our concerns are valid and serious too.

Our duties as parents are to provide love, support, compassion, and nurturance. But it doesn't stop there! The other
equally important side of the coin involves guidance, responsibility, accountability, limits, and constraints.

This isn't a simple question of right versus wrong. There
are temptations elsewhere that make your own lifestyle less
attractive to your daughter. But your values and principles
are important for her to learn, and to resent, and even to
rebel against. She is in the process of maturing and may
not appreciate your restrictions now, but she will come to
appreciate them eventually. Of course, if conflicts take over
the family, outside guidance is sometimes wise, but I doubt
this will be necessary in your situation. Who said parenting
was easy?

EIGHT:

School

Personally, I think none but stupid children should be sent to school till they are at least twelve years old.

Marie Carmichael Slopes,
Sex and the Young (1926)

I n our society, until the age of, say, twenty-two, there is nothing outside the family that dominates our lives more in terms of sheer hours, energy, and other demands than school. School is our first foray into the outside world, where we learn much about ourselves, friends, and strangers. Here we learn how to relate both to peers and to those who wield the power. We learn how we stack up, where our major strengths and deficiencies lie.

In this relatively rigid arena, problems can arise over difficulties with the work or conflicts with other people. In overcoming these problems, we learn lessons that will last a lifetime. Part of our success or failure here depends on our own attitudes. If school is seen as the enemy rather than an opportunity, we are setting ourselves up for trouble. This may sound like a paradox, but we have to *work* at learning how to have fun and to derive some pleasure or meaning in any situation.

Dear Dr. Levine: I am a seventeen-year-old male, and although everybody tells me how wonderful I am (bright, attractive, popular), I feel like a failure because of my poor school grades (I am in tenth grade). No matter how hard I try, I can't seem to get my marks out of the 60s. Sometimes I luck out and get near 80, but I know it's a fluke. My parents aren't on my back, but I can tell they're disappointed. I feel like I've let everybody down. This has been going on

ever since I was a child; at that time, we were told that I had a learning disability and I got special help. I don't think that I've been any other trouble to my parents.

Yours is a sad letter. I can hear your unhappiness around your school performance, and you obviously feel guilt-ridden about how you've burdened your parents. Saying that you have a "learning disability," a very common label nowadays, doesn't tell me any specifics about where your difficulties lie: reading, writing, concentration, spatial, perceptual, or memory problems can be implicated and need different kinds of attention. The fact that you got special help as a child tells me that some investigation was done at the time, but it may well be time for a good re-evaluation.

You haven't been a behavior problem. I just comment on this because it is not unusual for a child with a learning disorder to be inattentive and hyperactive. Some kids who have repetitive experiences with school failure react by giving up or rebelling. It seems that you have been able to overcome some of these problems.

While school is not going as well as you would like, you *are* in your proper grade, you have friends, and you are recognized as a bright young man. Your parents also are close to you and supportive.

You obviously have a lot going for you, in spite of the learning problems. An assessment with an educational psychologist would be useful (again) at this time. New directions or approaches might be suggested. Also, you'll get a better idea of where specifically your difficulties lie and, more important, what your strengths are and how you can exploit them.

It could also make sense to talk to your parents about your feelings of guilt. I'm sure they would tell you they are *not* disappointed in you, and that their concern is for your happiness. My prediction is that you will be successful in whatever you choose for yourself.

254

Dear Dr. Levine: I'm a fifteen-year-old girl with a mild language disability, in written language mostly. Many people think I have a problem in English because I haven't been in this country long, but it's not true. I have been here for more than ten years, and I have problems with all languages.

But that's not the real problem. Coming from a family of overachievers, I'm always being called the

**disgrace of the family and useless because I'm not
doing as well in school as everyone else in the family. I don't think I'm doing too badly with a B average in the honors program despite my disability.**

**I've been constantly compared to very smart or
talented kids. My parents think I'm lazy. They don't
believe I have a disability, although all the test results said I have a lot of difficulty in language. I really
tried hard.**

**I tried family counseling once, but it was hopeless.
I really want to leave home but I can't because I want
to finish and, I hope, go to college.**

Sometimes parents who are preoccupied with their children's success and achievement lose sight of inherent obstacles, like disabilities, or of their kids marching to the
beat of a different drummer. Their children appear to them
to be purposely frustrating their efforts.

Your mother and father most likely want you to be as high
an achiever as your siblings or other kids they know. They
may recall poverty and deprivation and may have made a
vow many years ago that their own offspring would never
know that experience.

You sound caught between your limitations and their
constant harangues. As it is, you seem to be doing extremely well, in spite of your "laziness," which obviously is
nothing of the sort. Your parents have to come to realize
that you are not irresponsible, and to appreciate your considerable strengths.

It is unfortunate that your first attempt at family counseling did not work. Perhaps you can speak to a counselor
in your school who can help you convey to your parents just
what your disability is all about, and that you are actually
working very well. I am not sure that will be enough, because words like "disgrace" and "useless" are remarkably
insensitive and brutal. You may have to try to get an advocate or personal counselor to advise and guide you. This
can be done through your school social worker or a staff
member at an adolescent clinic.

**Dear Dr. Levine: I'm a thirteen-year-old girl who is
very insecure. I'm in eighth grade, and first term was
terrible. I thought eighth grade would be real easy. I
thought I was smart. You see, my parents are very
proud people. They were born in Greece and didn't**

255

have much education. But they give me more than I can ask for.

They give me so much, but ask me for only one thing in return—to be good in school. I promised them that I would try hard. I've been doing extremely well, until eighth grade. I guess I was on a losing streak. I failed four tests in one term. Now I'm afraid of doing it again. Sometimes I want to kill myself but never have the nerve. I had to get the tests signed. My parents were so disappointed in me. Now whenever I take a test I get real scared. I love my parents more than anything in this world. But I'm scared to take tests.

This is a very poignant letter. I feel your sadness and frustration. I also feel your intense love for your parents and your guilt over having "let them down." But did you really? Your mother and father are indeed lucky people to have you as their daughter.

They may not be formally educated, but surely they will understand your anguish and pain. They will tell you not to worry. They will reassure you that we all falter at times and come back stronger another day. They will remind themselves and you of their own failures—and successes.

I recommend that you speak to your teachers and see if they can make any suggestions. You might also talk to your school guidance counselor or social worker to explain your predicament and difficulties. He or she might advise you on how to improve scholastically, but perhaps more important, might help you overcome your feelings of guilt toward your parents.

You might consider showing your mother and father your letter and this response, if you find it difficult to speak to them directly. Above all they want you to be happy, and surely they know how much you love them.

256 **Dear Dr. Levine: I'm a nineteen-year-old female with a disturbing problem. I have mental blocks while taking tests. No matter how hard I try not to panic, I get anxiety attacks. I have tried self-hypnosis and tranquilizers, but nothing seems to control these blocks in which my memory just goes blank. Will I always be nervous and have no confidence in myself? Everyone else seems to do better than me. Is there a way to overcome these feelings?**

You certainly aren't the only one who gets mental blocks when taking tests. There are few stimuli that raise as much anxiety in as many people as tests do, or even more so, final examinations.

Anxiety can actually be a help when we have to face a crisis of some kind. It gets us to muster our thoughts and energies and to act resolutely and efficiently. But the level of anxiety must arouse us while still permitting performance. Once it gets past the point of positive energy, the anxiety starts to have deleterious effects, as it is obviously doing in your case. In these circumstances, thinking, efficiency, remembering, concentrating, and performing all suffer.

It is something like a phobia, in which whatever is feared becomes so overwhelming and grotesque that we can no longer talk ourselves out of it by calm reasoning. And, like any other phobia, it *is* amenable to training and treatment. There are methods of desensitization and relaxation that can be learned and used before and during exams. Techniques involving schedules, notes, "tricks," and self-acceptance abound. Tranquilizers can be self-defeating, since they often have sedating properties, themselves interfering with good thinking.

You *can* get help. Speak to a school counselor or your family doctor, who can refer you to an appropriate psychologist or a learning center. I am sure that things will improve.

Dear Dr. Levine: I'm a fifteen-year-old girl who's fairly attractive. The first time I set eyes on a certain person, I found myself drawn quite close. I know very little about this person, whom I have known only three months. The problem is that this person is a woman, and she's also my favorite teacher. Her features are not what I am drawn to; just her, personally. The mention of her name makes me numb.

My feelings are hard to explain. I want to become much closer to her and hope I do by the time I graduate in three years. Yet, this is too far away. I want to become part of her important life now! I'll do anything to be near her. Once I thought of falling down the stairs, hoping to break my leg so she could help me to the hospital. My friends say I talk too much about her, and they even say I sound as if I'm in

257

love. I don't think so, but could I be? Should I tell
her now how much I care about her? Or should I let
nature take its course in the hope that in three years
we will be the best of friends?

Do you think I am sick, being so fond of another
woman? I'm so confused because I also like a boy I
see on the bus. What's wrong with me?
No, I don't think you're "sick," as you put it. You are young,
romantic, and overwhelmed by this female teacher who represents to you many wonderful things. It is a form of love,
an intense crush. But it doesn't mean you're gay or strange.
All it means is that your teacher makes you feel warm and
excited.

While you teacher most likely thinks that you are a lovely
girl, she would probably be unnerved by your intense at-
tachment. You'll look back on this crush in a few months
with fond memories, a little chagrin, and even some amuse-
ment.

258 Dear Dr. Levine: My problem is that I don't want to
go to the high school that I went to last year. I was
overly depressed and had social problems there. I am
really afraid to go back, because my mind will not be
on my work. I have tried to get into another school
close by, but they have too many students. I am going
into my last year of high school, and it seems there
are no more schools I can go to. Please tell me what
can I do!
You *must* get advice and guidance from someone in the
school system. There is no doubt that some schools are better environments for some students than for others. Some
are more rigid, some more lax. Some schools have a heavy
concentration of drug abuse or behavioral problems; others
represent different social classes or social groups.

I know nothing about the problems you are confronting
in your own high school, but since you are entering your
final year I take it that you are not expressing impulsive or
poorly thought out concerns. I urge you to speak to your
school social worker or guidance counselor. He or she is there
for that specific purpose: to help students with problems
within the school system that don't necessarily entail academic difficulties.

A transfer of schools might be the solution, or perhaps
something else can be worked out satisfactorily for you. But

you have no choice but to address the problem directly and immediately. I am optimistic that something can be done to make your final high school year a rewarding one.

Dear Dr. Levine: I am in tenth grade and attending an excellent public school. I am told I am very pretty. I don't think so. My problem is, I feel everybody at the school hates me.

259

What I mean by "hate" is calling me vulgar names that refer to me as cheap and easy. I am a very decent girl, I think. My mother would not let me out of the house if I was not decent. The girls at school also ignore me. When I go to talk to one of them, they all walk away.

I talked to my mom, and she said, "They are jealous of you." I don't believe her. I have nothing to be jealous of. This is really depressing. I really want some friends. Please help.

It's obvious that you are in a very painful situation. Your mom may well believe what she is saying to you, but she is also trying to make you (and herself) feel better.

For some reason your relationship with your schoolmates has got off on the wrong foot. The fact that they ignore you or call you names suggests that they are offended or annoyed about something. That something can be real or imagined. As you know, people can be quite cruel to each other, and this is a perfect example.

Sometimes parents get in touch with the school principal to see if he or she can ascertain just what is going wrong. At times school authorities can intervene, talk to the class, confront the troublemakers, or enlist their help in achieving a solution. I don't know if you are ready for such an experience.

You could speak to a counselor in an effort to discover how to cope with this problem and also to see if there is anything you do to bring it on.

See 57.

Dear Dr. Levine: I have left school and am looking for employment. I keep replying to advertisements in the newspapers, and after some interviews I keep being rejected.

260

I'm getting so depressed and feel my life has met a standstill. I don't plan to go back to school. I'm

living at home and my mom is constantly on my back, asking me where I'm going in my chosen career. The way things are now, I don't know where I'm headed. I know where I'd like to be, but with a job, I could begin my career much faster.

How should I begin to dust myself off and try again? How can I begin to get things together in my mind when things look so downhill?

Yours is a common story: a young man or woman with no specific skills to offer employers, in a depressed job market, and not able to find work. The result? Frustration, futility, and demoralization.

While we *do* have a major youth unemployment problem, the main sufferers are those without adequate schooling or vocational training. I urge young people to stay in school or to get into one of the many vocational programs offered by various school boards or different levels of government.

I don't know enough about your own situation—such as what schooling or job training you have had—to give specific advice. But if it is at all possible to complete one or both of these, I recommend that you pursue this course of action. Other young people have gone to vocational counselors to assess their interests and aptitudes and have found new directions to explore. Others have gone to employment agencies, government employment agencies, or bulletin boards.

I don't want to minimize your suffering, but eventually many people like you do get jobs. I am assuming from your letter that your mood of melancholy stems directly from your inability to find gainful, meaningful employment. If the mood persists even after you have a job, or if it preceded your wanting one, you might consider other kinds of counseling.

NINE

Social and Psychiatric Problems

Melancholy begins with frequent attacks of de-
spondency—what are commonly called "the
blues," which may in many cases be overcome
by the use of Lydia E. Pinkham Vegetable Com-
pound, with proper rest and cheerful surround-
ings. . . . Food should be given in large
quantities.
Lydia E. Pinkham's Private Textbook *(ca. 1885)*

Who said life is easy? It just ain't so. Problems and predicaments are as much a part of everyone's life as are excitement and joy.

Some people tolerate troubles better than others. They don't break, they bend; they surf on the waves. Of course they get hurt, but their sense of adventure in living remains. It's not that their lives are problem-free, but their attitude remains optimistic and hopeful, even in the face of inevitable trials and tribulations.

While we can learn to develop a more positive view of our lives, our relationships, and even ourselves, and to take some responsibility for improving any of these that may be in trouble, there *are* certain psychological problems that defy simple "emotional tinkering."

Today when words like "stress" and "burnout" seem to be applied to every emotional ache and pain, it is important to remember that there are specific psychological conditions such as anxiety, phobias, depression, and psychosis that can and do afflict large numbers of teenagers. While not a panacea, psychiatry and associated professions offer help for many of these disorders. The first prerequisite is that the suffering person recognize that he or she needs that help. Once we admit that to ourselves, we have crossed the most important barrier.

Dear Dr. Levine: What is the difference between a psychiatrist, a psychologist, a therapist, and a coun- **261**

selor? How expensive are they on average? Are the
Yellow Pages the best place to find one? Is there a
cheaper way to get help and, if there is, is the quality
of help inferior? I don't know how to start.

You are asking important questions. Psychiatrists are physicians trained to diagnose and treat so-called abnormal behavior; they are graduates of a medical school and have
completed a residency program in the specialty. They are
taught to diagnose and treat emotional disorders and major
mental illnesses, working with problems affecting both mind
and body, and to prescribe medication.

Psychologists have a Ph.D. or a master's degree in clinical
psychology. This specialty overlaps with psychiatry, but
usually psychologists are adept at applying specific written
tests, have a better research background, and are usually
more expert in therapies involving specific approaches, like
behavior therapy and cognitive therapy. They are not allowed to prescribe medication.

Counselors can have master's or doctoral degrees and may
have received training in specific kinds of counseling methods. Social workers have graduate degrees and are trained
in a variety of psychotherapies. There are other professionals who provide psychological help too, such as chaplains.
There is considerable overlap between the professions, which
leads to collaboration, cooperation, and sometimes competition.

Costs vary. Some health insurance plans cover at least
part of the cost of any kind of psychotherapy or counseling.

The Yellow Pages are certainly a source of names. But so
are the various state professional associations; departments of psychiatry, social work, or psychology in most
hospitals; and various social agencies.

Perhaps the best place to start is with your family doctor,
who can refer you to an appropriate therapist. Not only are
the therapist's professional background and credentials important but also his or her interests, skills, experience, and
personality. So too are *your* personal characteristics, motivation, and specific problems. The "chemistry" between you
and the therapist is also crucial.

Bottom line? Help for you is available.

262 Dear Dr. Levine: I was told that a girlfriend I haven't
seen for three months was hospitalized for psychiatric reasons. What exactly is a nervous breakdown?
Is it the same thing as going crazy?

I'll attempt to give you a short course in psychiatric termi-
nology with all its limitations. I compare a person who has
a nervous breakdown to an overloaded machine that breaks
down because of extraordinary pressure. Every machine, and
for that matter every human being, has a breaking point.
We can all get overheated by internal and external forces
that cause us to develop symptoms of an emotional disorder. No one is immune to that possibility. The word "crazy"
is used colloquially nowadays to describe any unusual,
aberrant, or unacceptable behavior. It is *not* formally used
in psychiatry at all.

Psychosis is a severe psychiatric disorder, such as schiz-
ophrenia, that affects how an individual perceives reality,
thinks, acts, and reacts to others. Neurosis is considered to
be a less severe disorder and has more to do with the lengths
to which we human beings go to protect ourselves from undue anxiety, fear, or inner conflict. There is a host of other
"categories" of psychiatric disorder that can afflict us, and
often there is considerable overlap between various diagnoses.

It is very likely that your friend found the pressure of continuing under major stress too much for her to handle. It is
also highly likely that she is out of the hospital and doing
quite well by now. Why don't you give her a call?

**Dear Dr. Levine: I am a fifteen-year-old girl with a
big problem. At any social gathering, I sit off to the
side and feel out of place. I always walk about two
steps behind my friends, even where there is enough
room to walk beside them. And at school I always get
this feeling of not belonging, even though I know I
have very good friends. Plus I'm always dwelling in
self-pity. My friends tell me to get help, but I don't
know where to turn. My parents aren't much help,
and I'm a bit frightened of my father. I feel so alone.**

263

What clinicians and social scientists refer to as "social anxiety"—more popularly referred to as shyness—is an extremely common and painful human experience. I know very
few people who have never suffered those excruciating mo-
ments when they feel their heart in the pit of their stomach,
their pulse racing, their skin sweating or blushing, for fear
of being embarrassed, humiliated, rejected.

Shyness, of course, is all of those things and more. It has
to do with lack of self-confidence in certain social situations
where other people who "matter" seem to be looking at you,

themselves obviously so cool and full of self-esteem. Little do shy people realize that many of the people they think of as confident are themselves uncomfortable in those same or similar circumstances. Of course, moderate shyness in new social gatherings is not only common but accepted. It is when the shyness becomes so frequent and intense that it is almost incapacitating that something must be done.

When the person with the problem is fifteen, I usually ask her to put her best foot forward, concentrate on her strengths, pursue interests instead of people. But all this may simply not be enough. Sometimes group therapy is very helpful in that it feeds back to a person just how he or she is functioning socially. Shyness clinics have sprouted up in many large cities, responding to the common needs of many people (look in the Yellow Pages).

Given your description of yourself and the comment you make about fearing your father, I recommend that you speak to a counselor at an adolescent clinic.

264 **Dear Dr. Levine: I feel extremely immature for my age (sixteen) and it really has me worried. I sometimes wonder if I am growing up normally. People have noticed this, and they treat me differently. I feel as though the world is growing up around me and I am being left behind in my childhood.**

Everyone seems so happy with their lives, and I feel as though I am the only one in the world with a problem. I have always been very shy, but I find it unbearable now that I am in high school. I am envious of people who are popular and seem to have it all.

I've never had a lot of friends, but now I have totally alienated everyone. They all think I am very boring and stupid, so they don't bother with me. I dread going to school each day, and when I'm home I just sit around, cry, and feel sorry for myself.

The concerns that you have written about so poignantly are probably the most common ones that preoccupy young people. Shyness, low self-esteem, loneliness—they are all excruciatingly painful and contribute to your picture of depression.

Another perception of people your age is that all the other kids have it better in terms of popularity, happiness, enthusiasm, etc. I assure you that many adolescents feel somewhat out of sync with most of their peers and feel that only they are experiencing these emotions. The problem is, because they isolate themselves, they never get to check it out with others.

Be that as it may, you have passed the point of being reassured merely by the news that you are in good company. You sound like you could benefit from a group therapy experience. Therapeutic groups can be a boon to people who have difficulties with relationships. You will get feedback on how you are coming across and learn how to overcome deficiencies and maximize your strengths. It can be an exciting learning experience.

If you feel intimidated by the idea of exposing yourself in a group situation, you are again in good company. Of course, you can seek individual counseling; your family physician can be of help in getting you a proper referral.

Dear Dr. Levine: I was wondering if a person could lose their shyness by going to a hypnotist. If possible, could you tell me whom I could see and how much it would cost to see one?

265

There are extents of shyness, and some people become shy only in highly specific situations. Hypnosis can be of some help to a few shy people, but I would expect that the majority will not improve significantly if hypnosis is the only therapeutic technique used. Ultimately, shy people have to face the problems that plague them by confronting their worst fears. It usually works.

Dear Dr. Levine: I can't stand life the way it is anymore. I am always alone, and I never have any fun. All I ever do is work and sleep. I never go out and I have very few friends, no close ones. I have seen my closest friend once in the past year. (He is in the air force.) The only people I know are those at work. I don't have a girlfriend because I don't know any girls. Life is just miserable. I can't take it anymore. It's been like this for two and a half years. If it doesn't change soon I will commit suicide.

266

Your loneliness and isolation come through loud and clear. And yet I am left with more questions. Why are you so alone? Do you have any interests? You say that you work and sleep; what sort of work? You have some relationships with people at work—can they not be cultivated? You do have at least one good friend; can he be of any assistance, offer any enlightenment? Why has it been like this for only two and a half years? What was going on before that time? Did you have friends before? Why the change?

You are frustrated and despondent, and I'd urge you to seek professional guidance: a course of group psychotherapy would more than likely help you. And yet, it is important that you take some responsibility for what happens to you. You don't mention family, interests, hobbies, activities, aspirations, hopes, or fantasies. It is not enough to bemoan the fact that you are alone; you have to make some things happen. By pursuing interests that just happen to involve other people, you will be meeting them inadvertently and spontaneously rather than artificially and by design. If all this is too much for you to contemplate, then I suggest that you get some help.

267

Dear Dr. Levine: I am a twelve-year-old girl who has an average of 89 percent in school. I am also quite mature. Except for one thing (please don't laugh). I have a problem with my mind or something. I have about fifteen stuffed animals that I love and cherish. I hug them and talk to them. Once in a while I even give them a pinch so they won't "get diseases"! At night I sleep with three of them, taking turns.

I could go on and on, but I'm getting embarrassed. We could never afford for me to see a psychiatrist. Actually, my parents know I like my stuffed animals, but they don't think I go this far. Also, I don't have any brothers or sisters, and I live with my grandparents. I certainly do need help, but I would never give my animals away.

You are the one concluding that you have a problem with your mind; you signed your letter "'Lonely and crazy." From what you have written, I would conclude that you are more lonely than crazy. People—especially children—often develop imaginary companions or give human characteristics to pets or inanimate objects when they need extra companionship. This seems to be what you are doing. Living with your grandparents may in fact enhance your sense of loneliness.

You are embarrassed about your secret friends and don't want to tell anyone about them. There really is no need to. You are young, and you will soon develop real relationships to supplant these.

As far as seeing a psychiatrist is concerned, health insurance might cover some or all of the cost. But frankly, I'm not at all sure you need one.

Dear Dr. Levine: I'm a fifteen-year-old girl. I'm very depressed, and I don't know why. I can't even express how depressed I feel. I'm the one always taking the blame. My sisters get away with murder, and I get stuck with the blame. It hurts me so much.

268

My mom says I'm a loser because I'm always alone, but I really enjoy my time alone. I read books all the time to avoid contact with people, because I've been rejected before and I have hardly any friends. I'm always afraid of being rejected. I've thought about suicide. The way I get rid of the hurt is by hurting myself. I know it's not normal to be so depressed, but I just can't talk to my parents.

A very sad letter from a very sad young girl. It bothers me that you feel so rejected at home and that your mother says horrible things to you, like calling you a "loser." But I am just as perturbed by your isolation, your withdrawal from social interaction, your loneliness and lack of friends.

You are right. It isn't "normal" to be so depressed, and I hope you can get some help to overcome the hurt that you feel so deeply. You don't mention any positive, redeeming features in your life. No interests, hobbies, or pleasures other than reading? Is your life totally depressing and futile?

You are so adamant in your certainty that you can't talk to your parents. I tend to see parents as a "first line of defense." Especially when there is difficulty, most people find more solace, support, and advice from their mother or father than from any other source. Ordinarily I would urge you to discuss your unhappiness with them, but you seem to be saying that this is out of the question. And your mother's remarks to you don't fill me with confidence.

Are there other adults whom you trust and in whom you could confide—a favorite uncle or aunt, a teacher, school social worker, or family doctor? They and others can act as intermediaries to bridge the gap between you and your parents. Given your degree of depression, you probably will need some kind of counseling, individually, with your family, or both. Your parents or one of the above adults can help you get the help that you sorely need.

Dear Dr. Levine: I am a fourteen-year-old girl who thinks she is going crazy. I can't control my emo-

269

tions. When I'm in class, I sometimes start to cry. I don't know what causes these outbursts. I went through four months of depression last year. I did not talk to anyone unless it was necessary. I don't want this to happen again.

I was adopted when I was a small child, and I have always wondered who my real mother is. Now that I am older, that emptiness has gotten stronger, and I would like to find her. But I am afraid I might find something I did not expect. Would this have anything to do with my emotions?

Feelings of depression are extremely common. They are experienced by everyone from time to time. Whether people get help for their depressive feelings often has as much to do with their tolerance for this pain and the degree to which it interferes with their lives—school, activities, relationships, etc. You are also in an age group when emotions are sometimes rapidly changeable and unpredictable. So I would not necessarily advise you to seek help unless you find your feelings of depression persistent, pervasive, prolonged, or increasing.

Space doesn't permit a complete answer to your second dilemma. You realize, of course, that most adopted young people wonder about their biological parents and that nowadays many begin a concerted search for them. You are going through the process of defining your identity, of finding out who you "really" are. Consequently you have concerns about your earliest experiences and background. It is normal for someone in your position to have these concerns and fears—and hopes.

270 Dear Dr. Levine: I am a sixteen-year-old girl. Two months ago, a dear friend of mine (I'll call him John) was killed in a tragic accident. I was having trouble dealing with it, but on top of that I'm having to deal with my best friend's (Mary's) feelings as well. John and Mary were very much in love. John had a lot of friends, and none of us has ever had to deal with death before. Now that I'm finally starting to get my life organized again, Mary can't seem to get over it. All she wants is to get John back. It tears me apart to see her so depressed. I don't know what to say anymore. She used to be so happy and was always laughing. I have talked her out of suicide a couple of times now, and I don't think she has the guts, but I'm still terrified she might.

One thing is sure: Mary is lucky to have such a good friend as you. She is obviously going through a rough mourning period. The loss of John has hit you both; he sounds as if he was a special kind of guy. But it is particularly tough for Mary, since they seem to have had a close, romantic relationship.

I can understand the pressure on you right now; Mary counts on you for all kinds of emotional support, and your own feelings are coming through in your interesting and caring letter. If you absolutely cannot "give" anymore, then you owe it to yourself, and to Mary, to tell her, ever so gently and in a most caring manner, that she will have to seek solace elsewhere. This is a tough message to receive, and to convey.

I just want to remind you that it has only been two months since John was tragically killed. You must understand that this is really a relatively short time. There is every probability that Mary will come around soon. What she needs for a while longer is the loving support of friends like you.

Dear Dr. Levine: I'm female and twenty years old. I just broke up with a guy I've been going out with for two years because we had a fight and he hit me. I met a new guy and he's really nice to me, but I'm afraid of him because I'm afraid of getting hurt again.

271

I have been drinking a lot and I've been taking drugs. Sometimes I get very depressed and I get thoughts of hurting myself. Sometimes I hear voices and I get really scared. I can't eat anymore. I'm 5 ft 6 in (168 cm) tall and I weigh 103 lb (47 kg).

I don't know why all of a sudden my life is falling apart. I get very lonely and depressed. Sometimes I feel really mixed up, and I feel like two people. I told my doctor how I was feeling like two people, but he didn't seem to believe me. This world is a sad place to live in—it is so frustrating.

This poignant letter is written by someone in deep emotional trouble. Violence, fears, weight loss, drinking, hallucinations, depression, and suicidal thoughts—these are just some of the unpleasant experiences in your recent life. Why your doctor didn't believe you is beyond me, unless you tried to hide your misery from him.

You *must* seek proper help. If your doctor does not take you seriously, you can go to one who will. You can also go to the emergency room of a general hospital and ask to see the doctor on call. My feeling is that you are in sufficiently dire straits that you could be considered a relatively urgent case. You can be helped, but you must seek out help actively.

272 **Dear Dr. Levine: I'm an eighteen-year-old female, and I'm terribly worried about my temper. When I have fights with my family or things upset me, I refuse to blow up. I become withdrawn, lock myself in my room, and turn on my stereo. The problem comes later while I'm alone. If I'm working on a hobby and it doesn't work right, or something else minor happens, I scream at the top of my lungs or throw chairs across rooms or punch walls. I never did things like this before, but lately I've noticed it occurring more frequently. These bursts last only a few minutes, and so far I haven't done any real bad bodily damage to myself or others.**

There's a lot of hate, hurt, and anger bottled up inside of me, and I'm worried about what may happen if one day it all erupts. Should I worry or forget it?

Rather than the two options you mention, why not try doing something about your pressure-cooker temper? Your pattern is now set—get angry, hold it in, then explode later when you're alone. As you so sensitively put it, the "hate, hurt, and anger" will become more of a problem unless you attempt to overcome these personally destructive emotions.

A few sessions with a psychotherapist (psychiatrist, psychologist, social worker) will clarify the whys of your unhappiness and, more important, help you start doing something about it. I would not recommend that you wait for this problem to take care of itself.

273 **Dear Dr. Levine: I have a problem with one of my friends. She has serious mood swings. One minute she's okay, and then suddenly she's down.**

Lately her depression has become very bad, and she mentions suicide. At first I thought she was joking, but today she was really down. I think she might

be serious. I've read that people who are intent on suicide don't mention it, so I don't worry too much, but I'm afraid she might slip into deep depression.

Her past seems to be the main problem. She had an alcoholic parent and a rough childhood. She also feels inferior to her friends, because she has to work harder than we do to get honors.

She doesn't think people want to notice her, and she's wrong, because if she seems to be down, they ask me what's bothering her. Some have even offered help, if I need any, in bringing her out of the depression.

We've talked to the school counselor, and he suggested that we make an appointment for her and he'll start off talking about options for next year and then ask about home, or mention that she has seemed a little down lately. Are we on the right track? Is there anything else we can do? The more we sympathize, the worse she gets.

I would say you are on the right track. Your friend is lucky she has friends as committed and interested as you are. She certainly has problems; your concern is warranted.

Many individuals have rapid or intermittent mood swings, some much more severe than others. At times it is a full-fledged psychiatric disorder, while at others it reflects certain kinds of actual changes in personality. In your friend's case, however, it may be due to certain problems in her life that are stressing her. You should know, by the way, that the idea that those who mention suicide won't do it is wrong, I'm afraid; I always take these threats seriously.

The counselor who has agreed to speak with her is to be commended. Not only is he interested in her school progress, but he is willing to go beyond that area and deal with her emotional concerns. If you can convince her to speak to him, it would be very beneficial. If she opens up, he can help her get appropriate help.

Dear Dr. Levine: I am a high anxiety sufferer and have a very difficult time concentrating and relaxing, even for a short period of time. How can I reduce this anxiety and be more productive? **274**

Anxiety is one of the most common, painful emotions that we have all experienced from time to time. You all know the sensations associated with anxiety. They are of two kinds, psychological and physical, although separating them in this way is really oversimplifying things.

Psychologically, one feels a vague discomfort increasing to a feeling close to fear and progressing at times to panic. The anxiety may not be closely associated with a specific fear but rather brought to the surface by certain circumstances. Anxiety can interfere with everyday activities that we take for granted, like eating, sleeping, and relaxing. Also our ability to concentrate, work, read, or study is reduced. There are many kinds of bodily symptoms that can be associated with anxiety, like headaches, sweating, diarrhea, dry mouth, dizziness, cramps, and palpitations, to name a few.

Anxiety probably has multiple causes, including early experiences (long forgotten but recalled to mind by current circumstances), "faulty learning" of how to cope with difficulties, and inherited characteristics. A touch of anxiety serves to keep us on our toes and actually increases our efficiency. It is when anxiety is prolonged or severe that it becomes truly destructive.

Treatment is largely effective. Various kinds of psychotherapy have proven useful. Relaxation exercises, behavior modification, biofeedback, hypnosis, exercise, and medication have also been very helpful. A wide variety of tranquilizers are also used, so much so, unfortunately, that these pills are the widest-selling medication all over the world.

If nothing works for you on your own, you may have to consult your family doctor for further advice.

275 **Dear Dr. Levine: I am a normal fifteen-year-old girl with a problem that turns me to tears sometimes. Ever since I can remember, I have been frightened of lakes. I love to swim and play all sorts of water games but only in pools. What scares me most is the bottom of lakes where I can see logs and rocks and dead leaves. I've never had a bad experience in a lake, and although I've seen the movie _Jaws_, it didn't affect me in any way.**

Many people develop specific fears for which they can identify no logical basis, and except for this fear they function normally and well. Such a fear can be called a phobia. Phobias (irrational fears) can arise from a variety of causes, but the bottom line involves overcoming that dreaded panic. By recognizing the negative effect this fear has on your life and by asking for help in eliminating it, you've taken an important step toward resolving the problem.

Speak to your family physician. He or she can help you or can refer you to a therapist who can aid you in unlearning your fear by using a technique called behavior therapy. It is very effective in eliminating phobias and can also help you generally by improving your ability to feel relaxed and comfortable.

Dear Dr. Levine: I am a thirteen-year-old girl. When I go to bed I always seem to think of things like werewolves or that something is going to come in and get me while I'm sleeping. I get terrified and go up and sleep with my sister. I can't even watch something scary on TV without thinking about it for weeks.

276

I am getting tired of having to go upstairs to my sister's room every night, and I'm not sure my parents would understand, so can you please help?
I wish my younger readers would trust their parents more. Unless your own mother and father are so insensitive as to defy imagination, I fully expect that they would understand.

Nighttime fearful fantasies are very common in younger children. There are a few *potential* reasons for this fear in your case. Perhaps it is covering up some other fears that your conscious mind is not aware of. Or maybe it is a fear that was originally triggered by viewing a movie or drama and has become embedded, very much like a habit. Perhaps the initial fear occurred at the same time something else very upsetting happened, maybe when you were very much younger. These are all just guesses but give you some idea of how these kinds of fears come about.

Whatever the cause, your fears are bothering you considerably. I think that, first and foremost, you should speak to your parents. Perhaps a visit to your family doctor or pediatrician will suffice. It might be that a few sessions with a psychologist or psychiatrist may be in order. There may be more questions to explore regarding other aspects of your life. And leave your sister alone; maybe waking her is a necessary part of the ritual that must be disrupted.

Dear Dr. Levine: I'm a nineteen-year-old male student who has an unusual but painful problem. It seems that whenever I venture outside my home environment, I have difficulty eating or can't eat. Pe-

277

riod! My stomach muscles contract and my throat
muscles tighten up, making it virtually impossible for
food to pass and remain in my stomach for any period of time before I vomit.

The problem seems to be getting worse because I'm
becoming more and more self-conscious, thinking
several days in advance about whether or not I'll be
able to eat at my girlfriend's, at banquets, at wed-
dings, etc. The problem occurs wherever I go and it's
really frustrating and I'm becoming really depressed.

Recently I visited a psychiatrist who suggested I
undergo systematic desensitization. Please explain
what this process involves and comment on my
problem, whether other people have it, or am I the
only one that's screwed up?

Systematic desensitization is a series of behavioral treatments usually directed by a clinical psychologist trained in
various forms of behavior therapy. It is a type of treatment
designed to remove specific symptoms, or groups of symptoms, like phobias, some forms of anxiety, uncontrollable
habits, or even more complex but maladaptive and painful
behavior patterns. It pays little or no attention to causation
or symbolic meaning or unconscious conflict. Its success
rate varies from problem to problem but in some instances
is impressively high.

Essentially, systematic desensitization is a process whereby
stimuli that provoke anxiety are presented repetitively and
gradually increased in intensity until the individual learns
to master his or her anxiety and react in a relatively relaxed
manner to the kind of stimulus that would ordinarily induce intense discomfort.

In your case, food and an unfamiliar environment appear
to be two characteristics that are crucial to your intense
reaction, which is a combination of anxiety, phobia, and
bodily distress. There may be a "cause" that one could work
out with sufficient time and exploration, but your psychiatrist has made an assessment and has recommended a highly
respected technique of intervention. I urge you to follow his
or her advice.

278 Dear Dr. Levine: I enjoy school very much and have
consistently achieved high academic standings. I can
easily express myself well on paper, but I find oral
expression an extremely difficult task. I become very

tense and nervous when faced with making speeches, preparing seminars, or any other type of oral presentation.

Whether I stand or sit, my heart rate increases until I feel it in my throat, and I feel my voice shaking as I speak. It's such a terrifying experience!
The experience you are describing is, in fact, a common one. The popular term for it, and quite an accurate depiction, is stage fright. It is the experience of symptoms of intense anxiety—which you describe so well—when having to make a presentation to other people.

The basic, ultimate fear is of humiliation. It is based on a lack of self-confidence, on a gnawing fear that what the presenter has to say or how he or she says it will be criticized or even laughed at. And trying to convince someone with stage fright that the fear is unfounded does not work, at least in severe instances.

This is a condition that is amenable to training, practice, and coaching. It is such a common condition that many techniques have been developed to overcome it. It is one that is responsive to repeated successful experiences, usually achieved in a gradually more intensive manner: for example, starting with familiar material in front of one person, progressing all the way to difficult material in front of a large audience. Behavior therapy, a psychological technique based on learning theory, can be very effective in treating this problem.

Most general hospitals' departments of psychiatry and psychology have units that can offer help.

Dear Dr. Levine: My problem first began four years ago when I was fifteen, when I had an anxiety attack in a shopping mall. I felt like I wasn't in the same dimension as everyone else. I was hearing what my friends were saying but it wasn't computing. I felt like if I didn't hold onto something I'd drift away. I got really scared and I started to panic. I got home okay, but I've never set foot in that mall again. I tried going in several times but I got those attacks every time.

279

Through the years my problem has worsened. I get a shortness of breath with these attacks now. Slowly my world has closed in on me. Now I'm confined to the house. I can't ride in cars or buses. Sometimes I

can't even make it upstairs to brush my teeth. The attacks come every half hour or so now. In fact, I had to stop writing this because I had one. I'm basically terrified of these attacks. My life is a living nightmare and my only escape is going to sleep.

The panic attacks you describe are in reality an explosion (implosion, to be exact) of anxiety, and they are remarkably common. For some reason the condition, known as agoraphobia (literally "fear of open spaces"), is much more common in females than in males. It is an irrational fear, not based on any realistic danger in malls or elsewhere.

You are in a proverbial catch-22. You can only get help by going out to get it. And you can't go out to get that help without inducing one of these attacks. So you remain in a state of emotional paralysis, sequestered in your home, fearful of venturing out.

Your agoraphobia *can* be eradicated. The condition is very amenable to treatment through a combination of psychotherapy, behavior therapy, and minor medication. Not doing anything about it is a travesty, because the phobia "spreads," as it has in your case, until the afflicted individual can do nothing.

You do not mention anybody you are living with—parents, a roommate or lover. Often it is helpful to have one or more of these individuals accompany you to the first session or two. You or your family or friends can find out who does this type of work by calling the department of psychiatry or psychology at any good general hospital. Support groups of agoraphobics are extremely effective (look in the Yellow Pages or phone the department of psychiatry or psychology of a local hospital).

280 **Dear Dr. Levine: Please help me resolve a difficult problem. People I know say I am emotionally disturbed, perverse, and sexually repressed because of my favorite pastime. For example, I enjoy taking pictures of people's faces and affixing them to the photographed bodies of voluptuous strippers, centerfolds, exotic dancers, and mud wrestlers and circulating my creative work. They say I am infringing on their rights and privacy.**

Now these people won't associate with me or trust me. Is this such a sick and disgusting hobby?

I don't readily use such words as "sick" and "disgusting." Taking pictures of your (female, I expect) friends and affixing them to the photos of voluptuous women probably says something about your sexual fantasies, needs, and perhaps insecurities regarding sexually approaching or relating to attractive women. Beyond that, I wouldn't hazard a guess, because I don't have enough information from you.

But circulating the photos is of more concern to me, as well as to your friends. Yes, it is most definitely an invasion of their rights and privacy and lives. It is crude, rude, and hostile. Their reaction is exactly what you should expect. And if you don't know this, you are indeed insensitive and callous. You owe them all an apology, and you should take some time to examine your motives and rationale.

Dear Dr. Levine: I sometimes hallucinate and hear voices when I'm alone. I have attempted to kill myself, but the strange thing is, each time I displayed little emotion and actually enjoyed these self-destructive actions.

281

I have talked with psychologists and I have seen a psychiatrist, but after seeing him I feel more confused and perplexed. I feel I have reached the point past sanity. I feel like the majority of my movements are monitored by some other being.
You are describing symptoms of a psychiatric disorder. You are confused and depressed and have been actively suicidal, although the mood that went with this was curiously devoid of "appropriate" feelings. You give evidence of auditory hallucinations (hearing voices when nobody is speaking), paranoid delusions (ideas that people are controlling you), and increasing withdrawal.

It bothers me to urge you to get help from the same kind of professionals you feel have failed you in the past. But that is exactly what I would like you to do. You should see another psychiatrist, who can assess your psychological state and determine what kind of intervention would be most suitable. Medication is certainly a possibility, but there are other helpful ways of reducing your level of distress and turmoil.

I obviously cannot comment on why you didn't hit it off with the psychiatrist you saw; sometimes it is nobody's fault. Be that as it may, you are perfectly entitled to seek another professional. If the exact same experience occurs, you might consider that your state of mind may play some role in the problems between you.

282 **Dear Dr. Levine: I'm scared that I'm going to die at an early age, and I want to live a long life. The problem is, every time I get a headache, I think of brain tumors; when I get a stomachache, I think of ulcers; and if I get a pain in my chest, heart attacks come to my mind. Sometimes when I go to bed at night I'm scared that I won't wake up, and because of this I lose a lot of sleep.**

Is this a common thing for people to think, or do I need help of some kind?

I wouldn't say that it is "common" for people to exaggerate physical symptoms, to fantasize serious pathology on the basis of flimsy evidence. While this kind of bodily preoccupation is certainly something that all clinicians have seen, it is by no means an everyday phenomenon.

The cause of this *psycho* (mind) *somatic* (body) disorder is obscure, or at least complicated. Sometimes it is based on a family pattern passed on from generation to generation. At other times the bodily preoccupations have some hidden or symbolic meaning to the individual: perhaps the seriousness of the imagined illness achieves for you some "denied" level of anxiety or fear. Perhaps it is nurturance you are after. Or is flirtation with illness or even death on your (unconscious) agenda? Obviously, these are all rhetorical questions, and considerable exploration would be necessary to achieve some answers.

I recommend that you see a psychiatrist. I seldom recommend members of my own profession in strong preference to psychologists or other well-trained psychotherapists. In this instance, however, you need a physician who is adept at recognizing bona fide physical symptoms and who can tell the difference between organic symptoms and those based on hysterical fantasies or phobic thoughts, for example. He or she would also know when to send you to a specialist to rule out specific physical disorders.

283 **Dear Dr. Levine: My problem is that I steal a lot. I don't know why I do it, because I never had money problems. I've been stealing since I was eight years old. This bad habit is getting worse. I can't seem to control it anymore. I steal money, mostly in the fam-**

ily. Sometimes I sit down and cry, and I hate myself for doing it, but I just can't control it.

Please help me. I don't want to end up in jail or caught stealing. I've been trying so hard to change but I just can't. Is there any way I can change? I really want to because I want people to believe in me again.

Just by virtue of admitting to yourself and to me that you have a problem, you have made a big step in the right direction. I can't tell you why you steal repetitively; there are many possible reasons, ranging from your feelings about yourself to your relationships with your parents or authority figures and the meaning of money to you.

I don't know how old you are, but I'd guess you are at least a mid-teenager, which means that this compulsion of yours has been going on for many years. It also sounds like you are not going to lick it by yourself. You are ashamed of the symptom but attached to it; it is now part of you.

You need help, and this is the first hurdle. Now you must get your parents to help you get to a psychotherapist; or if you don't want them to know, you can get referred by your school social worker or an adolescent clinic. I hope that your relationship with your parents is such that you can confide in them. They may surprise you with their support and advice. You are ashamed of the symptom, but you should know that it is amenable to psychotherapy. Stealing seldom occurs as an isolated problem; you will be dealing with other personal issues and feelings as well.

Dear Dr. Levine: I am writing in regard to my sixteen-year-old sister. Since Barb was thirteen, she has had what you might call "sticky fingers." It started with money, and she is now stealing clothes, jewelery, etc., from her family. Her whole attitude is bad. Helping out around the house is not important to her, and she's the biggest liar. She really doesn't give a damn about anything.

I am the eldest daughter and work full time. I work hard to buy clothes and don't fancy the idea of having to lock all the rooms in the house so Barb doesn't take something. Recently Mom was missing some expensive earrings. She asked Barb if she had them, and Barb said no. A month later they were found hidden in Barb's room.

284

The entire family attended sessions with a family counselor but to no avail. The counselor's attitude seemed to be, "Let her grow." The problem has caused a lot of arguments and strife in the family. My parents are at a loss what to do. Could you please help? It sounds as if your sister is not being treated for her problem; nor is she being punished for her misbehavior. In the meantime your family has to deal with the tension and upheaval her stealing causes.

She has been stealing for long enough now to convince anyone that this not a passing phase. She is doing it for some unknown reason, but it's now part and parcel of her personality. The reasons I could offer are many and varied, but I would only be guessing at this point.

Sometimes people like your sister can easily convince authorities that "there are no problems" or that "it won't happen again"—and yet it does. I would suggest that your parents consult another psychotherapist to try to deal with your sister's problems—and the family's role in all of this. It would be a major help for your sister to be able to trust and confide in someone. If this proves to be impossible for some reason, your parents may have to follow an unpleasant course: pressing charges against your sister. This sometimes "forces" a resolution of the problem very quickly.

285 Dear Dr. Levine: I have a problem that started a year ago when I started to go with my boyfriend. For the first three months we got along well. But then he became violent. He hit me, leaving me bruised and scared. So I broke up with him. Then I went back with him because he promised not to hit me. But he broke his promise and started to hit me again.

We broke up again, and then he wanted to go with me again. I did because he beat me until I said I would. But this time he had been with a girl during our breakup, so I lost my trust in him. He promised he wouldn't go with another girl, but he did, so now we've broken up for good, as far as I am concerned, and I don't think he will hurt me anymore. He says I am crazy or stupid. What should I do? Yours is a sad and frustrating letter. It makes me want to yell at you: "Why in the world do you take this? Why do you come back for more?" It makes me want to forget my clinical understanding and give your boyfriend (and I use the term loosely) a taste of his own medicine.

Violence has no place in a relationship and is a serious danger sign of problems both in the relationship and within the person inflicting the injury. At the first sign of violence, your relationship with that boyfriend should have ended. No one has the right to hurt another person.

You need help if you can't extricate yourself from this incredibly demeaning, brutal relationship. No person is worth the degradation and pain brought about by violence. You should get professional attention to overcome your feelings of low self-esteem and self-hatred. You are hanging in there because you hate yourself and feel that you deserve it.

Well, you don't. Drop him—forever—and get help. You need some expert counseling from someone who can work with you not only to help resolve the current crisis but to make sure you never have similar problems again.

Dear Dr. Levine: I am a seventeen-year-old girl with a fifteen-year-old brother who has a serious problem. It's probably just adolescence, but I am convinced he needs help. He has been to two specialists, but it did no good. He is physically violent, he is irritating to people around him, and he tries to get attention by damaging people's property. **286**

I told my parents about this because he was physically hurting me. I would fight back, but it went nowhere, and my parents did nothing to stop it but shout. It has gotten to the point now that he figures he is getting no attention from my parents when he hits me, so he takes things of mine or puts them out of use altogether. The other day I found a butcher knife on my bed and my eight-tracks rearranged and my stereo not working.

I have to take this into my own hands because my parents are simply tired of having to discipline him every time I complain to them. I don't know how to handle the situation. I figure if I damage his property, my parents will make me pay for it. I told my parents about my stereo, and they told me not to involve them anymore in our problems.

Nevertheless, I have to realize he is my brother,

and however I plan to seek revenge, I have to be cautious that I don't kill him.

I'm afraid that it isn't just adolescence that accounts for your brother's problem. I think you know that yourself. Your brother is engaged in destructive, antisocial behavior.

As a rule, young people whose personalities permit them the license to indulge in these kinds of behavior are notoriously resistant to traditional forms of intervention. The fact that he has already been to two specialists who failed to make any inroads in his behavior is evidence of that.

Why the specialists didn't follow through with management suggestions or referral elsewhere is beyond me—but not nearly as much as is the inactivity of your parents. We all, at times, tend to use denial when we don't want to face an unpleasant truth. But your brother's behavior is so blatantly offensive and dangerous that their lack of action borders on irresponsibility.

If matters continue, I worry about escalation or the miscalculation of a temperamental fifteen-year-old in an impulsive, uncontrollable rage. I urge you to try again to convey to your parents how desperate the situation is. Chances are they are quite concerned but are confused as to where to take it from here. Your brother has to be taken back to one of the specialists for guidance and evaluation.

Frankly, if your parents still refuse to take action, you may want to move out with the help of a relative or even the Children's Aid Society.

287 **Dear Dr. Levine: When I was a young girl, I was a victim of child abuse. The people at the Children's Aid never talked to me or asked me what happened. They always talked with my parents. I developed a wall and now I'm older and I've still got this problem.**

I've seen social workers and psychiatrists and because of an overdose spent months in a hospital ward. They even plugged me full of drugs to relax me and open me up. I now see a therapist who is really warm and caring and very strong. But I am still stuck. What am I supposed to do? I'll never be able to accomplish what I want. I can't even go to school because of my emotional disability.

The question you ask is an extremely difficult one to answer. You have obviously had a rough life so far—abuse, placements, hospitalizations, medication, psychotherapy, the works! It is indeed a sad story.

But you are young and working with someone whom you trust and respect. While you may feel stuck, this is still an opportunity to use this relationship to grow. Our lives are not cast in stone; there is still time for you to make major gains and changes in your outlook and performance. Expect more of yourself than you are doing, but don't set your sights so high that they are unattainable. Your therapist can be of major help to you.

Dear Dr. Levine: Last year you answered my letter in your column. I was a child abuse victim. Well, I thought I would write to let you know that I'm still fighting my way with the same therapist, and I'm in college now. I'm even averaging 87 percent. I never thought I could do it. Thank you very much for your sound advice. I still have a lot of problems in and out of school, but at least I'm on the right track. It'll take a few more years of therapy, but I'm more optimistic about succeeding.

288

Please print this letter so it will show others like myself and all your readers that your advice is sincere and honest and, above all, helpful.

I appreciate your sentiments, but I am even more pleased at how well you are doing. You can show our readers that, no matter how tough the going gets, there is always hope.

Dear Dr. Levine: I am a twelve-year-old boy. My parents are really good friends with our next-door neighbor. He is like my uncle, and I've been going to his house every Friday when my parents go out. He has been babysitting me this way since I was little. I always fall asleep there, and I spend the night. In the morning I wake up and I have no clothes on or I am half undressed. I used to think maybe I changed really late and I just couldn't remember.

289

I wanted to find out, so I pretended to be asleep. It was him who did it and some other terrible things too. It didn't hurt, I just didn't like it. I can't tell you what happened. I feel sick and embarrassed. Luckily, I haven't had to go to his house since then. I still like the way he was, but I don't trust him now.

I don't trust my parents now either, so I didn't tell

them. If I tell them they will make a big fuss. He will
go to jail or something, and everyone will think I'm
funny too. I think his craziness is rubbing off on me.
I'm afraid to fall asleep and I don't like anyone getting near me. Will it go away, and can he get better?

I have to go to his house for a whole weekend soon.
I'm so scared I feel like I'm going to die. I'm going
to run away if I can't get out of it any other way. I
can't tell my parents, my teachers, or the police, only
my scout leader maybe. Should I tell him? Am I a
homosexual now?

This is a very serious and difficult letter. Let me start by
reassuring you that you are not a homosexual on the basis
of these experiences, nor are you crazy, but you have developed some problems that you may well get over on your own.
If not, you can arrange to get help.

But you have to share your secret with somebody, if only
to protect yourself and others. The man next door has a
problem that should be treated. He has been molesting you
for a long time now and will continue to do so unless you
stop going over there.

I can understand how you feel about exposing him; the
furor caused will be very upsetting to everyone. Your parents will be outraged—justifiably—and you will feel guilty,
at least for a while. The man may, in fact, be arrested.

You cannot go back to this man's house; if you can manage it, you could tell him that you know what he's been doing
and you will never go there again. Speak to your scout leader,
or any close adult you trust, about your predicament. You
need advice, but it has to come from somebody who knows
you and the situation in more detail.

There are no perfect answers to your complicated situation. There are certainly many people who would feel that
your neighbor should be punished for his destructive acts.
I am just saying that you will need guidance, advice, support—in a mature way—if you decide to blow the whistle.

290 Dear Dr. Levine: I am a nineteen-year-old man. When
I was ten years old, I was sexually assaulted by a
woman in her late twenties. She coaxed me into her
company by buying me a toy, then volunteered to
drive me home. She didn't take me home, however,
but away from the city, so I cried after she had started
to come on to me. She stopped off in a dead-end road.

Then she started to take off my clothes, and I panicked, but that was no use. Then she started hurting me, scratching me. It was just horrible. She eventually drove me home, and I woke up in my backyard on the seat of the picnic table with my clothes over me.

When I was twelve, my sister-in-law forced herself on me when nobody was home. She locked my bedroom door and took off her clothes and did all kinds of weird things to me (like throwing knives and cups and things at me). If I didn't do what she wanted, she said she would tell my family that I molested her children, which I didn't. So I did what she wanted. Years later she told the family that I had molested her children, and the family up to this day won't have anything to do with me.

Now I am terrified of being involved with women in any way. I cry for no reason, get flashes, and sometimes almost lash out in anger.

I have been seeing a psychiatrist for two years but to no avail. He won't do one thing to help me. He hardly talks to me. Why can't psychiatrists treat people with human compassion and act like psychiatrists instead of computers? Do you think I should continue? What can I do? I really need some answers fast if I am to get on the right road to becoming a human, functional male in a world that is demanding!

Yours is an unusual letter, for a number of reasons. For one thing, it is quite uncommon for a male child to be sexually molested by an adult female. For this to happen to the same youngster on two separate occasions and at the hands of different predatory female adults is downright rare. Be that as it may, you are now left with problems involving your relationship with the opposite sex. To make matters worse, you have sought professional help to overcome these problems and are disillusioned with that process.

You are wise to seek psychological help for your problems, but I don't want to oversimplify by attributing all of these to the sexual attacks. There is too much that you haven't said about yourself for me to know whether other circumstances may also play a part. This should be explored with your psychiatrist. Although you feel he is impassive and nonresponsive, that doesn't necessarily mean he is inadequate; he may be an adherent of a specific school that puts more of the onus on the patient to be verbally productive. The fact that you are uncomfortable with the process does not invalidate its potential effectiveness. But if you feel this approach does not work for you, tell your psychiatrist, or go to someone new.

291 **Dear Dr. Levine: I am a nineteen-year-old female. When I was thirteen, my stepfather kept molesting me. Once his friend was babysitting me, and as soon as I went to bed, he got in with me and started trying to take my clothes off. I started to cry and he stopped.**

I am now terrified of men. I think they will try the same thing. I still live with my parents, but I go nuts if my mother goes out and leaves me with my stepfather. I never told her because I was afraid she would not believe me.

I have just recently been able to talk about it to my fiancé and close friends, but it doesn't help much. I could never be afraid of my fiancé and grandfather because I know they really care. What can I do to overcome this fear?

I have a little sister and am keeping a close eye on her in case my stepfather tries anything with her. We are pretty close so I think she might tell me. I would like to tell my mother, but she would probably not believe me since I waited this long. Also, I wouldn't want to cause trouble in the family.

You are left with two problems: the first involves your fear of men and the second relates to any possible course of action regarding your stepfather.

You are fortunate that there are at least two close men in your life whom you know you can trust. Surely they prove that some men are loving and caring. Only more positive experiences with the opposite sex will enable you to shake your fear. If not, then try some sessions with a psychotherapist. Certainly, what happened to you is sufficient to have caused your problem, but there may be other issues that contribute to it and should be explored.

As for exposing your stepfather *at this point,* that course of action is controversial. If there is *any* suspicion that your stepfather is molesting your sister or harassing you, I feel you have no choice but to tell your mother or someone in authority. But be aware that the revelation may well bring about upheavals and conflict in the family. If he has stopped his former misdeeds, consider what is to be gained risking that now. Some people would demand retribution. But only you can make that decision. Perhaps this is one of the things you can discuss with your therapist. Certainly, it should not be taken lightly.

Dear Dr. Levine: I am a twelve-year-old female. I am having a problem that concerns my aunt's boyfriend, Gerry. Last summer, while I was sleeping, he started molesting me. I woke up, but I didn't do anything. I was so frightened after that and I dislike him and I don't trust him anymore.

292

    Later I found out that this had also happened to my cousin, my aunt's daughter. I don't want to tell my parents, even though they would understand, because I am afraid of what might happen.

It sounds like Gerry has a serious problem. Not only is he unfaithful to your aunt, but he sexually abuses young women against their will. I hope that you tell your parents and that they deal with it maturely and carefully. Gerry should be "reported." Most states have specific offices for reporting child abuse, sexual abuse, or domestic violence. The police can also be used for this purpose. Gerry should then get appropriate help; he should receive corrective psychotherapy and should be carefully monitored by a probation officer/counselor.

    Just be prepared for some emotional outcry, yelling, and threats. This is not inevitable, but I have seen it occur in many such instances. You want to protect other girls from being molested, and you want to ensure that Gerry gets treated and rehabilitated. But your aunt will be very upset, as will others who are involved. So be deliberate, go slowly and surely, and think in terms of your goals.

Dear Dr. Levine: I'm a fourteen-year-old girl who would like your help. There is incest in my family, this being between me and my father. This happened three times, a year ago. I felt terribly guilty, thinking maybe this was my fault. This guilt haunted me every single day until I watched a program about incest. It helped me realize I'm not guilty. My father hasn't touched me for a year, but still every time I'm with

293

**him alone I tense up and feel very nervous. My fa-
ther is a very good and emotional man. He often tells
me he loves me. I always answer "Me too" without
really meaning it. He (I think) senses this and one
day told me, "Maybe one day you'll be able to tell me
you love me." This remark hurt me very much. Why
do I feel this way? How do I bring myself to forgive
him?**

Your experiences are, tragically, all too common and involve
complexities that make it hard to decide what to do. I wish
I could tell you to open the whole subject up with your parents, but I've too often seen families torn asunder by this
type of revelation. Fathers often deny, mothers are critical,
and the girls feel terribly guilty about having exposed their
fathers—as if they were responsible for the whole ordeal.

Your father may well have given up the incestuous behavior. It sounds like he feels some remorse and that he recognizes that he hurt you. He also may be aware that your
difficulty in expressing love for him is related to his sexual
misadventures.

If he truly has stopped his destructive behavior, I can't
see the point of blowing the whistle on him. You might try
talking to him—at the right time—and sharing your concerns about his actions. But frankly, I feel that he knows
how you feel. It will take a considerable amount of time for
you to forgive and forget. Your father will have to earn your
love this time around.

In any case, I would strongly urge you to get some professional counseling. An adolescent clinic or Family Service
branch will have counselors who can help you.

294

Reply to readers: I have been taken to task by a number
of readers who were upset by my seeming indifference to
the plight of a fourteen-year-old girl whose father had been
sexually molesting her. I had urged her to speak to a counselor at a Family Service branch or an adolescent clinic. I
also told her to be prepared for a possible unpleasant reaction in her family if she did blow the whistle on her father.

This is a highly complex issue. As much as readers demand retribution, punishment, and treatment for the father, and protection for the child, the cruel irony is that
professional intrusions often create major problems. The very
people we want to protect often end up being further victim-
ized.

I have recently been made aware of a number of similar

cases in which the daughter's telling all has led to a jail
term for the father (in one case), removal of the girl from
the family (in three cases), rallying of the mother to the defense of her husband (in most), denial on the father's part
(mostly), and massive conflict and upheaval in the family.
More often than not, the daughter was blamed!

Some readers wanted me to tell all girls caught in this
trap to expose their fathers for what they really are—sick,
disturbed, sadistic, etc. That way, they reason, the fathers
will get help or deserved punishment, the parents will get
marital therapy or will split, and the victims will stop feeling guilty and fearful. Frankly, I'm not sure they are wrong.
I just want readers to know that things don't always work
out "happily ever after."

Incest is the worst catch-22, and it does not lend itself to
glib solutions. Whatever else the young victims do, they would
be wise to seek counseling and support from the agencies
I've suggested or from the Children's Aid Society or a rape
crisis center.

**Dear Dr. Levine: I am a fifteen-year-old boy. Since
I was very young, I've been sexually abused by my
father. There was never any physical damage done
to me. My father doesn't seem homosexual, and
I do not think he is. I never understood what was
going on.**

**My mother has problems of her own, and if she
found out it would destroy her. I have never told
anyone.**

**I have not had sexual contact with anyone other
than my father. I never talked to him about it. I was
never forced or blackmailed. When I'd stay away from
him, he sensed that I didn't want to anymore, and
we haven't had sexual contact for about a year now.**

**I like girls and have gone out on dates, but some-
times I have sexual desires for someone of the same
sex. I'm not sure if I'm gay or not, and the thought
that I am makes me mad.**

**My grades are very good. I get along with most
people and have lots of friends. But I can't stop my
feelings, and I don't know what to do. I have tried
reading books but they don't say much. I don't want
to see counselors because I'm afraid. Children really**

295

don't have protection against this type of incest, and
what the abusers might not realize is the mental anguish the children face as teenagers. I would deeply
appreciate your advice.

You are partly correct. Some adults who sexually abuse young
children don't realize the emotional pain they are inflicting.
But most abusers *do* understand and still persist. I don't
want to let them off the hook—they need help, counseling,
and controls—but my own list of priorities tells me that protecting and helping the children comes first by a long shot.
I still have difficulty swallowing my anger at child abusers
of any kind.

I've gotten into trouble for responding to this type of letter. According to the law, a responsible adult, especially a
clinician, *must* report to the proper authorities that this kind
of behavior is going on. The problem *sometimes* is that the
child victim gets into even more difficulty as a result, unless
the whole thing is handled cautiously and sensitively.

You are only fifteen, but you have gone through a lot of
painful stuff that merely confuses the issue of sexual orientation. There is no reason, even on the basis of your experiences, to think you are homosexual.

I am going to recommend to you the very thing that you
fear: I urge you to speak to a counselor at a teen drop-in
center or adolescent medical clinic; or your doctor, school
social worker, or guidance counselor might be worth a try.

296 Dear Dr. Levine: I'm a fifteen-year-old girl who needs
help badly! A boy at school, whom I shall call Rick,
raped me. I was so terrified I let him do it. It was
painful, but I didn't scream because I was scared of
what people would think if they found me there na-
ked. Everything was okay until the next time. Rick
knows I will let him get away with anything. Since
then he has raped me six times.

After the fourth time I stopped getting my period
and thought I was pregnant. I wasn't. Things started
getting so bad I attempted suicide. I've only told one
person about all this, and he didn't believe me. If he
didn't, who will? I can't stand to live with myself
anymore. I feel like a slut.

My parents cannot find out about this! They can't,
it's out of the question. I tried speaking to a social
worker and a rape crisis center, but they both told

me if I didn't tell my parents there was nothing they could do. I definitely can't report it to the police; I allowed him to do it to me.

I'm afraid that I agree with the people at the rape crisis center. Because you are so young, your parents are legally responsible for you. Surely they will have to know what happened and why you are seeking much-needed help. But the rape crisis center should still be prepared to help.

You are protecting either Rick or yourself or both. And I think you're wrong on all counts. If you are worried about him "getting into trouble," then you have some justification. But he's already in emotional trouble and will cause a lot more harm to others before he's through. He has to be stopped. Period. Yes, he may be charged by the police, but that may be the only way he will be stopped from hurting you and will get the proper help for his terrible problem and behavior. Moreover, it is probably the only way that society can be protected from this dangerous young man.

As far as your "reputation" is concerned, if this is done properly—with your parents' help—your name need not be released. But even if it is, you have suffered grievously at the hands of a disturbed individual, and it is most important that you don't blame yourself. Rape has become too common in our society to be seen as anything other than what it is: a terrible, violent act perpetrated by a sexually insecure and generally inadequate male. There is no way that it should be condoned.

You have already sought help, and for that I commend you. I urge you to take the necessary next step. If you can't bring yourself to tell your parents, then perhaps you should get in touch with a local branch of the Children's Aid Society. A counselor there will help guide you through the difficult but important journey ahead.

Dear Dr. Levine: When I was fourteen years old, I was raped by four guys. This all happened while my two ex-friends sat downstairs and watched TV. In the five years since then, I have been very afraid to let any guys come near me.

A year ago I met a guy whom I fell deeply in love with. We could talk about everything, and I felt comfortable with him. This guy tried to make love to me three times, and I wanted him to, but at the last minute I would turn cold and it would upset him terribly. We ended up breaking up.

297

I still talk to him regularly, and occasionally we go out. I was wondering if maybe you thought I should tell this guy what happened or maybe it might make things worse between us.

You went through a terrible experience, and your reaction to men since then is entirely understandable. Luckily you met a young man who showed you that the violent louts who raped you are exceptions to the rule. Most guys are as appalled as you by these unconscionable and cruel actions.

As far as your specific question is concerned, I urge you to speak openly and honestly to this fellow. If he is as kind and mature as you describe, he will be very understanding when he learns of your experiences. I don't know if this will suffice to rekindle the romance, but it will surely cement the friendship. If your love relationship with him doesn't get off the ground, there will doubtless be others.

298 **Dear Dr. Levine: I'm fourteen and have two brothers, twelve and eighteen. My father is constantly finding fault with everything, which he never used to do. He often calls us lazy, inconsiderate, incompetent, useless, spoiled, etc. He never asks us a simple question, but his tone always insinuates that we are at fault. I have always been the outcast at school, with no more than one or two friends and always a few really bad enemies.**

I found myself thinking about how I could commit suicide. I started hearing voices, which kept repeating my father's insults over and over. I have never been afraid of death.

I went to a psychologist once, and he suggested a family session. An appointment was scheduled, then canceled, and no new appointment was made.

I feel as if my parents don't want to face the problem. I've tried to bring it up, but they won't listen. What do I have to do to make them notice?

A very sad letter from a very troubled person.

Your father sounds like a guy with some problems who is taking them out on the family, perhaps especially on you. But he is not the only one with whom you have difficulties. You call yourself an outcast and tell us that you have "a few really bad enemies." This makes me think that you are lonely, isolated, insecure, and depressed.

You are contemplating suicide, which will end all of these

problems and destroy you in the process too. Surely there are other alternatives. Have you enlisted the help of your older brother? Is there an adult whom your parents respect who could speak to them on your behalf?

It is unfortunate that the last appointment was not rescheduled, but it is not too late. Perhaps an initial visit to your local Family Service branch might be in order. If your parents cannot be persuaded to seek help with you, you may have to speak to a staff member at an adolescent clinic, your school guidance counselor or social worker, or your family doctor.

Dear Dr. Levine: I would really appreciate if you would print this letter so that Mom and Dad will understand why I did what I did. I am an eighteen-year-old girl who has not been very happy for about three years. I really tried to talk my feelings over with many people, but no one ever picked up my hints.

299

I really loved you, Mom and Dad, but I just couldn't go on as unhappy as I was. Pregnancy was the last straw. School was no help either. I just felt so lonely. I can't explain why I decided to end it, but I suppose it took a lot of courage.

By the time this is printed, I will already be gone. Please say goodbye to all my friends and relatives, especially my best friend, Stan. The reason for me using the method of pills and alcohol is because I knew that when I took them it would be final. I had a lot of time with you both away. By the way, don't worry—the pills didn't hurt.

P.S. If anyone ever feels so lonely, don't keep it inside, talk to someone. Don't let it go too far, like I did. I had nowhere else to turn. Talk to someone! Also, I would like the Youth Clinic to write a little something to help my parents accept this decision of mine. Tell them that I will be happier wherever I went. There is no doubt that this young woman was filled with sadness and futility. She was—I hope still is—going to school, had friends and a seemingly intact, caring family; yet she felt so "lonely." When she became pregnant her pessimism was enhanced and she saw no recourse but to end it all. Her attempts at seeking help were either too feeble to be noticed or were presented to individuals who were too busy or not sensitive enough to her inner pain. Perhaps she hid it better than she knew, better than for her own good.

So many of our letter writers tell about having no one to talk to. Yet when they're in deep emotional trouble, even those who *do* have people who care and are available often don't talk to them.

There *are* people out there who will listen and try to help. It is a kind of arrogance to write people off as uncaring; who among our readers would describe themselves as uncaring and rejecting? Yet this sad girl does just that, in a sense, by not making her feelings known. Sometimes we have to "cry for help." And I don't necessarily mean to professionals. Parents, friends, and family can be used as sounding boards, supporters, advisers, or just plain close, caring people. Certainly, if trained psychotherapists are needed in any of these situations, it is easier to arrange when one is not acting totally alone. Family doctors, ministers, school counselors, staff at drop-in centers, etc., can also be used as a "line of defense" and can help you get appropriate help.

I hope with all my heart that this writer delayed her suicide plans and got the attention of some of those who care for her.

300 **Dear Dr. Levine: I am an eighteen-year-old male. A few years ago I attempted suicide three times. The next two years were spent getting help: psychiatrists (two on a regular basis), eleven months at a youth development center, plus five months at a halfway house, and so on.**

Nothing's changed. I really did try to turn my life around, but it just didn't. And now, as I see it, the only way for me is suicide. I don't want to hurt my family, yet I don't know what else to do.

Why I'm writing is to ask you to help me be remembered. I don't want to end up on page twenty-one of the newspaper below an ad for some acne cream. My life was that way. I don't want to die that way. I want to go out with a bang. Maybe I'll be remembered a little longer. I don't want to die a nothing. As each minute goes by, I get more scared. But I know this is what I have to do.

Look, young man, you have me over a barrel. I have no way of getting in touch with you, and you are more or less threatening to end your life. I know very little about you, except that you've had a rough few years and that you obviously want to make some noise, some splash. You are angry, frustrated, and now quite desperate.

What can I do to convince you otherwise? I urge you to get in touch with a counselor or staff member of the youth development center you were at. You must not allow yourself to give in to your misery and pessimism. I know many young people who have felt as you do and who have overcome their problems after a long, hard struggle. It won't be easy but it will be well worth it. When I speak to young adults who have gotten over that major hurdle, they all are relieved that they didn't give up hope.

Don't give up.

TEN:

Abusable Drugs

For in modern society there is a widespread yearning for unnatural stimulants, which finds gratification not only in the abuse of alcohol but also in the excessive use of opium, chloral, and other narcotics.

H. Lyman et al.,
The Practical and Home Physician *(1890)*

We live in a world of chemicals, some naturally occurring and some manufactured, and many, such as antibiotics, necessary for our well-being. It's also a world of stress and turmoil from time to time, and in that state we often look to some of those chemicals to provide a shortcut to feeling better. In fact, many of the chemicals "work": for at least a short time we feel better, more alive, happier.

So what's the problem? The problem is real and has many levels:

- *All* drugs have potentially undesirable and dangerous side effects.
- *All* drugs can be abused, overused, used destructively.
- *All* mind-altering chemicals can cause dependence (psychological or physical), and many can lead to serious addictive disorders.
- Chemicals *never* solved anyone's problems.
- Even if chemicals work for a while, the effects are *always* short-lived and can become a crutch. Even if they make us feel better, they fool us into believing that we cannot do without them, and worse, that we cannot solve our problems on our own.

Our message? Treat drugs very gingerly, even suspiciously. Seek other ways of turning yourself on to life.

301 **Dear Dr. Levine: We are a group of kids in ninth and tenth grade who have had an argument about drugs.**

Some say that marijuana is dangerous and addictive, others not. Some say it is as addictive as cocaine. Who is right?
How to put this gently? All of you are wrong! Marijuana, a potentially destructive substance, is not addictive. Cocaine, an extremely destructive substance, is also not addictive. Alcohol, a fairly dangerous substance, is definitely addictive. Has this confused you? Let me try to clarify.

An addictive substance is one that causes the cells of the body to develop an actual physiological *need* for the drug, that must be taken in increasing doses to produce the same physical and emotional effect, and, finally, that causes a severe and potentially dangerous bodily reaction when it is abruptly stopped in an addicted individual (abstinence syndrome). Substances that do not meet all these criteria are not considered addictive.

However, they can *still* be dangerous. Marijuana causes some physical changes and can develop a kind of psychological dependency in certain vulnerable and needy individuals. These people become apathetic and withdrawn, and their schoolwork and relationships can suffer. Cocaine is one of the most destructive substances around and is very expensive. It induces an extraordinary craving and dependence in many susceptible users. It creates the illusion of well-being and power while providing just the opposite.

In fact, all of these (and other) drugs, when abused, allow the user to escape from a painful reality in an unrealistic and ultimately destructive way.

Dear Dr. Wilcox: My girlfriend is always bugging me to quit smoking. I don't smoke pot, just cigarettes. Is it really that bad for you? **302**
Tobacco is indeed a powerful and dangerous drug, and in fact the list of health problems linked to smoking grows longer every day. A very common but not serious problem is that smokers catch more colds and have more respiratory infections than do nonsmokers.

More serious is the way tobacco increases the risk of heart disease, heart attacks, strokes, chronic lung disease (such as emphysema), ulcers, and cancer of the lung, mouth, and esophagus. It also contributes to the development of cancer of the bladder, kidney, and pancreas and may also increase the risk of stomach and even cervical cancer.

Smoking is actually considered to be a major factor in 40 percent of all cancers in men, and it's been said that 85 percent of all lung disease could be eliminated if everyone stopped smoking.

303 **Dear Dr. Wilcox: My parents have smoked all my life. It never seemed to bother me before, but lately I notice my clothes smelling terrible and the air really musty. I've been told you can get lung cancer from just living with a smoker. This really worries me. I've tried talking to my parents, but they just get defensive and yell at me to stay out of it. I realize they're not going to stop smoking, because they are both very heavy smokers and they enjoy it. I can't do anything about it without getting in trouble. I've given up on trying to save their lives, but now I'm going to save mine. What can I do?**

It is very frustrating and painful when you see people you love engaging in self-destructive behavior. You have told your parents how much their cigarette smoking worries you, and their response is probably an indication that they know you are right, that it is very damaging to their health. You've done all you can do. You might ask your family doctor to intercede, but the ultimate responsibility is theirs.

Studies have shown that health risks increase for non-smokers exposed to smoke from smokers' cigarettes, but the risks are not nearly as great as for the smokers themselves. Children who grow up in a home with smokers tend to have far more respiratory (breathing) problems, such as colds and bronchitis, than do children in families where no one smokes. The greatest risk is for infants less than one year of age who are constantly with a smoking mother. These babies actually have measurable amounts of nicotine in their saliva and urine.

It has been estimated that 18 to 34 percent of all cases of asthma in children are attributable to maternal smoking. And children living with smokers also tend to be shorter than children of the same age and sex who've been in non-smoking families.

Your major concern, however, is the risk of cancer. Be reassured that there have been *no* studies that have shown any increased risk of cancer among children whose parents smoke. What can you do to protect yourself from cancer? Continue to do just what you are doing: don't smoke.

304 **Dear Dr. Levine: I would like your opinion. My friends and I are full-grown, sixteen-year-old boys. For about**

a year we have gone out about once or twice a month. We get drunk and go to a movie. Afterward, we sober up at about eleven P.M. or midnight, then go home. None of us has a car, so we use the bus. None of us gets a bad hangover.

I am wondering if we are doing anything really harmful. I have noticed no change in my friends or myself at all, and none of us is anywhere close to being an alcoholic. I know you cannot promote this activity, but I would like your opinion.

The kind of behavior you are describing is, as you probably know, quite common. I don't think that having a couple of beers a few times a month will cause you any harm. Where I draw the line, however, is in your statement that you "get drunk." I am relieved that you and your friends don't have cars, because booze and driving is a lethal combination. But drunkenness can get you into all kinds of trouble (not to mention the possibility of getting really sick to your stomach). Guys with too much booze in their system tend to be raucous and rough and occasionally get into fights.

I am pleased that none of this happens to you (does it?). Just cut back on the amount—don't go out to get drunk! Besides, who is selling you the beer, anyway? It's illegal at your age, the last I heard.

305

Dear Dr. Wilcox: I am a fifteen-year-old girl, and I think that I might have a drinking problem. Every time I go out with a guy or to a party, I feel dependent on alcohol to loosen me up so I can be more relaxed around other people. I know people usually do drink at parties, but I wish I could be one of those who don't need to drink.

I'm too young to be drinking, but I already feel kind of hooked on it. I don't like beer, only vodka and whisky, and I've been drinking for only two years. Lots of times, I've been getting too drunk and wind up making a fool out of myself. But if I don't have any, I shut up and don't say a word around people (mostly guys), and then I feel I am being a drag because I'm so shy. Could you tell me what you think I should do?

From what you have described, you are right; you do have a problem with alcohol. But your letter says more than this.

It also shows you have the maturity to recognize the problem, and this maturity and recognition are the necessary foundations for successfully dealing with your problems.

As you undoubtedly realize, there is a multitude of medical, social, and psychological problems associated with alcohol abuse, which is increasing in the adolescent age group. Statistics vary, but one reliable survey states that one in three adolescents can be classified as an infrequent or light drinker but almost one in four is a moderate-to-heavy drinker. Moderate-to-heavy drinkers drink two to four drinks at least once per week or larger amounts three or four times per month.

Why do people in your age group say they drink? Usually the reasons given are similar to yours: alcohol makes them feel and appear more sociable and less anxious.

Problem drinkers (30 percent of adolescent drinkers) are usually defined as those who have been drunk at least four times per year and/or have encountered two or more negative social consequences of drinking (difficulties with friends, criticism by dates, driving while impaired, or trouble with family, teachers, or police). From what you say, you probably would fit into this category—which, it is apparent, is not what you want.

Your reasons for drinking are not unusual, but you could better and more healthfully fulfill these needs (to be sociable, to be more relaxed) by increasing your self-confidence. Right now, your drinking is actually chipping away at any positive feelings you have about yourself—and this will ultimately make the situation worse. One way to start working on the problem is to find someone in whom you can confide and who can help you build your self-esteem. Your doctor or school nurse can help direct you to the appropriate counselor.

306 **Dear Dr. Levine: I am so frustrated I feel as if I'm headed for a nervous breakdown! My father is an alcoholic, but he won't admit it. He scrounges money or borrows it whenever he can to buy beer. He hasn't worked in a long while and has no desire to. I'm embarrassed to have my friends over in case he's going to get drunk that day.**

When he is drunk, he is rude and obnoxious. He has kept my mom and me up late in the night when I have to go to school the next day and my mom has to go to work. He makes long-distance phone calls

**at night, which we can't afford, and once our phone
was cut off for a few months, which was utterly embarrassing. In the few days when he is sober, he is
grouchy and inconsiderate. When he buys food, he
does not let anyone else eat it. I cannot stand him
when he is sober either. He acts just like a little kid
and not like other fathers!**

**I'm afraid that he is driving my mom to be an al-
coholic or have a nervous breakdown. She tries to
drink whenever he does because she says that's the
only way she can tolerate him. I've tried to persuade
her to kick him out and divorce him. My mom does
not deserve this at all. We cannot live a normal life
with him.**

Your letter sounds like so many others I have received over
the years from young people living at home with an unpredictable, unreliable, offensive alcoholic parent. There is fear,
depression, guilt, anger, frustration, humiliation, and phenomenal helplessness expressed. It is fairly certain that your
father will not seek help on his own. Ideally, he would get
into a treatment center, join Alcoholics Anonymous, admit
his rather serious problems, and get to work alone and with
the family on repairing emotional bridges and overcoming
major psychological and family issues. But it's not going to
happen that way.

You and your mother have to be aggressive about seeking
help. You should speak to your family doctor, or the two of
you should go to the nearest Family Service branch and enlist the aid of a counselor there. You should also contact
Alcoholics Anonymous or their offshoots Al-Anon (for family
members) and Alateen (for teenage children) for advice and
help.

At some point your father is going to have to come to grips
with the fact that he's going down the tubes. If that happens, the arduous road to recovery will begin. If it doesn't,
you and your mother may well have to leave him, as callous
as this sounds. Better one person destroyed than three.

**Dear Dr. Levine: I am fifteen years old and very, very
upset about my mother. She started drinking heavily
when I was ten and has told me and the rest of my
family that she will quit. She hasn't. She doesn't drink
as much anymore, but she's addicted to drugs and
takes them all the time.**

307

She's a nurse and still doesn't know any better. I personally don't touch any liquor or drugs because I'm so afraid I'll be like her. I want her to get help, and I would like to go to a psychiatrist and talk to him/her. I think it would help me. Could you give me some suggestions on how to help her and myself? The rest of my family keep it inside them and won't let their hurt feelings show. Is there any hope for her?

Yes, there is hope for your mother, but it will take work and time. Usually an alcoholic or drug addict will not benefit from help until he or she admits to having a problem. I don't know if your mom is at that point—yet. I also don't know if she really is an addict.

Does she drink alone? Does she regularly increase the amount of alcohol or drugs she needs? Does she physically crave the substances and suffer when she doesn't have them? Are the substances addictive? What kind of drugs does she use? These and many other questions would have to be answered before a label of "addict" is applied. But she sure has severe problems.

Who is "the rest of your family" to which you refer? Is your father in the home? With your help, they might be able to help your mother finally accept the fact that she needs professional attention. But you also seem to want psychiatric help. Your depression may be largely related to your mother's problems but may also be due to a number of other issues. That is, if you do see a psychiatrist, your relationship with your mother will be just one area that you can expect to work on.

308 **Dear Dr. Wilcox: I was introduced to marijuana when I was sixteen. Before I tried pot, I was dead against it, but with a lot of coaxing I finally tried it—and loved it. For a while, that is. But recently I've been getting depressed, paranoid, overweight, and low on money. My friends don't want to hang around with me anymore because they say I'm burned out. Also I've been coughing a lot, making my parents suspicious of me.**

I want to quit smoking pot. Telling me how marijuana can hurt my health may help get me to quit.

Marijuana is the third most common drug used by young adults. Tobacco and alcohol rank Nos. 1 and 2. Light users smoke it once per week or less; a heavy user smokes it two or more times per week.

The negative effects of marijuana use vary with the amount used and the frequency of use. The list of marijuana's ill effects is extremely long. Common short-term problems include irritation of the eyes, nose, and lungs; decreased memory, coordination, and ability to learn; and, for some people, emotional effects such as depression or panic. A very serious effect is that hours after the high is gone, one's ability to drive is still badly impaired. Obviously, this can be extremely dangerous.

Consistent heavy use can also interfere with your body's ability to fight infection, although this effect appears to resolve once you stop using it. Long-term effects can persist as long as the abuse continues. These include poorer performance on tests that measure learning and thinking, loss of motivation, and chronically irritated lining of the lungs.

Risk of lung cancer increases for long-term marijuana smokers even more than it does for those who smoke cigarettes. The cancer-causing agents are 70 percent more concentrated in marijuana than in tobacco.

It sounds as though you are feeling very low, and the marijuana abuse may be a symptom of your unhappiness—and is actually making you feel worse. You may have a lot of feelings to sort through, and a supportive counselor can help you get through them and get back in control of your life.

Dear Dr. Wilcox: I am a sixteen-year-old girl. I smoke pot quite often (an average of three days a week or more), and I was wondering if you could tell me if it will have any effect on my bearing children when I'm older. Please don't say it will just so I won't smoke drugs, because I may not stop because of that. **309**

Marijuana is not known to affect a woman's ability to bear children or to damage her chromosomes or genes. Thus, marijuana smoked now would not lead to genetic birth defects of a child born to you in the future. There is, however, evidence that smoking five or more joints per week during pregnancy may cause subtle changes in a baby's nervous system. The effects are suggested by the baby's tendency to startle when tested shortly after birth. These babies also tend to be smaller than those born to non–marijuana users.

Heavy users who are male, however, do show changes in their reproductive systems, although these effects resolve approximately one month after stopping smoking. The changes include decreased size of the testicles and decreased production of normal sperm.

310 **Dear Dr. Levine: My best friend in the world is getting herself so badly into drugs that it's unreal.**

She doesn't realize it, of course, but I can see through her so easily. It's getting to the point where she gets high for classes at school, and now she even gets high for exams. The problem is, I'm too afraid to discuss the subject with her, because any time I bring it up she tells me to shut up and says I don't know what I'm talking about.

The thing is, I _do_ know what I'm talking about. To put it simply, my best friend is screwing up her life, and she doesn't even realize it.

You are absolutely right to be seriously concerned about your friend.

I doubt that she is—as yet—on cocaine or heroin. She is probably stoned on grass and hash, and perhaps booze. But no matter, because she can end up destroying herself even on these substances. It is not only the drugs that worry me. It is perhaps even more significant that she is using them to conquer her unhappiness and pessimism. The combination is deadly. If she won't or can't stop on her own, or if she won't get outside help, she will end up wrecking her schooling and friendships (like yours)—and her life.

I am not surprised that she resents your concern. She knows she is playing with fire but doesn't want to hear it from you or anyone else. You have tried caring, concern, compassion—to no avail. One suggestion is to show her your letter and my response. Perhaps you can speak to her parents about your concerns.

311 **Dear Dr. Levine: I am a sixteen-year-old boy from a good family. My older brother (he is nineteen) took some LSD last week with some friends, and one of them was hospitalized overnight (he became panicky). Is this a common reaction? I thought that LSD was harmless. What about PCP? There is someone at school who is selling this stuff, as well as anything else we might want. Should I take a chance, just for the experience?**

You are asking all kinds of important questions. LSD stands for lysergic acid diethylamide. It is one of a group of drugs known as hallucinogens or psychedelic substances. When taken orally they induce hallucinations, or perception of colors, images, and figures in our vision that really are not there. LSD (and mescaline, peyote, etc.) were common in the 1960s when their virtues were extolled and their dangers downplayed. We have learned over the years that almost *anything* can be abused; that street drugs are often impure (adulterated), so one doesn't know what he or she is really getting; and that psychedelics can cause severe psychological reactions (like those of your brother's friend). PCP (phenycyclidine, also known as angel dust) causes similar hallucinations but is more damaging to the emotional and physical state of the user.

As far as the seller (dealer) in school is concerned, he should be tossed out on his derrière. I would not recommend that you purchase drugs for the experience, any more than I would urge you to do anything else that can be detrimental.

Dear Dr. Levine: I'm an eighteen-year-old female, and for the past two and a half years I've been taking bennies, uppers, or beans on a regular basis, and when I say regular, I mean every day. I take eight to ten a day. Sometimes I get bad headaches, and I have been forgetting stuff.

312

Sometimes it has to do with my weight. Sometimes I feel fat, and I figure if I take a few more bennies I'll lose weight fast and quick. Sometimes I feel I need them to get through the day at work. Do these things have any effect on my body or brain?

These "things," as you refer to them, the uppers or bennies, are either amphetamines (also called speed) or some drug related to them. They are dangerous, emotionally and physically, and what makes matters worse, they don't do the job. People have used amphetamines in attempts to overcome depression or to reduce appetite and lose weight. Unfortunately, the "rebound" tends to be stronger than their initial effect. That is, the user usually ends up being more depressed and anxious afterward, and appetite returns with a vengeance. More and more is required to achieve the same level of relief, so that we end up with an ever-increasing cycle of use—and eventual abuse.

Amphetamines are not classically addicting, but they do engender a kind of psychological dependency. They play havoc with sleep, reduce resistance to illness (often because of fatigue and poor nutrition), can cause cellular damage, and can certainly precipitate serious psychological disorders.

You must stop taking them immediately! Go to your family doctor for a checkup; he or she will advise you as to the best course to follow for counseling or psychotherapy, if necessary.

313 **Dear Dr. Levine: I am a fourteen-year-old boy, and my friends think that I have a serious drug problem, but I think they are wrong. For the past six months I have been sniffing glue from tubes used for model building. I love the smell, and it makes me feel terrific (I usually feel low). Is this dangerous? My parents don't know about this, and I'm scared to tell them, but I'm not sure they care.**

I'm afraid that your friends are completely right. Sniffing glue is a dangerous habit, not only because it affects the way the user feels or acts but also because it can cause permanent brain damage. The gas given off by the glue is a potentially lethal chemical. As a matter of fact, the manufacture and sale of these glues (and other related substances) have been greatly curtailed by law in many areas.

Getting off the glue is extremely important and, believe it or not, not that difficult. The major problem for you will be getting over your low moods, which make you look for an easy answer.

You have mixed feelings about your parents. On the one hand, you don't think they'd care; on the other, you fear that they'll be upset. I expect that they *do* care. If you feel that you can't talk to them, show them your letter and this answer. They might contact your family doctor, who can refer you to a teen counselor.

314 **Dear Dr. Levine: I am a sixteen-year-old girl who is very confused. I have a father who is constantly beating up my sister and me. About three years ago I got mixed up with the wrong group (my dad hated them, so I hung around with them on purpose) and some heavy drugs and drinking. In the past six months things have gotten even worse. Now I am doing speed and cocaine every day (I have to steal to**

get the money). I am constantly drunk and all my teachers know.

I don't have to tell you that you are in sorry shape indeed and in fact in a precarious situation. You *must* get help before you allow yourself to be severely and/or permanently damaged. Your family situation and your destructive use of drugs are more than enough reason to get professional attention, and, frankly, I feel that you have no choice.

You can go to an adolescent clinic, your family doctor, or a drug treatment clinic, or even speak to your school social worker. Any of these sources can make sure that you get proper treatment for your many serious personal problems, not to mention your father's abuse. Do not delay.

Dear Dr. Wilcox: I have a girlfriend who has something called endometriosis. She was taking some very expensive medication that I noticed made her very moody. She claims, however, it made no difference to her condition, and she was still in pain.

315

She has had this pain for almost two years, and in the past ten to eleven months has been taking large doses of over-the-counter painkillers. I've told her it must be harming her. Can she have become dependent on them, or is she really in a lot of pain?

Endometriosis is a condition in which the lining of the uterus is found not only inside the uterus but also in other internal locations. *(See 139.)* Pain is a prominent symptom. Available treatments include the use of hormones and of analgesics (pain relievers).

Drug abuse is defined as the use of prescribed or unprescribed drugs in such a way that it results in impairment of the individual's physical, mental, emotional, or social well-being. Overuse of over-the-counter painkillers such as aspirin or acetaminophen can cause medical problems. Overuse of codeine-containing preparations can lead to dependence.

In answer to your question, then: yes, she *could* cause herself physical harm or, with certain medications, become dependent, and yes, she really could also be in a lot of pain.

Because I don't know what medication she is taking in what amount, I can only make some general comments about the complications that can be associated with analgesic overuse or abuse.

With aspirin overuse, possible problems include gastritis (irritation of the stomach) or ulcers, possibly leading to internal bleeding and anemia; temporary hearing loss when blood levels of the drug are high, and a vitamin C deficiency. With acetaminophen abuse, chronic hepatitis (serious liver disease) is a dangerous possibility. Interestingly, cases of acute liver damage have been reported in alcoholics who combined relatively low doses of acetaminophen with alcohol.

Your girlfriend needs to discuss with her doctor the types and amounts of painkillers she's taking and should make sure all other avenues of treatment have been explored. Her overuse of painkillers could cause her harm; she needs to make sure she uses them as carefully as possible to give her the relief she needs with as little risk of serious side effects as possible.

316 **Dear Dr. Wilcox: I would like to know if a person can be awakened while under the effect of a sleeping pill.**
Yes. And if the person *can't* be, something is wrong—either they've taken too many pills or for some reason the dosage is far too strong for them. If you can't awaken someone, you should consider it a medical emergency, and that person should be taken to the hospital. People should also be aware that sleeping medication (also called tranquilizers or sedatives) should never be combined with any other drug that also depresses the nervous system (increases drowsiness), because such a combination can be deadly. Alcohol and antihistamines (contained, for example, in allergy medications) are two such products that should never be taken with sleeping pills.

317 **Dear Dr. Levine: I am a nineteen-year-old girl with emotional problems. I see social workers and a psychiatrist, and I live in a group home. My problem is that when I become extremely upset I take antihistamines. Sometimes I take up to thirty pills in one day. Twelve is usually the minimum. I'm really scared because I don't have much control over this and it has been going on for months.**

I would like to know what effect these pills could have on my body and how serious this is. I'm also wondering if antihistamines are addictive, because I feel a strong need to take them.
We must be doing something awfully wrong. "We," in this case, refers to the mental health profession. Here we have a

young woman close to being addicted to a potentially harmful drug, abusing her mind and her body, who regularly sees a child care worker (in a group home), a social worker, and a psychiatrist, and *still nobody knows*! This is truly mind-boggling and depressing.

Antihistamines are not addictive in the classic sense of the word, but like any other substance they can be dangerously abused. You can and *must* get off this stuff, which, I can assure you, is not doing you any good and is going to destroy you if this goes on much longer. Surely you are working on—or should be with all this help available—how to deal with your states of upset without resorting to chemicals and other dangerous pursuits.

Dear Dr. Wilcox: Would you please tell me the long-term effects that purging and taking large amounts of laxatives have upon one's body. **318**
Long-term or excessive laxative use is a very dangerous practice that can lead to a variety of problems.

Laxatives may be divided into different types based upon the way they work. Each type has particular problems associated with its abuse.

So-called stimulant laxatives work by irritating the lining of the intestines and "speeding up" their activity. They also alter the way fluid is handled by the intestine. Used excessively, these laxatives can cause dehydration and serious imbalance of so-called electrolytes such as potassium and sodium. Severe deficiencies of water or electrolytes can be fatal. Long-term use may lead to a condition called cathartic colon, where the large intestine's normal function has been damaged so that it can no longer work on its own. Treatment aimed at retraining the intestine to function normally can be long and difficult. Some patients with this self-induced problem end up needing a colectomy, or surgical removal of the intestine. Although most such patients have been abusing laxatives for thirty to forty years, several have been less than thirty years old.

Specific chemicals used in certain laxatives may also cause damage to the lining of the intestine, irritation of the stomach, or inability to absorb calcium well (this will weaken bones), or can cause unusual skin conditions and allergic reactions.

So-called lubricant laxatives, containing mineral oil, coat the stool to make it easier to pass and also keep more water in the intestine. Prolonged use, again, can lead to severe side effects. Vitamin A and D deficiencies may develop; if the oil is absorbed into surrounding tissue or organs, the body attacks these deposits as "foreign," and inflammation occurs.

INDEX

The numbers in this index are not page numbers. They refer to the large marginal numbers that identify each letter and answer.

Homosexual community ser-
vices, 197
Homosexuality, female, 200,
201, 228, 229, 257
Homosexuality, male, 194–
199, 289, 295
and AIDS risk, 144
Hormones, female. *See* Estro-
gen; Progesterone
Hormones, male. *See* Andro-
gens
Hymen, 163, 164
Hyperactivity, 253
Hyperhidrosis. *See* Perspira-
tion, excessive
Hypnosis, 34, 265, 274
Hypogonadism, 130

Impotence, 194. *See also*
Erections
Incest, 293, 294, 295
Infatuation, 257
Infertility. *See* Fertility
Intercourse. *See* Sexual inter-
course
Internal exam, 138
Intertrigo, 72
Inverted nipples, 14
Iontophoresis, 83
Irritability, 231
Isotretinoin, 64, 65
Itchy anus, 133
IUD, 189

Jealousy, 215, 230

Keratosis pilaris, 76
Kissing, 153
and AIDS, 144
Kleine Regel, 23
Kleptomania, 283, 284

Labia, *See* Genitals, female
Laparoscopy, 139
Larynx, enlargement of, 119
Laxatives, abuse of, 48, 52,
54, 55, 318
Learning disabilities, 253
in language, 254

Leaving home, 239
Legs, heavy, 44
Loneliness, 208, 264, 266,
267
LSD, 311
Lumps. *See* Swellings
Lying, 226
Lymph nodes, swelling of,
122

Makeup
for covering scars, etc., 62,
66, 68
and eye irritation, 109
Marijuana, 301, 308, 309
Marriage, 217
premarriage classes, 162
Masturbation, 155, 156
Melanin, 67, 69
Menarche, 1. *See also* Menstruation
Menstruation
and anemia, 18
blood loss in, 18
cessation of, 20, 52, 53
and hirsutism, 94
and cramps, 21
and endometriosis, 315
delayed onset of, 7
frequency of, 17, 18
irregularity of, 17, 173
mid-cycle symptoms, 23
onset of, 1, 2, 16
and percentage of body fat,
20
periods
anovulatory, 22
ovulatory, 22
premenstrual syndrome, 25
prolonged bleeding, 19
Mescaline, 311
Milia, 80
Minoxidil, 99, 100
Mitral valve prolapse, 116
Mittelschmerz, 23
Moles, 77
Molluscum contagiosum, 148
Monilia infections, 141, 143
Mononucleosis, 121
Mood swings, 273